T0360767

Regenerative Strategies

In the current climate emergency, it is no longer enough for businesses to simply employ environmental strategy typologies focused on 'greening the business' and maintaining the 'business-as-usual' logic. Gregorio Martín-de Castro and Javier Amores-Salvadó argue that disruptive business models and solutions are now required, and they propose a new regenerative strategy linking climate science to management studies. The main features of this strategy are cutting-edge climate science solutions (capturing and utilising atmospheric carbon dioxide to produce net zero or net negative emissions and positive environmental externalities) and a redefined firm purpose under an ecological, ethical and moral paradigm (integrating eco-emotional wealth, environmental performance, systemic socioecological resilience, wider stakeholder management and a very long-term perspective). They demonstrate that, by applying this strategy, companies can not only reduce their negative environmental externalities and create positive environmental externalities, but also reverse current environmental degradation through a new sustainable capitalism.

GREGORIO MARTÍN-DE CASTRO is Professor of Management at the Complutense University of Madrid. His research focus is on the intersection between business strategy and the natural environment. He is currently the President of the Business & Society Division of ACEDE – The Spanish Academy of Management.

JAVIER AMORES-SALVADÓ is Associate Professor in the Management Department at the Complutense University of Madrid. His research focus is on the study of firms' environmental strategy and environmental innovation from the strategic management perspective.

Organizations and the Natural Environment

The increasing attention given to environmental protection issues has resulted in a growing demand for high-quality, actionable research on sustainability and business environmental management. This new series, published in conjunction with the Group for Research on Organizations and the Natural Environment (GRONEN), presents students, academics, managers, and policy-makers with the latest thinking on key topics influencing business practice today.

Published Titles

Potoski, *Environmental Strategy for Businesses*
Matisoff and Noonan, *Ecolabels, Innovation, and Green Market Transformation*
Rivera, Oh, Oetzel and Clement, *Business Adaptation to Climate Change*
Crow and Albright, *Community Disaster Recovery*
Grabs, *Selling Sustainability Short?*
Sharma and Sharma, *Patient Capital*
Marcus, *Strategies for Managing Uncertainty*
Marcus, *Innovations in Sustainability*
Bowen, *After Greenwashing*

Forthcoming Titles

Gouldson and Sullivan, *Governance and the Changing Climate for Business*

Regenerative Strategies

Exploring New Sustainable Business Models to Face the Climate Emergency

GREGORIO MARTÍN-DE CASTRO
AND JAVIER AMORES-SALVADÓ
Complutense University of Madrid

CAMBRIDGE
UNIVERSITY PRESS

Shaftesbury Road, Cambridge CB2 8EA, United Kingdom

One Liberty Plaza, 20th Floor, New York, NY 10006, USA

477 Williamstown Road, Port Melbourne, VIC 3207, Australia

314–321, 3rd Floor, Plot 3, Splendor Forum, Jasola District Centre,
New Delhi – 110025, India

103 Penang Road, #05–06/07, Visioncrest Commercial, Singapore 238467

Cambridge University Press is part of Cambridge University Press & Assessment,
a department of the University of Cambridge.

We share the University's mission to contribute to society through the pursuit of
education, learning and research at the highest international levels of excellence.

www.cambridge.org
Information on this title: www.cambridge.org/9781009261937

DOI: 10.1017/9781009261920

First published 2024

A catalogue record for this publication is available from the British Library

*A Cataloging-in-Publication data record for this book is available from the
Library of Congress*

ISBN 978-1-009-26193-7 Hardback

Contents

Figures

Tables

Foreword: Reversing Course

In June 2023, the average global surface temperatures were 1.05°C above the twentieth-century average, making it the warmest June ever in the Earth's recorded history. The temperature kept going up in July 2023, breaking previous records. Canadian forest wildfires began to burn in May 2023 – earlier than ever before, more widespread than ever and more severe than ever due to excessive heat. The resulting smoke from these wildfires blanketed the United States and reached European skies and continued to do so for all of summer. The summer of 2023 saw the second consecutive month of record low sea ice in Antarctica; global accumulated cyclone energy that was twice the past annual average; water temperatures off Miami reaching 6°C above the average, stressing corals and sea life; cactus plants under stress and beginning to die due to over three weeks of consecutive temperatures in the US Southwest over 43°C; and the heat index reaching 67°C in the Middle East, beyond the human body's ability to cool (US NOAA, 2023). The world is literally burning and, as the authors of this book rightly point out, this is not climate change but a climate emergency.

The time for mitigation and reduction is long past and there is an urgent need to reverse the accumulated CO_2 and other greenhouse gases in the atmosphere to enable the survival of the Earth's species including humans and the ecosystems that support the species. At this critical time, this book on regenerative environmental strategies is a welcome addition to the growing discussions about a shift in thinking towards net positive (Polman & Winston, 2021) if the planet has to have any hope of achieving the goal of keeping temperature increases to below 1.5°C, as agreed by most countries at the 2015 Paris climate conference (COP, 2015).

This book reviews the extant environmental strategy literature and argues that businesses need to focus on regeneration as the strategy that goes beyond mitigation and reduction of environmental damage. Regeneration involves reversing the outflow of greenhouse gas emissions by capturing them from the atmosphere and either sequestering them or using them as feedstock for industrial use. The authors elaborate a case study of direct air capture by the Canadian company Carbon Engineering as an example of regenerative strategy.

As discussed in the opening paragraph of this foreword, the challenge we face is so daunting that we not only need to identify many more such examples and case studies if we are to inspire businesses from different sectors and countries around the globe, but also examine and elaborate on other pathways to tackle the climate emergency. Direct air capture is a costly technology that may take decades to be widely adopted in a viable manner. This technology can at best reduce only a small proportion of the approximately 35 billion tons of CO_2 that humans pump into the atmosphere every year. While this is a promising technology, given our climate emergency, it will only make a miniscule dent in the short term, given the magnitude of the problem. We need many more technologies, business models, processes, products and services that *do not* generate CO_2 and other greenhouse gases in operations. Regeneration is a pollution control strategy of cleaning up after the pollution is created rather than a pollution prevention strategy that redesigns the industrial enterprise to eliminate the generation of emissions (Russo & Fouts, 1997).

In Chapter 7, the authors outline a set of guidelines for companies seeking to develop regeneration strategies. These range from redefining the purpose of the business to wider (and fringe – Hart & Sharma, 2004) stakeholder engagement for knowledge generation. At the same time, the authors state that these firms should be prepared for returns in a *very* long time frame. However, it is not clear how businesses can change expectations of returns to the *very* long term without any guidance. Business operates in capital markets that provide the engine of commerce in terms of funds from investors and shareholders. Even funds from angel investors and patient investors will not be forthcoming unless they generate a reasonable return within a reasonable period of time. Family enterprises are an exception and many have transgenerational survival and performance expectations (Sharma & Sharma, 2011, 2019, 2021).

Hence, there is a major role for governments and institutions to create the conditions that motivate and facilitate the deployment of patient capital (Sharma & Sharma, 2019) that can allow for returns over a very long-term time frame. The current US government's

Inflation Reduction Act (US Congress IRA, 2022) has created incentives and subsidies for investments in technologies that address climate change. However, the climate problem is global and the actions are local and politically motivated. Positive actions by one country to reduce emissions are compensated negatively by actions of another country that subsidise the use of fossil fuels and the building of coal-fired power plants. At the same time, the developing economies face a choice of the most effective allocation of their limited resources: do they use these resources immediately to fight diseases and infections that kill millions of their citizens and reduce malnutrition, or invest them in renewable energy and deforestation that will generate returns in the long and very long term? Both are necessary and hence there is a major role for the rich world to enable the poorer developing countries to tackle climate change. Since the problem is global and affects our commons, it is in the self-interest of the developed countries to help the developing world, as climate change is mainly the result of two centuries of industrialisation by the developed world. Many such agreements have been reached in global forums, but there is little or no action and insufficient technology, aid and funds transfer from the developed to the developing world.

Drawing on the family enterprise literature's concept of socio-emotional wealth, the authors present the concept of eco-emotional wealth as a possible driving motivation for businesses to adopt regeneration strategies and accept patient, very long-term returns. However, the concept of socio-emotional wealth has at its roots the need for family harmony that is as important as financial returns for family enterprises focused on transgenerational success. Without harmony, conflict jeopardises succession and the survival of family enterprises. Eco-emotional wealth does not have the same level of urgency and it is difficult to permeate throughout larger organisations – especially those with multiple operations in multiple countries and contexts. Hence, genuine progress to avoid climate disaster would require coordinated action not only between countries at a global level, but also between governments, communities and businesses at a national and local level. The world has been coming together to discuss climate change and sustainable development every few years and recently every year ever since the 1972 United Nations Conference on the Human Environment in Stockholm. At the same time, at the local level communities pull together and help each other after climate-induced floods and hurricanes. In spite of all these efforts, after more than fifty years of global meetings and conclaves, the climate problem has grown and accelerated and reached the tipping point of an emergency. This book is a welcome addition to the discussion about an alternate pathway to achieve net positive emissions. Building on this discussion, the world needs an explosion of technologies and business models that will eliminate emissions rather than just cleaning and/or capturing emissions after they are generated.

Sanjay Sharma

References

COP 2015. (2015). United Nations Climate Change Conference. https://en
.wikipedia.org/wiki/2015_United_Nations_Climate_Change_Conference.

Hart, S. L., and Sharma, S. (2004). Engaging fringe stakeholders for competitive imagination. *Academy of Management Executive*, 18(1): 7–18.

Polman, P., and Winston, A. (2021). *Net Positive: How Courageous Companies Thrive by Giving More Than They Take*. Cambridge, MA: Harvard Business Review Press.

Russo, M. V., and Fouts, P. A. (1997). A resource-based perspective on corporate environmental performance and profitability. *Academy of Management Journal*, 40: 534–559.

Sharma, P., and Sharma, S. (2011). Drivers of proactive environmental strategy in family firms. *Business Ethics Quarterly*, 21(2): 309–332.

Sharma, S., and Sharma, P. (2019). *Patient Capital: The Role of Family Firms in Sustainable Business*. Cambridge, UK: Cambridge University Press.

Sharma, P., and Sharma, S. (2021). *Pioneering Family Firms' Sustainable Development Strategies*. Cheltenham: Edward Elgar.

US Congress IRA. (2022). Summary: H.R. 5376—117th Congress (2021–2022): Inflation reduction Act of 2022. www.congress.gov/bill/117th-congress/house-bill/5376/text/rh.

US NOAA. (2023). Climate change impacts. www.noaa.gov/education/resource-collections/climate/climate-change-impacts.

Acknowledgements

We would like to express our thanks to Prof. Paul Adler, from the University of Southern California, for his insightful advice in the very early stages of this research, and to Prof. Sanjay Sharma, from the University of Vermont, for his advice, comments and help during a research stay in Vermont in 2022.

Also, we would like to thank both Prof. David Keith, Harvard Professor, environmental entrepreneur and former CEO of Carbon Engineering, and Daniel Friedmann, current Carbon Engineering CEO, for their interviews and insights on atmospheric carbon dioxide capture and utilisation technologies, and Carbon Engineering's initial and current steps and main challenges.

Finally, we would like to thank for financial support the Spanish Ministry of Economy and Competitiveness research project # CO2015-65251-P, 'Conocimiento, aprendizaje organizativo y emprendimiento: antecedentes eimplicaciones sobre la innovación tecnológica medio-ambiental y los resultados empresariales'; the Spanish Ministry of Science and Innovation # PID2020-117564GA-I00, 'Estrategia e innovación medioambiental: una perspectiva desde el conocimiento y el capital intelectual'; and Complutense University-Banco Santander research projects # PR26/16-15B-1, 'Desarrollo sostenible, empresa y gestión medioambiental: hacia una visión multidisciplinar desde la economía, la ciencia y el derecho', and # PR108/20-01, 'Estrategia e innovación medioambiental: una perspectiva desde el conocimiento y el capital intelectual'.

1 | *Introduction*

Look deep into nature and you will understand everything better.

Albert Einstein

To what is common to the greatest number gets the least amount of care.

Attributed to Aristotle

1.1 Why This Book

The effective fight against the climate emergency calls for overcoming the traditional and extant divide between natural science and management silos. In doing so, we propose a disruptive business regenerative strategy that can change the economy and business by putting cutting-edge climate and natural science at the service of humanity through the economic and business sphere on a planetary and emergency scale.

The latest scientific evidence (IPCC, 2023) offers a pessimistic picture of current and future trends in the climate emergency, which corroborates the general state of the planetary emergency introduced to the reader in Chapter 5. Via global warming, surface temperatures reached 1.1°C in 2011–2020, unequivocally due to human activities, such as unsustainable energy use, land use and land-use change, lifestyles and consumption and production patterns across countries, and through the emission of greenhouse gases. The general state of planetary emergency (Ergene et al., 2021) and the widespread and rapid changes occurring in the atmosphere, ocean, cryosphere and biosphere have a disproportionate impact on the most vulnerable communities, precisely those who are least guilty.

Despite the Paris Agreement in 2015 concerning the current mitigation progress (IPCC, 2023), the efforts made by mitigation policies and laws supporting solar energy, the electrification of urban systems and infrastructure, energy efficiency, demand-side management and so on – although they are becoming cost-effective – are not enough.

Table 1.1 *Greenhouse gas (GHG) and carbon dioxide (CO_2) emission reductions in 2019, median and 5–95 percentiles*

		Reductions in 2019 emission levels (%)		
		2030	2040	2050
Limit warming to 1.5°C	GHG	43 [34–60]	69 [58–90]	84 [73–98]
(>50%) with no or	CO_2	48 [36–69]	80 [61–109]	99 [79–119]
limited overshoot				
Limit warming to 2°C	GHC	21 [1–42]	46 [24–63]	64 [53–77]
(<67%)	CO_2	22 [1–44]	51 [36–70]	73 [55–90]

Source: IPCC (2023:22)

In addition, the adoption of low-emission technologies in developing countries lags due to financial restrictions. Overall, it is likely that warming will exceed 1.5°C during the twenty-first century and that it will be difficult to limit warming below 2°C.

If we want to stop global warming and the related, intensifying, multiple and concurrent planetary hazards, deep, rapid and sustained reductions in greenhouse gas emissions via strategies and actions are necessary within the next two decades (IPCC, 2023). Although current levels of greenhouse gas emissions have already made many changes to natural ecosystems irreversible (risk of species losses, heat-humidity risks to human health and food production impacts, among others), these can be limited by deep, extensive, rapid and sustained global greenhouse gas emissions reduction. In fact, limiting global warming to 1.5°C or 2°C requires net zero carbon dioxide (CO_2) emissions via determined reduction, undertaken during this decade through immediate gas emissions reduction, as Table 1.1 shows.

As the recent IPCC report argues, limiting warming to 1.5°C or 2°C requires immediate CO_2 reductions in all sectors during this decade to achieve global net zero emissions by 2050 or 2070, respectively. In this sense, and since other mitigation options such as afforestation or production of biomass crops can have adverse socioeconomic and environmental impacts if implemented at large scales, global mitigation pathways reaching net zero CO_2 and greenhouse gas emissions give great prominence to the transition from fossil fuels without carbon capture and storage to very low- or zero-carbon energy sources, such as renewables or fossil fuels, with carbon capture and storage complementing CO_2 removal methods (IPCC, 2023).

Nevertheless, only a small number of globally modelled pathways limit global warming to 1.5°C by 2100. If warming exceeds 1.5°C, it could gradually be reduced by carrying out net negative global CO_2 emissions – or positive environmental externalities – which would require the additional deployment of CO_2 removal (IPCC, 2023) or atmospheric CO_2 capture.

Taking that into consideration, this book calls for a disruptive shift in business models towards a regenerative strategy capable of reversing the current climate emergency. For that purpose, it is essential to provide scientific evidence and convince business leaders, governments and policy-makers, as well as global citizens, of the need for immediate, proactive and globally coordinated action. As the latest IPCC report (2023) advises, there is a rapidly closing window of opportunity to secure a liveable and sustainable future for all. Mitigation and regenerative strategies require increased international cooperation among the business sphere, civil society and governments, particularly in vulnerable countries and industries. A planetary green deal includes coordinated political actions, laws and regulations in well-aligned multilevel governance, as well as access to finance and climate science technologies. Immediate coordinated action is mandatory because the decisions made during this decade will have impacts now and for thousands of years.

However, some questions arise: Why is it so difficult to address the climate emergency? Is it technically feasible? Economically? The next section aims to provide some answers to these questions.

1.2 The Tragedy of the Commons and the Climate Crisis

In the context of the natural environment, the tragedy of the commons is a well-known situation in which individuals who have open access to a natural good or resource, unhampered by shared social structures or formal laws and regulations that control access and use, act independently, according to their own self-interest, in an uncoordinated way, do not take into account the common good of all users and ultimately cause resource depletion. Hardin (1968) links this problem to a technological solution and a fundamental change in human morality. Coined by the British economist William Forster Lloyd (1833) to explain the hypothetical effects of unregulated grazing on common lands – termed 'the commons' in Britain – the tragedy of the commons encapsulates Aristotle's thought: 'that which is common to the greatest number gets the least amount of care'.

The climate emergency can be framed as an extreme consequence of the tragedy of the commons (Hardin, 1968). For traditional capitalism, human selfishness – individual incentives – and the existence of environmental externalities are inherent to business and economic development and prosperity, whereby companies, citizens, governments and countries pollute the air – the commons – due to different human activities and in an uncoordinated way, leading to the current climate emergency. However, atmospheric pollution, especially CO_2 air concentration, is distributed around the globe, conferring special complexities to creating an effective response due to the inexistence of atmospheric national borders and extreme difficulties in fostering worldwide coordinated action to address the climate emergency.

Concerning environmental degradation and pollution, although the tragedy of the commons is shared by soils and spring water, rivers and lakes, in ocean degradation and especially atmospheric pollution, the tragedy of the commons manifests in its maximum expression because the atmosphere belongs to the whole population on Earth, without any national borders.

In Hardin's (1968) analysis of the tragedy of the commons, applied to population growth or nuclear war problems, he advises that these dilemmas had no technical solution but required a fundamental extension of human morality. Currently, in the twenty-first century, climate science-based solutions, as previously noted regarding atmospheric decarbonisation, can help address the climate emergency; however, as Hardin reminds us, a planetary joint solution guided by a 'human green or natural' morality is needed; that is, changing this way humans behave towards the natural environment. This is precisely the core of our regenerative strategy concept and the difficult path to regeneration we aim to illustrate with the pioneering Canadian company Carbon Engineering. This requires two main complementary elements.

First, a science-technical solution is atmosphere decarbonisation through CO_2 air capture and utilisation, such as Carbon Engineering's Direct Air Capture and CO_2-based synthetic fuel AIR TO FUELS™ cutting-edge technology and other technologies. The latest scientific evidence (Schäppi et al., 2022) has confirmed the technical and economic feasibility of atmospheric CO_2-based synthetic fuels. Both technologies, according to the latest IPCC report (2023), are new, disruptive solutions that can effectively address the grand climate emergency, achieving net zero and even net negative emissions, which are necessary to stop climate warming in an immediate and planetary way. These are technical and economically feasible solutions, ready to be adopted right now and compatible with the existing gas and oil, industrial and transportation infrastructures; more importantly, they are ready for the immense majority of nations, industries and the world population, especially affordable in developing countries and the Global South (Hart, 1995) to address the grand challenge of sustainable development.

Second, there is a new human morality, where value is conceptualised beyond its economic nature, recognising both social and ecological values and restraining the view of individualistic, selfish and indulgent benevolent affections as the perfection of human nature, harmonising human sentiments and passions, just as Adam Smith analysed in his pioneering book *The Theory of Moral Sentiments* (1790). A new green deal where people intrinsically recognise this natural value is what we encapsulate in the emerging concept of 'eco-emotional wealth', a necessary driver of environmental entrepreneurs, managers and investors, allowing a regenerative strategy that implies three main disruptive changes in business models: (1) a new emphasis on transparent environmental performance and a company's contribution to 'systemic socioecological resilience', the resilience of our planet as a whole; (2) new and wider stakeholder engagement, including market and fringe stakeholders (Sharma & Vredenburgh, 1998) – communities, the natural environment, and so on; and (3) a very long-term perspective, which includes future generations.

1.3 General Approach in This Book

This book aims to present the reader with a comprehensive and realistic view of the climate emergency we are facing from the point of view of management science and business practice. In this sense, it shows how scientific evidence has been pointing to the existence of the climate crisis for decades and elaborates the responses that scholars in the field and firms have provided to the problem.

To address the climate emergency, the work clearly advocates the development of regenerative strategies by firms in which the corporate purpose is redefined (with an emphasis on a humanistic conception), where other stakeholders that were not taken into account until now (e.g. the natural environment itself) are taken into consideration, and where a very long-term vision is adopted. All of this is driven by cutting-edge climate science and disruptive technology.

The concept of a regenerative strategy aims to provide a realistic and balanced view of the focal problem. This is a balanced position because on the one hand, it shows evidence that technology alone will not solve the problem – there are no magic solutions – and on the other hand, it indicates that unfortunately, neither society nor companies are willing to drastically change their living standards today. This requires a lot of education and time, which are precisely what we do not have.

Thanks to science, we know that the climate emergency is rooted in the energy-intensive nature of our societies and based on the increasingly intensive consumption of fossil fuels; therefore, regenerative strategies aim to facilitate the transition to the economy of the future, where companies are embedded in the natural environment in which they operate and adapt their activity to the regenerative capacity of socioecological systems.

However, achieving the ideal of regenerative strategies cannot be done in the short term, as this is a radical change that requires drastic modifications not only in a company but also in society (through environmental education, for example, as we show in the last part of the book), under the premise that it is neither possible nor desirable to pursue indefinite growth, because the planet's resources are limited.

In this book, we also offer a clear example of how difficult it is to put the ideals of regenerative strategies into practice through the case of the Canadian company Carbon Engineering.

Carbon Engineering is a unique company that develops cutting-edge technologies that enable carbon removal and carbon capture and sequestration on a large scale, thereby eliminating the greenhouse gases that cause global warming. These advances in themselves are relevant enough, but they are not the only ones. Carbon Engineering has also developed a technology that makes it possible to create synthetic fuel from captured carbon, which could allow a qualitative leap in the fight against the climate emergency, with truly significant implications for some important sectors on a global scale. It is, then, a company that is perfectly equipped to develop regenerative strategies into their ultimate consequences.

However, the challenge of regeneration is not simple. Along with technological capabilities, it is necessary to make a series of decisions involving risks and uncertainties that may jeopardise the company's core business, preventing it from realising its full regenerative potential.

Carbon Engineering thus faces a dilemma: to bet everything on technologies close to its core business – generating immediate profits – or to leapfrog, to use its technological advantage to truly and fully adopt the regenerative strategy. In this book, the reader will be able to assess the nature of this dilemma, illustrated through the case of Carbon Engineering, and will also be able to see how in these times of climate emergency, the decisive impulse of the public initiative and governments – which could allow companies to make qualitative leaps in the field of regenerative strategies – is more necessary than ever.

1.4 Book Structure

The book is structured in two distinct blocks. The first block, which includes Chapters 1–5, elaborates the context of the climate emergency we are experiencing and the extant responses from academia and business practice. This first block of content serves as a starting point for addressing what constitutes the key concept of our proposal: regenerative strategies.

Therefore, in the second block, which includes Chapters 6–8, regenerative strategies are addressed in depth, both from a theoretical and from a practical point of view through a case study. This block concludes with an analysis of the elements that must accompany regenerative strategies to achieve their full realisation. Both blocks are described in more detail next.

1.4.1 First Block of Content

First, following this brief introduction in Chapter 1 where we set out the reasons for writing this book, the nature of the climate challenge we face and the general approach we apply, in Chapter 2 we outline the early scientific evidence on climate change and the impact of this evidence on both academic and business discourse. In Chapter 3, we delve into the academy's responses to the problem of the climate emergency through the concept of environmental strategy. Thus, from a longitudinal perspective, we analyse the evolution of that term and deconstruct environmental strategies, differentiating conventional or business-as-usual strategies from the regenerative strategies that are the central element in our book.

In Chapter 4, we move from strategy to capturing and delivering value in the context of the climate emergency. Thus, starting from the business model concept, we analyse social and environmental business models to demonstrate that both these models are embedded in the logic of the regenerative strategies already discussed. Chapter 5 delves into the relationship between humans and the natural environment, paying particular attention to the concept of the Anthropocene, the reason for its popularity and significance, and to the effects of intensive human intervention on the biosphere.

1.4.2 *Second Block of Content*

In Chapter 6, we address in depth the concept of the regenerative strategy, highlighting its main characteristics via a special emphasis on technology foresight and the more humanistic aspect of this type of

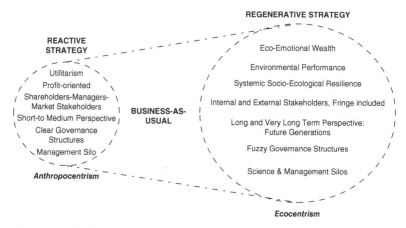

Figure 1.1 Anthropocentrism versus ecocentrism: the regenerative strategy's main features
Source: Authors' own elaboration

strategy in relation to the redefinition of firms' purpose and a new way of understanding not only their relationship with stakeholders, but also their time horizon. In Figure 1.1 we illustrate the main features of regenerative strategies.

In Chapter 7, we put the theory of regenerative strategies into practice by discussing the pioneering case of Carbon Engineering, which, as already mentioned, is developing cutting-edge technologies such as Direct Air Capture and AIR TO FUELS, capturing, sequestering and, most importantly, applying the captured CO_2 in the production of synthetic fuel.

Finally, in Chapter 8 we address some key aspects that are necessary to bring regenerative strategies to their full potential: on the one hand, the environmental and value-based education of future generations of business leaders – offering concrete examples of good practices; on the other hand, the essential role of public initiative in addressing global problems, among which the climate emergency is certainly prominent.

References

Ergene, S., Banerjee, S. B., and Hoffman, A. J. (2021). (Un)sustainability and organization studies: Towards a radical engagement. *Organization Studies*, 42(8): 1319–1335.

Hardin, G. (1968). The tragedy of the commons. *Science*, 162(3859): 1243–1248.

Hart, S. L. (1995). A natural-resource-based view of the firm. *Academy of Management Review*, 20(4): 986–1014.

IPCC. (2023). *AR6 Synthesis Report: Climate Change 2023*. Geneva: Intergovernmental Panel on Climate Change. www.ipcc.ch/report/ar6/syr.

Lloyd, W. F. (1833). *Two Lectures on the Checks of Populations*. Republished in 2017. North Charleston, SC: CreateSpace.

Shäppi, R., Rutz, D., Dähler, F. et al. (2022) Drop-in fuels from sunlight and air. *Nature*, 601: 63–81.

Sharma, S., and Vredenburgh, H. 1998. Proactive corporate environmental strategy and the development of competitively valuable organizational capabilities. *Strategic Management Journal*, 19(8): 729–753.

Smith, A. (1790). *The Theory of Moral Sentiments*. London: A. Millar (6th ed. 2006. São Paulo: Metalibri.)

2 | Assessing the Response to the Climate Grand Challenge

Institutions, Governments, Business Practice and Management Research

You will achieve a good reputation by striving to be what you want to look like.

Attributed to Socrates

2.1 Introduction

Since the 1980s, climate science has alerted us, with data and evidence, to the serious effects that human intervention is having on the climate. The intensive use of the resources that the planet offers and a continuous obsession with growth at all costs, above all via fossil fuels, has placed the advancement of civilisation before the grand challenge of climate change. This grand challenge constitutes 'a global problem that can be plausibly addressed through coordinated and collaborative effort' (George et al., 2016:1880); its solution requires the decisive involvement of governments, supranational institutions, companies and, of course, management academics, who must provide solutions and alternatives that help companies face a challenge of such magnitude.

In the following sections, we first address how climate science sent the first warning signals of the problem of climate change and how multinational institutions and governments initially perceived the problem.

We then delve into the reaction of industry to this evidence, paying special attention to the fossil fuel industry because of the visibility given to it by its prominent role in the generation of greenhouse gases. Finally, we analyse the role of academia in addressing this challenge. In particular, we show the role played by academics dedicated to the organisation and natural environment field.

2.2 First Evidence and Early Warnings: Science, Governments and Institutions

The evidence that the climate is being altered, for its effects and for its causes, due mainly to human activity, has been known for a long time; the first to point out the problem, along with warning messages, and to complete outreach work were a handful of pioneering scientists (Fueyo, 2022).

One of the most important milestones in climate science in this respect is the work of the Swedish scientist and 1903 Nobel Prize winner for Chemistry, Svante Arrhenius, who established, as early as 1896, the relationship between the amount of carbon dioxide (CO_2) in the atmosphere and the Earth's temperature. Subsequently, Charles David Keeling, at the end of the 1950s, showed through measurements, using the so-called Keeling Curve, the variation in the level of CO_2 on the Earth over time, making it possible to clearly appreciate the correlation between the level of CO_2 and the increase in the use of fossil fuels in the production of energy. Keeling provided the first documented example of climate change with his accurate measurements of atmospheric CO_2 concentration at the Mauna Loa mountain station in Hawaii (Heimann, 2005).

Taking the torch from Keeling, in 1967 Manabe – Nobel Prize in Physics 2021 – and Wetherald used mathematical models to warn that if the CO_2 content of the atmosphere doubled, it would increase temperatures by approximately 2°C (Manabe & Wetherald, 1967). Thus, if CO_2 were to increase from 300 particles per million to 600 particles per million – in 2021 CO_2 levels exceeded 416 parts per million – the temperature would rise by 2.36°C. The same authors demonstrated in 1975 (Manabe & Wetherald, 1975) that the temperature in the Arctic was rising faster than in the tropics. In 1978, John Mercer went a step further in his *Nature* article (Mercer, 1978), predicting increased CO_2 emissions, melting Antarctic ice and rising sea levels, and warning of the need for civilisation to shift from fossil fuels to other energy sources.

According to these authors' evidence, such events would not occur in the foreseeable future were it not for the fact that humanity had injected massive amounts of industrial CO_2 into the atmosphere. Subsequently, and to corroborate all the foregoing, in 1981 Hansen and his collaborators adopted this extant evidence in climate models in an article published in *Science* (Hansen et al., 1981) relating global warming, the greenhouse effect and the increase in the probability of occurrence of extreme climatic phenomena. The authors thus warned that, in the twenty-first century, extreme weather events would lead to the creation of drought-prone regions in North America and Central Asia, the erosion of the West Antarctic ice sheet, with a resulting rise in sea levels across the globe, and the opening of the Northwest Passage.

The evidence from climate science left no room for doubt. Hansen himself, who was also director of the Goddard Institute for Space Studies, appeared before the US Congress in June 1988 to state that he was 99 per cent certain that the actual warming trend was linked to human activity. It was time to stop questioning the scientific basis of the problem (Klein, 2015).

Meanwhile, at the institutional level, steps began to be taken that revealed the problem had gradually moved from laboratories and universities to decision-making offices. Thus, in 1979 the first World Climate Conference was held and in 1988 the Intergovernmental Panel on Climate Change (IPCC) was created to advise, from a science-based perspective, on the risks and consequences of climate change, as well as on adaptation and mitigation options.

The IPCC was founded by the United Nations (UN) through the United Nations Environment Programme (UNEP) and the World Meteorological Organization (WMO). Its main task is to compile and examine the relevant data and work published by the scientific community and, on the basis of this information, to draw up recommendations. These have insistently pointed out that climate change exists, that it is due to the greenhouse effect, and that this is due to human action.

In the meantime, the UN has developed legal instruments to protect the climate system from human intervention. Hence, in 1992 the first Earth Summit was organised in Rio de Janeiro (Brazil), where the world's governments signed the UN Framework Convention on Climate Change. This has been the basic document for all subsequent climate negotiations.

In 1997 the Kyoto Protocol was adopted, to which 192 countries are now party and which established the first binding emission reduction targets. The initial commitment period of the protocol covered the period from 2008 to 2012 and the second period ran from 2013 to 2020.

In 2015 the signatories of the framework convention committed, in the Paris Agreement, to intensifying the actions and investments needed to achieve a low-carbon future in which the global temperature in the twenty-first century is kept below 2°C above preindustrial levels, with a commitment to continue efforts to further limit the temperature increase to 1.5°C. The Paris Agreement remains a historic international treaty; it was signed by more countries in a single day than any other (www.un.org/es/global-issues/climate-change) and serves as a reference for the Climate Change conferences that the UN organises periodically. Moreover, the last of these, held in November 2022 in Egypt, explicitly sought to renew the commitment to comply with the Paris Agreement.

However, all this institutional concern contrasts with government support for the fossil fuel industry, which receives between $775 billion and $1 trillion globally in annual subsidies (Klein, 2015). As the IPCC notes in its April 2022 report (IPCC, 2022), global financial flows are still not aligned with the goals set out in the Paris Agreement, with public finance playing a key role in this worrying situation.

In this regard, Rodel and Tucker (2022), drawing on data from the recently launched Public Finance for Energy Database, note that in 2018–2020 G20 countries, development institutions and major multilateral development banks provided at least $63 billion each year to coal, oil and gas projects, more than doubling the financial support these same institutions devoted to clean energy in the same period.

As Tucker, De Angelis and Van der Burg (2021) point out, although in global terms international public funding for fossil fuels has fallen from $91 billion annually (in 2012–2017) to $63 billion per year (2018–2020), the amount of public money still dedicated to these industries remains astronomical and does not seem to indicate that these public institutions consider the current situation a climate grand challenge. Specifically, countries such as Canada, Japan, Korea and China provided the most public funding to fossil fuel industries in 2018–2020, with $11, $10.9, $10.6 and $7.3 billion, respectively, while Germany, France and Japan provided the most funding to renewable energy in the same period, at $2.8, $1.4 and $1.3 billion, respectively.

Nor do the extant trade liberalisation agreements, which were forged long ago, help in compliance with the Paris Agreement; they are not useful today in responding to the environmental challenge. In this sense, policies that favour local industries are considered discriminatory within the World Trade Organization and are frequently challenged. As Klein (2015) argues, the United States, for example, has filed complaints against subsidies for local renewables in China and India, while the European Union and Japan have also been reluctant to require a percentage of local production of renewable energy-generating material, considering this a violation of international trade rules. Very successful instances of the launch of the renewable energy industry, such as the public policies implemented by Denmark in the 1980s – before the start of global trade liberalisation – would be incompatible with current trade rules.

In other words, efforts to promote clean energy in the public sector are relatively scarce and often come up against significant barriers, which do not allow a clear and consistent line of action in this direction.

Despite repeated calls from both the scientific community and multinational institutions, governments still do not treat the climate problem as a grand challenge, and any efforts made (if any) are very limited. In Section 2.3, we briefly discuss the role played by business and management science academics (specifically those specialising in organisations and the natural environment) in the reception of the arguments put forward by climate scientists and the degree of penetration of the latter's repeated warnings about the catastrophic consequences of climate change.

2.3 Business Practice and Management Research Response

The responses of firms (especially those belonging to the most polluting industries) and management academics to the environmental challenge are fundamental, as both can either aggravate the problem or, on the contrary, be part of the solution. Businesses, as one of the main actors in society, have an important responsibility because they offer goods and services to the public; the nature of those goods and services is a determining factor not only in quantifying their impact on the natural environment, but also in guiding the public's consumption decisions. Academia, for its part, must therefore offer companies a framework for discussion and dialogue that proposes solutions to the problems that afflict them, among which the problem of climate change stands above all others.

Accordingly, the following sections analyse these issues.

2.3.1 Business Response to the Climate Grand Challenge

The ways in which companies adapt to environmental challenges have been clearly explained by Wright and Nyberg (2017). These authors show how companies go through various phases or stages in the process of accommodating their discourse and practices to the evidence of the threat posed by the climate crisis.

In their work these authors clearly distinguish three stages, 'framing', 'localising' and 'normalising', each with distinct nuances and peculiarities. Thus, in the first stage companies place the problem of climate change in their discourse in what the authors call *framing*. In other words, a process of interpretation takes place within an organisation, whereby the company can link itself to or disassociate itself from the problem as if it were an issue outside its sphere of action. The company can therefore 'take the blow' by considering the climate challenge an opportunity to be seized, a risk to be managed or a moral imperative to be taken into consideration, a responsibility to society. Wright and Nyberg call this way of acting 'association'.

However, in this first stage of framing the company can also disengage by considering climate change a matter that completely exceeds its responsibilities and that other agents or institutions should be in charge of managing. The authors call this position 'disassociation'.

After an initial framing stage, companies try to operationalise their initial positioning on the climate challenge through practices that on the one hand respond to this initial positioning, but adapt it to their markets and business interests on the other. These practices constitute what Wright and Nyberg call *localising* and are articulated through 'incorporation', whereby organic structures and new responsibilities are created within a company that allow its environmental commitment to be metabolised, and through 'commensuration', which establishes its ways of measuring environmental actions and practices from a quantitative point of view.

Companies then move on to 'proselytisation', which leads them to publicise their environmental achievements both internally and externally. Notably, this localising phase can lead to 'splitting', which consists of adopting a purely rhetorical stance once a company realises it is not capable of putting into practice the environmental commitment reflected in its initial stance.

Finally, the 'evaluation' phase takes place, in which the success of the environmental practices implemented is measured. This process generally results in a *normalising* realignment of practices to accommodate the interests of the dominant stakeholders in an organisation. This realignment typically results in 'purification', whereby the interest in fulfilling the company's original mission re-emerges with intensity and the subsequent 'dilution' of its environmental commitment in favour of the fulfilment of other lucrative objectives in which the climate challenge does not play a leading role.

The mode of action suggested by Wright and Nyberg also seems to replicate beyond their focal cases. Thus, reality appears to corroborate that some important companies with great impact have gone through these stages and have arrived at the same place (business as usual) suggested by these authors.

In this sense, the behaviour of some companies in the fossil fuel industry is paradigmatic and very representative; they have gone through the stages described here. The fossil fuel industry is an appropriate point of reference in this matter, as it is one of the industries most involved in the emission of greenhouse gases.

Next, we explore some of the stages through which some of the most important companies in this industry have passed in their relationship with the problem of the climate crisis. The example in Sections 2.3.1.1–2.3.1.3 is very illustrative of the framework proposed by Wright and Nyberg.

2.3.1.1 Framing

Initially, in the face of the scientific evidence that was beginning to accumulate and become public opinion, the fossil fuel companies approached the problem in a cautious manner, making it clear that their responsibility for global warming was exactly the same as that of the rest of the world. In other words, it was a problem that we had all created together and that was mainly due to prevailing lifestyles. In this sense, the companies in this industry presented themselves to society as neutral actors whose responsibility was diluted among the responsibilities of the rest of the population.

This initial reaction is characterised by a refusal to consider global warming as an issue of exclusive concern for the companies in an industry. This attitude is in line with Wright and Nyberg's 'disassociation' practices.

As an example of this first phase of framing, we can mention the campaign by British Petroleum (BP) to promote its 'carbon footprint calculator' in 2004. As *The Guardian* points out, this multinational oil company actually coined the term carbon footprint and hired the advertising, marketing and public relations firm Ogilvy & Mather to promote its invention (Solnit, 2021). With this manoeuvre, the company set in motion a process of decoupling whereby, while admitting the existence of the problem of climate change, it implicitly rejected the idea that companies in its industry had a greater share of responsibility than any other organisations or citizens.

The logic behind this manoeuvre is that companies are 'neutral actors' in this matter. They are simple agents that only provide citizens with the goods and services they demand. Thus, if every citizen calculates his or her carbon footprint, it becomes clear that the problem is not the fault of the big oil companies but of every citizen because of his or her lifestyle (Hoffman & Ely, 2022).

However, over time and despite these 'diversionary manoeuvres', the pressure on such companies (from both supranational institutions and the public itself) and the cascade of scientific evidence pointing to the urgent need to take decisive action to avoid future climate catastrophes led them to rethink their initial approaches and to take the lead in the fight against climate change. They therefore redefined their initial framing and embraced the environmental dialectic, launching their 'association practices'.

As a result of this reframing, on 12 February 2020 BP published a press release (Looney, 2020) stating: 'BP today set a new ambition to become a net zero company by 2050 or sooner and to help the world get to net zero.' In this press release, the company's chief executive officer (CEO) conveyed the following messages:

The world's carbon budget is finite and running out fast; we need a rapid transition to net zero. We all want energy that is reliable and affordable, but that is no longer enough. It must also be cleaner. To deliver that, trillions of dollars will need to be invested in replumbing and rewiring the world's energy system. It will require nothing short of reimagining energy as we know it…

This will certainly be a challenge, but also a tremendous opportunity. It is clear to me, and to our stakeholders, that for BP to play our part and serve our purpose, we have to change. And we want to change – this is the right thing for the world and for BP.

These messages show how BP set this 'association' in motion, portraying climate change not only as a challenge but also as an opportunity.

Unsurprisingly, this new positioning was echoed in the mainstream press. As *The Guardian's* Global Environmental Editor pointed out:

This is a clear recognition of the scale of the challenge ahead and it is encouraging that the Irish CEO states oil companies can no longer simply justify themselves as providers of reliable, affordable energy. This has been their fallback position for many years. (Watts, 2020)

2.3.1.2 Localising

Thus, once the companies in this industry had established their initial positioning, it was time to put in place the appropriate actions to put this into practice in their day-to-day operations by carrying out 'localising' activities. Therefore, there was a need to address the initial positioning with more conventional objectives, which were supported by these companies' traditional stakeholders.

Thus, the main step was to convince BP's shareholders to take the right steps towards decarbonisation and the initial net zero framing enacted by its chief executive. As reported by *Reuters* on 12 May 2022, its investors endorsed BP's climate strategy at its annual meeting (Bousso & Nasralla, 2022).

However, this localising phase, as Wright and Nyberg point out, involves making compromises and establishing difficult trade-offs between business as usual and any new climate commitments. This complicated balance is referred to as 'incorporation' and is not without its problems.

In this sense, tensions have come to light. As reported in *The New York Times* in relation to the investigations carried out by the US House Committee on Oversight and Reform into the climate disinformation that companies in the oil industry were promulgating, such efforts contravened the commitments that the industry had already made.

In its reports, *The New York Times* (Tabuchi, 2022) reveals the existence of internal documents whereby companies in this sector established guidelines for their employees, asking them to exercise restraint in their environmental discourse. Particularly relevant in this regard, then, is a statement that has come to light from the internal documents of the oil company Shell: 'Please do not give the impression that Shell is willing to reduce carbon dioxide emissions to levels that do not make business sense' (Tabuchi, 2022). This indicates that in addition to increasing tensions, an incipient greenwashing strategy was being pursued, marked by a double discourse: between the external projection of the environmental commitment and the internal reality of the company. This reality is rather starkly evident in the communications to which the newspaper has had access, in which a Shell employee states, in relation to the announcement of the company's net zero emissions target, that it 'has nothing to do with our business plans' (Tabuchi, 2022).

2.3.1.3 Evaluation

Finally, there is the assessment phase, which analyses whether a response to the environmental challenge also meets the value creation expectations of shareholders. As a result of this analysis, a company can pursue its path towards decarbonisation without addressing internal pressures, realign its environmental practices to better respond to the dominant discourse within the organisation by 'normalising', or even return to its core business fundamentals by ignoring the environmental positioning of 'purification'.

For companies in the fossil fuel industry, everything points to a normalisation that is a consequence of a failed process of localising, as previously analysed. In view of these considerations and the apparent initial successes of incorporating environmental commitments among a company's shareholders, the logic of business as usual has finally prevailed, as seen in the latest movements within the industry. In this sense, the recent reformulation of BP's emissions targets, whereby it has reduced its initial CO_2 emissions reduction targets from 35 to 40 per cent to a more modest 20–30 per cent, is very illustrative. As *The Washington Post* pointed out on 7 February 2022:

BP is scaling back its climate goals and deepening its investments in oil and gas, casting new doubts on big oil companies' promises to embrace clean energy.

The companies are under increased financial pressure to tap the brakes on their clean power plans to focus more heavily on the core business.

Shareholder resolutions demanding the companies align their business activities with the commitments in the Paris accord on climate change won less support in 2022 than they did in 2021. In the case of Shell, for example, such a resolution from the Dutch shareholder activist group Follow This won just 20 percent of the vote, compared with 30 percent a year earlier. The group's proposal had the support of just a third of the shareholders at Chevron, after a similar proposal won 61 percent support in 2021. (Halper & Gregg, 2023)

Accordingly, the fossil fuel industry has adopted a path that follows, quite closely, the course set by Wright and Nyberg (2017), ultimately conducting business as usual, in which the short-term priorities of ownership end up being imposed over a more long-term vision adapted to the intergenerational nature of the climate challenge that threatens our civilisation.

Having analysed the way in which one of the industries most involved in greenhouse gas emissions is managing the threat of climate change, we now explore how academia, in particular scholars in the field of management dedicated to analysing the relationship between organisations and the natural environment, have managed the problem.

2.3.2 Academia's Response to the Climate Grand Challenge

Given the environmental challenge, it is also interesting to analyse the degree of penetration that climate claims have had in academia, particularly among organisations and natural environment scholars. Thus, to assess the interest aroused by climate change in this field and the ways in which the problem has been dealt with by the academy, the concept of environmental strategy is very useful. Through it, a company projects its corporate behaviour in the face of the environmental challenge, as well as the objectives and means it uses to provide an adequate response.

The response of academia to the environmental challenge has fundamentally been based on three dominant theoretical perspectives or frameworks, namely resource-based logic, institutional logic (Bansal, 2005) and the microfoundations of strategy. Resource-based logic is rooted in the resource-based view (Barney, 1991; Newbert, 2008). Fundamentally, for business and environment scholars, this was defined in the seminal work of Hart (1995), which constituted the main turning point in the field by demonstrating the integration or cross-fertilisation of strategic business management and environmental studies. Here, Hart develops the so-called natural resource-based view (NRBV), marking the beginning of a very fruitful tradition of research on organisations and the natural environment. Based on the NRBV, scholars have proposed that companies that possess environmentally oriented resources and capabilities are in a better position than their competitors to discover new business opportunities, obtain new competitive advantages and position themselves in new and emerging markets.

Hart (1995) also articulates the steps companies need to take to implement environmentally proactive strategies, ranging from *end-of-pipe* measures through pollution prevention and product stewardship to sustainable development strategies. Overall, then, Hart's visionary work constitutes a brilliant turning point in the field for several reasons:

- It alerts management scholars to the problems arising from the scarcity of natural resources and to how companies must deal with them. This fact, although today it seems obvious to almost all scholars within this field of research, was a visionary and courageous approach to the problem in 1995.
- As already mentioned, it unites the traditional strategic management literature with the field of environmental studies.
- It articulates the response of companies to the environmental challenge in a framework of several progressive, linked stages.
- It breaks down the boundaries of what were traditionally considered a company's stakeholders to evaluate, in the last phase of sustainable development, the future role of companies operating in unconventional markets, in which Western competitive dynamics do not apply and which, as we have seen, constitute the main source of natural resources for the companies that make up so-called developed economies.

Second, the term environmental strategy has been analysed from the perspectives of stakeholder theory and institutional theory. As argued by authors such as Bansal and Roth (2000) and Delmas and Toffel (2004) in the field of organisations and the environment, the stakeholders surrounding a firm play a major role in the development of its environmental strategies. The pressures that certain interest groups, institutions or regulations exert on business decision-making that affect the firm–natural environment relationship are the focus of the literature that adopts this theoretical framework. Thus, companies develop environmental strategies to accommodate stakeholder demands, environmental legislation and the environmental demands of society in order to gain legitimacy and the necessary 'licence to operate' that allow them to extend their influence in their respective industry and institutional framework (Etzion, 2007).

As mentioned by Bansal and Gao (2006), according to both the NRBV and institutional theory, the deployment of environmental strategies can be directed at improving the environmental performance of firms, achieving specific organisational objectives, or both; firms, at their discretion, decide to which type of objective they assign the highest priority. In this sense, the achievement of improved environmental performance can be seen as an end in itself or as a by-product of an environmental strategy leading to the achievement of specific competitive advantages and, subsequently, improved business performance. As Berchicci and King (2007) argue, the balance of these two streams will determine the extent to which environmental concern is integrated into an organisation.

Third, following the microfoundations of strategy (Felin et al., 2012), we highlight individuals' novel environmental ethics and morals, embodied in the features of CEOs and top management – key driving forces in seeking corporate sustainability, complementing the organisational level of the NRBV and the industrial and country levels of institutional theory's reasoning. Microfoundational studies thus emphasise the influence on firm heterogeneity of key organisational members' features, beliefs, actions and interactions (Devinney, 2013; Molina-Azorín, 2014; Linder & Foss, 2018; Contractor et al., 2019), helping us to obtain a complete understanding of corporate environmentalism (Montiel et al., 2020).

Delgado-García and De la Fuente-Sabaté (2010) have empirically analysed the key role of a CEO's affective traits in the decision-making process, defining it as the effect on a firm's strategy and performance of the CEO's long-term tendency to experience positive or negative emotions. They find that positive affection conditions processing strategies, rendering them simple and intuitive, promoting creativity, the search for novel information and non-conservative behaviours and decisions. In contrast, negative affection leads to careful, error-avoiding and conservative behaviours and decisions. More recently, the empirical research of Wang et al. (2023) has also positioned CEOs' emotions and affectivity as the antecedents of firms' corporate social responsibility (CSR).

Having briefly outlined the extant theoretical frameworks with which environmental strategies are explained, based on the work of Martín-de Castro et al. (2023), we now discuss how the concept of environmental strategy has been received in the specialised literature, from its emergence in the early 1990s to the present day. By analysing the evolution of the concept of environmental strategy over time, we are able to reveal the degree of progress in the understanding of the phenomenon of climate change in the specialised literature, and to check whether organisations and natural environment scholars have followed parallel or different paths to the business reality.

2.3.3 *Exploring the Evolution of the Environmental Strategy Concept*

The term 'environmental strategy' could be said to have entered the world of management in the early 1990s. The truth, however, is that the view of the environmental problem in the world of management and business practice is far from the approach taken by climate science researchers. Thus, while climate science, as we have already pointed out, has not only determined the impact on the climate of greenhouse gases and the disastrous consequences that could arise, but has also empirically demonstrated that the main cause of this change in the climate is humans, management science has dealt with the phenomenon from another point of view. This, of course, is one far removed from the concept of the climate grand challenge that is always present in this work, and also confirms the little or almost nil interaction between these areas and the lack of interdisciplinarity. In the following sections, we explore this notion in more detail.

To analyse the orientation of the academic management literature when addressing the problem of climate change, a valid approach is to delineate the main terms used in the definitional landscape of environmental strategy, which will provide us with an idea of the key concepts and concerns thus far among the scientific community in the field of organisations and the natural environment.

For example, the bibliometric research of Martín-de Castro et al. (2023) analyses the evolution of the conceptualisation of the core term 'environmental strategy' in the specialised literature, identifying fifty-three definitions and forty-three keywords in 1992–2020. Thus, as argued by Martín-de Castro et al. (2023), the treatment of the concept of environmental strategy between the early 1990s and the beginning of the second decade of the 2000s can be divided into two clearly defined stages, as Figure 2.1 shows.

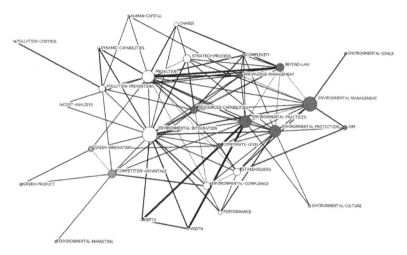

Figure 2.1 Cluster analysis of the 'environmental strategy' period, 1992–2010
Source: Reprinted from Martín-de Castro et al. (2023:14), with permission

In the first stage, from the first works on environmental strategy in 1992 until the first decade of the 2000s, the terms used to shape this concept revolved around the idea of the environmental business case and profit maximisation (Sharma, 2000). In other words, these concepts related to the search for the integration of firms' environmental issues, competitive advantages, performance, resources and capabilities; knowledge management within the company and stakeholders were the central concerns in the literature on environmental strategy. These were, therefore, concepts inherited from traditional management theory that have been used to respond to environmental issues. Thus, in this first stage, the priority was to integrate environmental concerns into the management and direction of companies to achieve greater environmental proactivity that would allow them to achieve competitive advantages, better performance or the legitimisation of stakeholders.

It is also interesting to note how in this stage, another series of terms were treated laterally or peripherally in the definitions of environmental strategy. Thus, it is striking how concepts that point more clearly to a rather environmentalist view of the problem, such as environmental innovation, environmental disclosure, environmental performance or global warming, were not considered central.

During this first stage, both kinds of terms – the central ones around which the literature on the subject revolved and the peripheral ones that played a secondary role – interacted to form compact theoretical ecosystems or clusters whose analysis shows us the theoretical currents in a more general way. Thus, during 1992–2010, three internally cohesive theoretical ecosystems, each with their own entity, were formed (Figure 2.1).

The first of these, the *environmental integration* cluster, brings together, on the one hand, the definitions of environmental strategy that seek to integrate environmental concerns into company strategy and thereby promote environmental proactivity and the subsequent generation of positive business outcomes; and, on the other, the definitions that emphasise the integration of influential stakeholder concerns into environmental strategy. While the relationship between environmental proactivity and firm performance has been analysed mainly from the perspective of resources and capabilities (Russo & Fouts, 1997), analyses of stakeholder pressure and firm environmental response have been underpinned by institutional theory (Bansal & Clelland, 2004; Delmas & Toffel, 2004).

The second theoretical ecosystem that emerged in this first stage is called the *environmental management* cluster, and the key words that comprise it revolve around the importance of environmental practices (Christmann, 2000) and the management of the resources, capabilities and knowledge (Sharma & Vredenburg, 1998) that are needed for the development of environmental strategies in a firm. This has important competitive implications and is also underpinned by resource-based theory.

Finally, the third cluster in this first stage is dominated by the concept of *competitive advantage*. This theoretical ecosystem is made up of those definitions of environmental strategy that seek to obtain competitive advantages through environmental innovations and, more specifically, those aimed at the creation and development of sustainable products. This sustainable innovation–business competitiveness binomial is rooted in the green and competitive idea formulated by Porter and Van der Linde (1995), among others.

In the second stage, covering the second decade of the 2000s, the academic literature on the subject incorporated some novel nuances, although the emphasis on the traditional business case and the relationship between environmental strategy, environmental proactivity

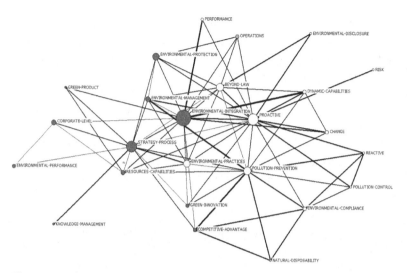

Figure 2.2 Cluster analysis of the 'environmental strategy' period, 2011–2020
Source: Reprinted from Martín-de Castro et al. (2023:15), with permission

and competitive advantage was still very much alive. However, here, and as the main novelty, the term 'green product', which in the first stage was peripheral – accompanying the concept of competitive advantage – also occupied a central place in the definition of environmental strategy.

The emergence of the concept of green product as a central construct in the definitions of environmental strategy can be interpreted as an important advance in the idea of environmental strategy, pointing, on the one hand, to environmental differentiation as a competitive strategy and, on the other, directly to the very heart of the operations function and the concepts of product stewardship, industrial ecology or circular economy.

However, such progress was very timid, as in this second stage the term 'global warming' also disappeared completely from the definitions of environmental strategy, while the concepts of green innovation or environmental performance were used in a residual manner.

During this second stage (2011–2020), the compact theoretical ecosystems or clusters that originated in the interaction of the different keywords used in the definitions of environmental strategy revolved around the constructs of environmental integration and proactivity, although they incorporated new nuances (Figure 2.2).

The *environmental integration* cluster maintains continuity with the first stage and incorporates the terms that in the first stage formed part of the *environmental management* cluster. There is, therefore, a fusion of theoretical ecosystems that gives rise to broader definitions of environmental strategy that reflect not only aspects relating to the definition of a company's environmental orientation, but also other aspects closer to the management of resources from an environmental perspective. Notably, the concept of environmental performance is also incorporated into the definitions of environmental strategy within this cluster. Although environmental performance is still a peripheral term, it is used together with the rest of the terms and seems to be, albeit cautiously, opening a path towards overcoming the exclusivity of the business case in the literature in the future.

The *proactive* cluster in this second stage brings together the terms that characterise environmentally proactive strategies aimed at improving business performance (Gilley et al., 2000; Shah & Soomro, 2021). In this cluster, concern for environmental performance is not present.

Thus, analysing both periods together, we can draw the following conclusions about the evolution of the terms that have been used to define the concept of environmental strategy since the management literature began to take an interest in the organisation and natural environment relationship.

Several terms considered central in the first stage (1992–2010) continued to be so in the second stage (2011–2020). This situation applies to the terms 'environmental integration', 'proactive', 'resources and capabilities' and 'competitive advantage', among others, corroborating the predominant influence of the business case in the conception of company environmental strategy and highlighting the arguments of researchers who have warned of the predominance and monopoly of economic-competitive objectives in company environmental positions (Alvarez et al., 2020; Barney, 2018; Ergene et al., 2021; Nyberg & Wright, 2022).

However, other terms have become less relevant over time in the definitions of environmental strategy and have come to be used in a residual or peripheral way. This is the case for the terms 'performance', 'knowledge management' and 'stakeholders'.

As far as 'performance' is concerned, its loss of relevance indicates above all that although business-as-usual logic still dominates the literature on the subject (e.g. the search for competitive advantage is still very present), the objective of business performance is not as intense, or at least not as explicit, in the definitions proposed by environmental strategy scholars.

The loss in relevance of the concept of knowledge management in definitions of environmental strategy is certainly surprising. Since the first works in the organisations and the natural environment literature analysed the environmental posture of firms from a resource-based perspective, knowledge management has been found to be a key element in environmental strategies (Hart, 1995; Russo & Fouts, 1997; Aragón-Correa & Sharma, 2003) and to play a fundamental role in the achievement of environmentally oriented resources and capabilities. However, based on the results obtained in this study, the term 'knowledge management' ceased to be central in the definitions of environmental strategy between 2011 and 2020.

This can be justified by the fact that 'knowledge management' can be understood as embedded in the term 'proactive', which increased in prominence in the second stage analysed. According to this argument, environmentally proactive companies are so because, among other things, they focus part of their knowledge on ends compatible with the generation of environmentally oriented resources and capabilities.

On the other hand, in the second decade of the 2000s, the specialised literature on organisations and the natural environment began to take into consideration concepts related to knowledge management but with a more specific nature, which ultimately had a substitution effect. Such is the case for the concepts of green intellectual capital and green social capital, which are related to environmental product innovation. In this sense, as argued by Delgado-Verde et al. (2014), the success of the environmental initiatives that a company implements depends to a large extent on the existence of fluid and cooperative relationships among its employees and key organisational members and their degree of environmental commitment, linking the NRBV and microfoundations of strategy. In the same vein, other, more recent, studies such as that by Asiaei et al. (2022) have analysed how the three components of green intellectual capital (green human capital, green structural capital and green relational capital) drive the creation of environmental resources and capabilities in and the environmental performance of a company.

Another concept that has also lost relevance in definitions of environmental strategy is stakeholders. The term 'stakeholders' played a central role in early contributions to the literature on organisations and the natural environment. From an institutional theory point of view (Delmas & Toffel, 2004), stakeholders have a central role because of the self-interested pressure they exert to implement environmental strategies (Sharma & Vredenburg, 1998). However, as the discipline has progressed, references to environmental strategies have focused more on the environmental proactivity discussed earlier than on the concept of the environmental response that was predominant in the early literature.

In addition, other terms have gradually become more widely used in definitions of environmental strategy, moving from a peripheral and residual role to become a central construct. This is the case for the green product concept, whose importance should not be ignored since, as mentioned, it can be related to growing interest in the circular economy, industrial symbiosis or more advanced developments in the concept of product stewardship. However, the importance of the green product concept can also be related to the instrumental character of environmental strategies and the proliferation of work on environmental certifications that emerged in the second decade of the 2000s. From this perspective, environmental certifications not only contribute to the improvement of business performance but also positively relate to the green image of a company, causing a differentiation effect (Martín-de Castro et al., 2016). This indicates that environmental strategies shift from initially having an internal dimension to subsequently acquiring an external dimension that allows them to gain legitimacy in the eyes of stakeholders.

There are also some peripheral terms whose use in the definitions of environmental strategy has hardly changed. This is the case for 'environmental performance', 'human capital' and 'green innovation'. Although in the first stage analysed this lack of relevance can be justified by the anecdotal role played by concerns unrelated to company performance within the field, the secondary role that these terms have continued to play in more recent times is an unmistakable sign that the management literature is moving too slowly towards a future in which environmental performance is considered an essential objective of a company's environmental strategy, implying the mobilisation of technological and human resources, in a coordinated manner, towards this end.

In this sense, the technological factor has hardly been addressed, and the technological difficulties that companies must address to implement environmentally proactive strategies do not play any role in the definition of environmental strategies. This is despite the fact that green technological distance – understood as the degree of separation between a firm's environmental knowledge and the prevailing environmental knowledge in its respective industry – is a determining element in a firm's environmental stance (Amores-Salvadó et al., 2021).

This evidence is reinforced by the fact that the concept of global warming, which was peripheral in the first stage, in the second stage does not even appear in definitions of environmental strategy, a clear sign of the distance between disciplines (in this case climate science and environmental management) and of the lack of awareness of environmental emergence that the management literature has demonstrated until very recently.

Finally, it is worth noting the appearance of emerging terms in the definitions of environmental strategy during the last period of analysis (2011–2020). These are the terms 'symbolic' and 'risk'. As mentioned in relation to the importance of 'green product', the phenomenon of certifications and the analysis of their motivations, effects and consequences have been recurrent in the specialised literature.

This proliferation has gone hand in hand with companies' extensive use of certifications and environmental information declassification programmes, to such an extent that, as the literature points out, the phenomenon of greenwashing and the widespread scepticism have been echoed by researchers on the subject (Bowen & Aragón-Correa, 2014; Ramus & Montiel, 2005; Delmas & Burbano, 2011). In some cases, they have even questioned to what extent these certifications were merely symbolic in nature. In this regard, recent studies have notably addressed whether a higher level of declassification of environmental information is correlated with better environmental performance (Aragón-Correa et al., 2016) and whether 'looking green' is economically profitable. Thus, as Amores-Salvadó et al. (2023) point out, financial markets reward companies that show a higher level of environmental communication, regardless of their environmental performance.

In parallel, and relatedly, the term 'risk' has also emerged in the literature and is undoubtedly a promising area of future research for scholars in the field. Indeed, recent studies have argued that the disclosure of environmental information reduces investors' information asymmetry and in turn corporate risk (Chang et al., 2021); hence, both the environmental risk of corporate activities and the reputational risk that firms face if they are environmentally irresponsible or engage in decoupling practices need to be taken into account in the literature (Martín-de Castro et al., 2020; Sharfman & Fernando, 2008; Truong et al., 2021).

In short, academia's response thus far has shown that the concept of environmental emergence has not permeated the arguments used by environmental scholars. Hence, a reductionist framework has predominated, with little mention of key issues related to concepts such as the strategic purpose of a company from an environmental point of view, the use of environmental innovation to address imminent environmental challenges, the broad conception of stakeholders (which even lists the natural environment as another stakeholder group to pay attention to) or the intergenerational time perspective that must be present in this context of the climate crisis. We thus devote a few lines to analysing these four aspects, which we consider essential and constitute the main limitations of extant studies on organisations and the natural environment.

2.3.3.1 Strategic Purpose

A common thread in the definitions of corporate environmental strategy since the early days of the discipline has been the absence of concepts that evoke the strategic environmental purpose of companies and the environmental values that govern their environmental positioning. As seen in the previous analysis, references to environmental values or to the microfoundations of the environmental action of individuals within a company have been virtually absent from conceptions of environmental strategy since the early 1990s. As we discuss further on, bringing analysis to the individual level can have enlightening value and explain much of the behaviour of companies and the redefinition of their profits with a purpose (Barney & Felin, 2013; Contractor et al., 2019).

Specifically, regarding a company's relationship with the natural environment, environmental values and the concerns or personal characteristics of those who make up the organisation are a key element in the implementation of environmental strategies (Montiel et al., 2020). It is significant, in this sense, to observe how the term 'global warming', which implicitly indicates the existence of an evident environmental concern, has gone from being treated in a residual manner to even disappearing from the definitions of environmental strategy among academics specialising in the field.

In addition to the absence of arguments relating to the microfoundations already noted, there is a clear lack of environmental purpose in the environmental strategy conceptions analysed earlier, as the absence of emotional aspects linked to a company's environmental stance is evident. These aspects fall under the generic concept of 'socio-emotional wealth' (Berrone et al., 2010; Sharma & Sharma, 2011) and reveal their environmental side under the emergent concept of 'eco-emotional wealth', which we propose and to which we will return later.

2.3.3.2 Innovation and Technology

The use of environmental innovation and technology to address the climate grand challenge is also absent from most of the environmental strategy definitions analysed here. Despite the important role that climate science, environmental technologies and innovation will play in the future in the development and implementation of environmental strategies, the concept of green innovation plays only a secondary role in these definitions.

In this sense, although since the early 1990s there have been very relevant and influential contributions on environmental technologies that – from a business case perspective – range from their precise definition as 'production equipment, methods and procedures, product designs, and product delivery mechanisms that conserve energy and natural resources, minimise environmental load of human activities, and protect the natural environment' (Shrivastava, 1995:185) to their classifications (Klassen & Whybark, 1999) and their applications in the operations function (Vachon & Klassen, 2006), the impact that these works have had on the design of environmental strategies has been very limited and markedly anecdotal.

This is undoubtedly an important gap, given that the environmental challenges that companies and humanity in general will face in the not too distant future will require disruptive technologies, strategies and business models (Bansal, 2019; Sharma, 2022; Montiel et al., 2021) to overcome the existing gap between climate science and management studies.

2.3.3.3 Stakeholders

As already mentioned, the concept of stakeholders has become less prominent in definitions of environmental strategy as the discipline has progressed. Thus, the pioneering academic contributions that made the concept a central construct in the environmental management literature (Sharma & Vredenburg, 1998) approached it from a perspective focused on the business case and the analysis of a company's responsiveness to the demands and pressures of its stakeholders. Subsequently, this conception of stakeholders, as drivers of environmental change in a company, gave way to another approach based on environmental proactivity in which a company plays a more active role in anticipating stakeholder demands, leaving the stakeholder concept a peripheral element in the definitions of environmental strategy.

Beyond this loss of prominence in the term, the specialised literature has a narrow conception of stakeholders that does not include the natural environment, as the current climatic context requires. This path towards a broad conception of stakeholders was put on the table by pioneering studies (Hart & Sharma, 2004), which first mentioned fringe stakeholders and even referred to 'non-human' stakeholders, such as endangered species or nature itself.

In this sense, the inclusion of the natural environment as a key stakeholder is fundamental not only from a strategic perspective (Haigh & Griffiths, 2009; Driscoll & Starik, 2004) but also from a broader perspective, whereby any visualisation of the network of stakeholders with which a company interacts must be embedded within the natural environment. As Laine (2010) suggests, this understanding of the natural environment does not depend on how a firm's stakeholders are defined, as any representation of them will be embedded within it. In short, the natural environment is not just another stakeholder or additional factor in this context (Bansal & Knox-Hayes, 2013).

2.3.3.4 Time Frame

Finally, it is important to highlight the total absence of references to the temporal scope in the definitions of environmental strategy analysed here. This lack of attention to the time factor is highly significant and reveals, as noted earlier, the lack of penetration that the concept of climate change has had among academics specialising in the business–environment relationship. In this sense, as Bansal (2019) maintains, the environmental challenge remains urgent, and it is vital to take into account the necessary interactions between social and environmental systems from a long-term perspective.

The relationship between time and the natural environment is relatively immutable in the physical world, yet this relationship is altered in corporate rhetoric, which tends to compress time through markets and financial instruments of various kinds (Bansal & Knox-Hayes, 2013). Therefore, management and the literature on organisations and the natural environment offer a distorted view of physical reality, which is, nevertheless, still out there and which, however much we try to materialise it through refined constructs, poses unavoidable limits that sooner or later organisations will have to face.

A more physically adapted conception of the time factor in organisation–environment relations allows companies to be aware of the limited nature of the resources the planet offers, to adapt their activity to the regenerative capacity of ecosystems – homeostasis – and to focus their decision-making processes on the long term, favouring intergenerational equity. In short, it allows for the reintegration and uniting of concepts that until now have been separate: humanity, nature and morality (Gladwin et al., 1995).

2.4 Concluding Remarks

In view of this analysis and having considered the stances adopted in both the world of business practice and academia in the face of the climate grand challenge, it is worth turning to Nyberg and Wright (2022). These authors argue that the traditional and majority business-as-usual logic impedes an adequate approach to frame the necessary, disruptive type of business to face current (and future) climate adversities.

From their perspective, along with the direct and explicit denial of climate change, there are other subtle forms of denial that are barely perceptible and that are mixed with the traditional and calculatedly ambiguous discourses maintained by much of industry and academia.

In this sense, and as Nyberg and Wright (2022) describe, there are three main forms of climate denial in the agendas of management research and business schools, ranging from literal denial to interpretative denial.

Literal denial implies an explicit rejection of the existence of both climate change and its anthropogenic – human-caused – nature. This has been a dominant logic in recent decades and has been promoted and funded by several gas and oil companies and associations.

In turn, *implicatory* denial practices assume the existence of climate change but deny its urgency. A great majority of management research carried out during the last three decades fits this logic, attempting to integrate environmental concerns and climate change into the dominant logic of capitalism and 'business as usual'.

Meanwhile, *interpretative* denial frames climate change as a relevant issue and a new context to consider in business strategies, threats and opportunity analyses. Resilience and sustainability logics modify business models, attempting to anticipate and prepare firms and industries for climate change-induced extreme weather events, but always emphasising Porter's well-known 'Green and Competitive' (Porter & Van der Linde, 1995) slogan by making the traditional profit-maximisation logic compatible with respect for the natural environment. At the heart of this, the 'business-as-usual' logic is maintained.

As this chapter has shown, the concept of climate denial is still very much alive and well, although it now takes much more subtle forms that with some exceptions do not involve a literal and direct negation.

On the one hand, the attitudes of companies to the grand climate challenge can be framed within what Nyberg and Wright (2022) call implicatory denial. Although it would be both unfair and untrue to say that all companies deal with the phenomenon in the same way, as far as the fossil fuel industry is concerned, implicatory denial is the norm rather than the exception. In this sense, it does not appear that the companies in this industry see an urgent need to address the issue with determination and speed. Nor do they seem to have a problem of sufficient resources to carry out disruptive measures to tackle the problem.

Rather, they simply prefer to continue exploiting their traditional businesses and gradually making improvements that are incremental at best. In light of the evidence, companies in the industry are changing their rhetoric and incorporating some innovations aimed at controlling the environmental impact of their activities; however, in essence, they maintain a logic centred on traditional business as usual. It could be said that they have chosen to apply the well-known aphorism 'change so that nothing changes'.

These companies have the technology and resources to tackle disruptive innovations, but they lack environmental purpose, long-term focus and a broad view of stakeholders beyond the dominant role played by shareholders.

In turn, academia's attitude towards the environmental grand challenge could be categorised as interpretative denial. Although the relevance of the problem seems to be commonly assumed among organisations and the natural environment academics and no one downplays its importance, the prevailing logic fits the previously mentioned slogan 'green and competitive'.

As indicated earlier, the environmental purpose or even the moral duty that companies have as key actors in society in the face of the climate grand challenge does not seem to be taken into consideration in the definitions of environmental strategy. The business case predominates, within which the ways in which companies can adapt to the environmental challenge to be more competitive have been analysed here. In general, the central aspects that are at the root of the environmental problem and that point directly to the conception of business that has predominated since the beginning of the discipline of management are not considered.

In this sense, the adaptation of businesses' activity to the regenerative capacity of the natural ecosystems on which they depend to develop their activity is an issue that has hardly been seriously addressed. Fortunately, there are some exceptions, and some recent works have taken this path (Hahn & Tampe, 2020), rethinking the current conception of business and proposing disruptive changes to reconcile business activity with the interests of the planet.

Some effective examples of the latter include Yu et al. (2023), who advocate abandoning the prevailing conception of the environment as a context in international business to embrace a new logic in which companies are embedded in the natural environment, and Hoffman and Ely (2022), who propose facilitating and accompanying the end of the fossil fuel industry through compassionate destruction and the application of triage, euthanasia and hospice measures. Triage identifies and separates environmentally unsustainable businesses, euthanasia compels corporations with businesses that are highly damaging to the planet to see their terminal condition and hospice accompanies the end of these industries.

References

Alvarez, S. A., Zander, U., Barney, J. B., and Afuah, A. (2020). Developing a theory of the firm for the 21st century. *Academy of Management Review*, 45(4): 711–716.

Amores-Salvadó, J., Cruz-González, J., Delgado-Verde, M., and González-Masip, J. (2021). Green technological distance and environmental strategies: The moderating role of green structural capital. *Journal of Intellectual Capital*, 22(5): 938–963.

Amores-Salvadó, J., Martin-de Castro, G., and Albertini, E. (2023). Walking the talk, but above all, talking the walk: Looking green for market stakeholder engagement. *Corporate Social Responsibility and Environmental Management*, 30(1): 431–442.

Aragón-Correa, J. A., Marcus, A., and Hurtado-Torres, N. (2016). The natural environmental strategies of international firms: Old controversies and new evidence on performance and disclosure. *Academy of Management Perspectives*, 30(1): 24–39.

Aragón-Correa, J. A., and Sharma, S. (2003). A contingent resource-based view of proactive corporate environmental strategy. *Academy of Management Review*, 28(1): 71–88.

Asiaei, K., Bontis, N., Alizadeh, R., and Yaghoubi, M. (2022). Green intellectual capital and environmental management accounting: Natural resource orchestration in favor of environmental performance. *Business Strategy and the Environment*, 31(1): 76–93.

Bansal, P. (2005). Evolving sustainably: A longitudinal study of corporate sustainable development. *Strategic Management Journal*, 26: 197–218.

Bansal, P. (2019). Sustainable development in an age of disruption. *Academy of Management Discoveries*, 5(1): 8–12.

Bansal, P., and Clelland, I. (2004). Talking trash: Legitimacy, impression management, and unsystematic risk in the context of the natural environment. *Academy of Management Journal*, 47(1): 93–103.

Bansal, P., and Gao, J. (2006). Building the future by looking to the past: Examining research published on organizations and environment. *Organization & Environment*, 19(4): 458–478.

Bansal, P., and Knox-Hayes, J. (2013). The time and space of materiality in organizations and the natural environment. *Organization & Environment*, 26(1): 61–82.

Bansal, P., and Roth, K. (2000). Why companies go green: A model of ecological responsiveness. *Academy of Management Journal*, 43(4): 717–736.

Barney, J. B. (1991). Firm resources and sustained competitive advantage. *Journal of Management*, 17(1): 99–120.

Barney, J. B. (2018). Why resource-based theory's model of profit appropriation must incorporate a stakeholder perspective. *Strategic Management Journal*, 39(13): 3305–3325.

Barney, J., and Felin, T. (2013). What are microfoundations? *Academy of Management Perspectives*, 27(2): 138–155.

Berchicci, L., and King, A. (2007). 11 postcards from the edge: A review of the business and environment literature. *Academy of Management Annals*, 1(1): 513–547.

Berrone, P., Cruz, C., Gomez-Mejia, L. R., and Larraza-Kintana, M. (2010). Socioemotional wealth and corporate responses to institutional pressures: Do family-controlled firms pollute less? *Administrative Science Quarterly*, 55(1): 82–113.

Bousso, R., and Nasralla, S. (2022, 12 May). BP wins shareholder support for climate strategy. *Reuters*. www.reuters.com/world/uk/bp-chief-says-uk-windfall-tax-would-not-affect-investment-plans-2022-05-12.

Bowen, F., and Aragon-Correa, J. A. (2014). Greenwashing in corporate environmentalism research and practice: The importance of what we say and do. *Organization & Environment*, 27(2): 107–112.

Chang, Y., Du, X., and Zeng, Q. (2021). Does environmental information disclosure mitigate corporate risk? Evidence from China. *Journal of Contemporary Accounting & Economics*, 17(1): 100239.

Christmann, P. (2000). Effects of 'best practices' of environmental management on cost advantage: The role of complementary assets. *Academy of Management Journal*, 43(4): 663–680.

Contractor, F., Foss, N. J., Kundu, S., and Lahiri, S. (2019). Viewing global strategy through a microfoundations lens. *Global Strategy Journal*, 9(1): 3–18.

Delgado-Garcia, J., and De la Fuente-Sabaté, J. (2010). How do CEO emotions matter? Impact of CEO affective traits on strategic and performance conformity in the Spanish banking industry. *Strategic Management Journal*, 31(5): 562–574.

Delgado-Verde, M., Amores-Salvadó, J., Martín-de Castro, G., and Navas-López, J. E. (2014). Green intellectual capital and environmental product innovation: The mediating role of green social capital. *Knowledge Management Research & Practice*, 12(3): 261–275.

Delmas, M. A., and Burbano, V. C. (2011). The drivers of greenwashing. *California Management Review*, 54(1): 64–87.

Delmas, M., and Toffel, M. W. (2004). Stakeholders and environmental management practices: An institutional framework. *Business Strategy and the Environment*, 13(4): 209–222.

Devinney, T. M. (2013). Is microfoundational thinking critical to management thought and practice? *Academy of Management Perspectives*, 27(2): 81–84.

Driscoll, C., and Starik, M. (2004). The primordial stakeholder: Advancing the conceptual consideration of stakeholder status for the natural environment. *Journal of Business Ethics*, 49(1): 55–73.

Ergene, S., Banerjee, S. B., and Hoffman, A. J. (2021). (Un)sustainability and organization studies: Towards a radical engagement. *Organization Studies*, 42(8): 1319–1335.

Etzion, D. (2007). Research on organizations and the natural environment, 1992–present: A review. *Journal of Management*, 33(4): 637–664.

Felin, T., Foss, N., Heimeriks, K., and Madsen, T. (2012). Microfoundations of routines and capabilities: Individuals, processes, and structure. *Journal of Management Studies*, 49(8): 1351–1374.

Fueyo, J. (2022). *Blues para un planeta azul: El último desafío de la civilización para evitar el abismo del cambio climático*. Barcelona: Ediciones B.

George, G., Howard-Grenville, J., Joshi, A., and Tihanyi, L. (2016). Understanding and tackling societal grand challenges through management research. *Academy of Management Journal*, 59(6): 1880–1895.

Gilley, K. M., Worrell, D. L., Davidson, W. N., III, and El–Jelly, A. (2000). Corporate environmental initiatives and anticipated firm performance: The differential effects of process-driven versus product-driven greening initiatives. *Journal of Management*, 26(6): 1199–1216.

Gladwin, T. N., Kennelly, J. J., and Krause, T. S. (1995). Shifting paradigms for sustainable development: Implications for management theory and research. *Academy of Management Review*, 20(4): 874–907.

Hahn, T., and Tampe, M. (2021). Strategies for regenerative business. *Strategic Organization*, 19(3): 456–477.

Haigh, N., and Griffiths, A. (2009). The natural environment as a primary stakeholder: The case of climate change. *Business Strategy and the Environment*, 18(6): 347–359.

Halper, E., and Gregg, A. (2023, 2 February). BP dials back climate pledge amid soaring oil profits. *The Washington Post*. www.washingtonpost.com/business/2023/02/07/bp-climate-emissions-oil-profits.

Hansen, J., Johnson, D., Lacis, A. et al. (1981). Climate impact of increasing atmospheric carbon dioxide. *Science*, 213(4511): 957–966.

Hart, S. L. (1995). A natural-resource-based view of the firm. *Academy of Management Review*, 20(4): 986–1014.

Hart, S. L., and Sharma, S. (2004). Engaging fringe stakeholders for competitive imagination. *Academy of Management Perspectives*, 18(1): 7–18.

Heimann, M. (2005). Charles David Keeling 1928–2005. *Nature*, 437(7057): 331.

Hoffman, A. J., and Ely, D. M. (2022). Time to put the fossil-fuel industry into hospice. *Stanford Social Innovation Review*, 20(4): 28–37.

IPCC. (2022). *Climate Change 2022: Mitigation of Climate Change. Contribution of Working Group III to the Sixth Assessment Report of the*

Intergovernmental Panel on Climate Change. P. R. Shukla, J. Skea, R. Slade et al. (eds.). Cambridge, UK: Cambridge University Press.

Klassen, R. D., and Whybark, D. C. (1999). The impact of environmental technologies on manufacturing performance. *Academy of Management Journal*, 42(6): 599–615.

Klein, N. (2015). *This Changes Everything: Capitalism vs. the Climate.* New York: Simon and Schuster.

Laine, M. (2010). The nature of nature as a stakeholder. *Journal of Business Ethics*, 96(Suppl. 1): 73–78.

Linder, S., and Foss, N. J. (2018). Microfoundations of organizational goals: A review and new directions for future research. *International Journal of Management Reviews*, 20(S1): S39–S62.

Looney, B. (2020, 12 February). BP sets ambition for net zero by 2050, fundamentally changing organisation to deliver. *BP Press Release.* www.bp.com/en/global/corporate/news-and-insights/press-releases/bernard-looney-announces-new-ambition-for-bp.html.

Manabe, S., and Wetherald, R. T. (1967). Thermal equilibrium of the atmosphere with a given distribution of relative humidity. *Journal of the Atmospheric Sciences*, 24(3): 241–259.

Manabe, S., and Wetherald, R. T. (1975). The effects of doubling the CO_2 concentration on the climate of a general circulation model. *Journal of Atmospheric Sciences*, 32(1): 3–15.

Martín-de Castro, G., Amores-Salvadó, J., and Díez-Vial, I. (2023). Framing the evolution of the 'environmental strategy' concept: Exploring a key construct for the environmental policy agenda. *Business Strategy and the Environment*, 32(4): 1308–1333. https://doi.org/10.1002/bse.3190.

Martín-de Castro, G., Amores-Salvadó, J., and Navas-López, J. E. (2016). Environmental management systems and firm performance: Improving firm environmental policy through stakeholder engagement. *Corporate Social Responsibility and Environmental Management*, 23(4): 243–256.

Martín-de Castro, G., Amores-Salvadó, J., Navas-López, J. E., and Balarezo-Núñez, R. M. (2020). Corporate environmental reputation: Exploring its definitional landscape. *Business Ethics: A European Review*, 29(1): 130–142.

Mercer, J. H. (1978). West Antarctic ice sheet and CO_2 greenhouse effect: A threat of disaster. *Nature*, 271(5643): 321–325.

Molina-Azorín, J. F. (2014). Microfoundations of strategic management: Toward micro–macro research in the resource-based theory. *BRQ Business Research Quarterly*, 17(2): 102–114.

Montiel, I., Cuervo-Cazurra, A., Park, J., Antolín-López, R., and Husted, B. W. (2021). Implementing the United Nations' sustainable development goals in international business. *Journal of International Business Studies*, 52(5): 999–1030.

Montiel, I., Gallo, P. J., and Antolin-Lopez, R. (2020). What on earth should managers learn about corporate sustainability? A threshold concept approach. *Journal of Business Ethics*, 162(4): 857–880.

Newbert, S. L. (2008). Value, rareness, competitive advantage, and performance: A conceptual-level empirical investigation of the resource-based view of the firm. *Strategic Management Journal*, 29(7): 745–768.

Nyberg, D., and Wright, C. (2022). Climate-proofing management research. *Academy of Management Perspectives*, 36(2): 713–728.

Porter, M., and Van der Linde, C. (1995). Green and competitive: Ending the stalemate. *Harvard Business Review*, 73(5): 120–134.

Ramus, C. A., and Montiel, I. (2005). When are corporate environmental policies a form of greenwashing? *Business and Society*, 44(4): 377–414.

Rodel, N., and Tucker, B. (2022, 28 April). We just launched a database to expose the institutions using our money to fund fossils. *Oil Change International*. https://priceofoil.org/2022/04/28/launched-public-finance-for-energy-database.

Russo, M. V., and Fouts, P. A. (1997). A resource-based perspective on corporate environmental performance and profitability. *Academy of Management Journal*, 40(3): 534–559.

Shah, N., and Soomro, B. A. (2021). Internal green integration and environmental performance: The predictive power of proactive environmental strategy, greening the supplier, and environmental collaboration with the supplier. *Business Strategy and the Environment*, 30(2): 1333–1344.

Sharfman, M. P., and Fernando, C. S. (2008). Environmental risk management and the cost of capital. *Strategic Management Journal*, 29(6): 569–592.

Sharma, P., and Sharma, S. (2011). Drivers of proactive environmental strategy in family firms. *Business Ethics Quarterly*, 21(2): 309–334.

Sharma, S. (2000). Managerial interpretations and organizational context as predictors of corporate choice of environmental strategy. *Academy of Management Journal*, 43(4): 681–697.

Sharma, S. (2022). From environmental strategy to environmental impact. *Academy of Management Discoveries*, 8(1): 1–6.

Sharma, S., and Vredenburg, H. (1998). Proactive corporate environmental strategy and the development of competitively valuable organizational capabilities. *Strategic Management Journal*, 19(8): 729–753.

Shrivastava, P. (1995). Environmental technologies and competitive advantage. *Strategic Management Journal*, 16(S1): 183–200.

Solnit, R. (2021, 23 August). Big oil coined 'carbon footprints' to blame us for their greed. Keep them on the hook. *The Guardian*. www.theguardian.com/commentisfree/2021/aug/23/big-oil-coined-carbon-footprints-to-blame-us-for-their-greed-keep-them-on-the-hook.

Tabuchi, H (2022, 14 September). Oil executives privately contradicted public statements on climate, files show. *The New York Times*. www .nytimes.com/2022/09/14/climate/oil-industry-documents-disinformation .html.

Truong, Y., Mazloomi, H., and Berrone, P. (2021). Understanding the impact of symbolic and substantive environmental actions on organizational reputation. *Industrial Marketing Management*, 92(Jan.): 307–320.

Tucker, B., DeAngelis, K., and Van der Burg, L. (2021). *Past Last Call. G20 Public Finance Institutions Are Still Bankrolling Fossil Fuels*. Washington, DC: Oil Change International and Friends of the Earth USA. https:// priceofoil.org/content/uploads/2021/10/Past-Last-Call-G20-Public-Finance-Report.pdf.

Vachon, S., and Klassen, R. D. (2006). Extending green practices across the supply chain: The impact of upstream and downstream integration. *International Journal of Operations & Production Management*, 26(7): 795–821.

Wang, L., Lin, Y., Jiang, W., Yang, H., and Zhao, H. (2023). Does CEO emotion matter? CEO affectivity and corporate social responsibility. *Strategic Management Journal*, 44(7): 1820–1835.

Watts, J. (2020, 12 February). BP's statement on reaching net zero by 2050 – what it says and what it means. *The Guardian*. www.theguardian.com/ environment/ng-interactive/2020/feb/12/bp-statement-on-reaching-net-zero-carbon-emissions-by-2050-what-it-says-and-what-it-means.

Wright, C., and Nyberg, D. (2017). An inconvenient truth: How organizations translate climate change into business as usual. *Academy of Management Journal*, 60(5): 1633–1661.

Yu, H., Bansal, P., and Arjaliès, D. L. (2023). International business is contributing to environmental crises. *Journal of International Business Studies*, 54(Aug.): 1151–1169.

3 | Business as Usual
A Review of Environmental Strategies

One can see from space how the human race has changed the Earth. Nearly all of the available land has been cleared of forest and is now used for agriculture or urban development. The polar ice caps are shrinking, and the desert areas are increasing. At night, the Earth is no longer dark, but large areas are lit up. All of this is evidence that human exploitation of the planet is reaching a critical limit. But human demands and expectations are ever increasing. We cannot continue to pollute the atmosphere, poison the ocean and exhaust the land. There isn't any more available.

Stephen Hawking

3.1 Introduction

Since the last quarter of the twentieth century, a growing concern among nations and societies for the preservation of the natural environment has emerged (Hart, 1995). At a business level, pressures come from different firm stakeholders, mainly derived not only from the increased legal and normative rules imposed by governments and public administrations, but also from the environmental pressures imposed by market agents, mainly customers, although competitors, suppliers, investors, non-governmental organisations and the media have all contributed to the greening of businesses and management (Henriques & Sadorsky, 1999). In academia, the seminal contributions of Porter and Van der Linde (1995) and Hart (1995) started a fruitful management and strategy literature debate about the inclusion of environmental postulates in a company's strategy formulation and implementation and their consequences for firm profitability and sustainability, which has very important implications and challenges for other ongoing academic and practitioner debates.

In response to this growing concern, several academic initiatives have emerged, devoted to the advancement of research and teaching in the area between organisations and the natural environment, such as the Division of Organizations and the Natural Environment (ONE-AOM) of the Academy of Management, the Group for Research on Organizations and the Natural Environment (GRONEN) or the Alliance for Research on Corporate Sustainability (ARCS).

In the management literature, and especially in the strategy tradition, a growing body of literature has emerged, mainly framed via institutional theory and the natural resource-based view (NRBV), to understand the drivers and implications of this new phenomenon, incorporating environmental concern into a firm's strategy formulation to make environmental respect and profitability compatible. Thus, from an institutional theory point of view (Bansal & Roth, 2000; Delmas & Toffel, 2008; Tashman & Rivera, 2016), many companies are facing environmental challenges and adopting corporate environmentalism postulates and compliance to gain and maintain legitimacy among their respective stakeholders and societies and thus their consequent licence to operate.

Other proposals, from the NRBV (Aragón-Correa, 1998; Hart, 1995), have explored the challenges, implications and potential economic and strategic benefits of adopting proactive environmental strategies in gaining and sustaining competitive advantages; that is, by making a firm's profitability compatible with environmental respect. These new proactive environmental behaviours imply the development of novel environmental resources and ways to develop environmental organisational capabilities and knowledge.

Focusing on corporate environmental commitment and proactivity, mainly from a strategic management point of view, during the last three decades several proposals have explored the environmental stance of firms, showing different typologies of environmental strategies, for instance Roome (1992), Hart (1995), Aragón-Correa (1998) or Henriques and Sadorsky (1999). These have shown a range of forms of strategic positioning, from reactive/compliance to proactive/ beyond compliance. Although much work has been done in this sense, a deeper understanding of environmental commitment and strategic positioning towards the environment is needed (Murillo-Luna et al., 2008; Potrich et al., 2019; Rivera & Clement, 2018), as well as proposals for more advanced environmental postures that go beyond the traditional reduction in negative environmental externalities.

For a deeper understanding of environmental strategies, in this chapter we deconstruct them by drawing on the connection between business strategy and the natural environment approaches within the well-known framework of generic strategies – reactor, defender, analyser and prospector – and their three main dimensions – engineering, administrative and entrepreneurship – proposed by Miles and Snow (1978). Originally, the term 'deconstruction' – as a type of thinking that criticises, analyses and revises words and their concepts – was used by the French philosopher Jacques Derrida. This typology has been extensively used by the literature and is the basis for one of the seminal works on environmental strategic proactivity, by Aragón-Correa (1998). In addition, due to the significance of technology and innovation in developing new proactive environmental strategies, we perform a more fine-grained analysis of the engineering and entrepreneurial dimensions by incorporating the exploitation–exploration dilemma proposed by March (1991) and Levinthal and March (1993), which reinforces the logic of the reactors, defenders, analysers and prospectors environmental strategic positioning. This approach has recently gained prominence among environmental management scholars (Demirel & Kesidou, 2019; Lin & Ho, 2016; Malen & Marcus, 2019; Orsatti et al., 2020) and emphasises the inclusion of the exploitation–exploration dilemma in any analysis of environmental strategies.

Nevertheless, governments, institutions and firms must face the grand challenge of climate emergency and natural environmental degradation (Independent Group of Scientists, 2019). As Lenon et al. (2019) have pointed out, scientific evidence for the threat of exceeding tipping points, such as climate warming, ice collapse and biosphere boundaries, indicates that we are approaching a global, interconnected cascade of tipping points, suggesting that we are in a state of planetary emergency: both the risk and the urgency of the situation are acute. The current levels of carbon dioxide (CO_2) in the atmosphere and soil as well as water pollution and degradation demand new disruptive innovations and business solutions that go beyond the traditional reduction in negative environmental externalities and are able to reduce current levels of atmospheric, soil and water pollution to create, in the new 'green capitalism', positive environmental externalities. New business models that include atmosphere decarbonisation or sea cleaning, among other initiatives, transforming pollution into the feedstock of productive activities, constitute pioneering responses to the current climate emergency.

Based on this theoretical approach and since most of the strategic positioning pertaining to the organisations and the natural environment literature has focused on the reduction in negative environmental externalities, giving prominence to a firm's profitability via a business-as-usual logic, we propose a new disruptive environmental strategy typology where the creation of positive environmental externalities plays a key role in a firm's mission and strategy. We name this the 'regenerative' strategy. In this sense, we draw on Hart's (1995) regenerative strategy not only to encompass sustainable development strategy insights, but also to incorporate a cutting-edge technological dimension into the environmental strategy portfolio that goes beyond the traditional (correction)/modern (prevention) approaches that have prevailed in the organisations and the natural environment literature.

The remainder of the chapter is organised as follows. In Section 3.2, some remarks about the most relevant environmental strategy typologies are provided. In Section 3.3, we deconstruct environmental strategies by connecting Miles and Snow's (1978) strategy typology with the environmental strategy typologies presented in the previous section and developing the relationships between environmental strategies and Levinthal and March's (1993) exploitation–exploration framework. In Section 3.4, we offer a critical review of the existing environmental strategies based on a 'business-as-usual' logic. Finally, we present our conclusions.

3.2 Environmental Strategies

How companies face environmental concerns determines their degree of proactiveness and commitment towards those concerns. As Henriques and Sadorsky (1999) state, firms' approaches to the natural environment started to be analysed and catalogued in the corporate social responsibility literature with the typologies proposed by Carroll (1979) and Wartick and Cochran (1985), who differentiated among reactive, defensive, accommodative and proactive postures.

With the emergence of the environmental management literature during the 1990s, additional typologies of environmental strategies emerged, ranging from reactive/compliance postures to proactive/ beyond compliance ones. Thus, the initial contributions pertaining to the new environmental management literature in the early 1990s (Hunt & Auster, 1990; Roome, 1992) shared common features while articulating different environmental strategy typologies, ranging from the basic dichotomy of reactive–proactive to the most sensitive five-stage typologies (Henriques & Sadorsky, 1999).

The distinction between reactive and proactive environmental positioning made by Sharma and Vredenburgh (1998) is one of the most widely disseminated. Based on eleven dimensions that can be grouped into three main themes – (1) stakeholder integration; (2) continuous higher-order learning; and (3) continuous innovation – they classify companies into reactive–proactive positions.

This clear and basic distinction between proactive and reactive postures lays the foundations for future environmental strategy typologies. Using a more demanding concept of proactivity, firms are considered environmentally proactive only if they show a consistent and general pattern across all company functions in the deployment of those environmental activities that are not required by environmental regulation and do not respond to isomorphic pressures.

To understand the heterogeneous nature of the different environmental strategy typologies and to conduct a more fine-grained analysis, subsequent research proposals developed and amplified the existing typologies. Thus, among the three-stage environmental strategy typologies, Aragón-Correa's (1998) contribution is one of the most popular. Aragón-Correa draws on Miles and Snow's (1978) generic defender, prospector and analyser strategies and Hart's (1995) environmental insights to propose a less demanding concept of environmental proactivity – in line with Hart (1995) – whose lower limit is established in the pollution prevention approach. Using a similar concept of environmental proactivity, Buysse and Verbeke (2003), via the NRBV, offer an alternative classification of environmental strategies, falling into three main categories: (1) reactive; (2) pollution prevention; and (3) environmental leadership. They apply the term 'environmental leadership' rather than Hart's 'sustainable development' because the latter includes the moral leadership dimension (Buysse and Verbeke, 2003:457). According to them, firms with a reactive strategy give high importance to government regulation – but only at the compliance level. In contrast, firms following a pollution prevention strategy create more sophisticated adaptive routines that include a learning component, although laws and regulatory pressures are the key drivers for resource allocation in various environmental management domains. Finally, companies with an environmental leadership strategy frame a firm-level creation of green competencies as a source of competitive advantage and economic and strategic opportunity, pre-empting competitors. These categories are empirically built via the following firm resources and capabilities: (1) conventional green competencies; (2) employee skills; (3) organisational competencies; (4) management systems and procedures; and (5) strategic planning processes.

The four-stage environmental strategy typologies (Hart, 1995; Henriques & Sadorsky, 1999; Murillo-Luna et al., 2008) do not cover all environmental strategic options, as five-stage models do, and differ in their scope of proactivity. In this sense, Hart (1995) devotes special attention to the development of proactive environmental strategies, showing three different stages in the proactive environmental stance (pollution prevention, product stewardship and sustainable development). In contrast, although end-of-pipe positioning is also mentioned, it does not play a key role in Hart's typology.

Henriques and Sadorsky (1999) use reactive, defensive, accommodative and a more demanding concept of environmental proactivity to test the sources of these environmental postures. Murillo-Luna et al. (2008) also identify four types of environmental response (passive response, attention to legislation response, attention to stakeholders response, and total environmental quality response), where more proactive environmental responses are characterised by high stakeholder involvement, investment in environmental research and development, environmental prevention and correction measures, environmental training and environmental responsibility allocation. Notably, both Henriques and Sadorsky's (1999) and Murillo-Luna et al.'s (2008) typologies do not use a detailed concept of environmental proactivity and do not establish different levels of environmental proactivity, as Hart's typology does.

Finally, five-stage environmental strategy typologies (Hunt & Auster, 1990; Roome, 1992) provide the most detailed and fine-grained analysis of the different strategic orientations that firms can develop to address natural environmental challenges. Thus, first, a reactive and non-compliant strategic posture can be identified, where a company is cost constrained and cannot react to changes in environmental laws. These beginners tend not to face up to environmental problems, avoiding their responsibilities. Second, a just compliance posture – for example, a reactive position towards the natural environment that is driven by commitment to the law – can be identified. As firefighters

(Hunt & Auster, 1990), environmental problems are not these firms' strategic priorities. Third is a compliance-plus strategy, which implies a proactive posture that considers a company a concerned citizen, and demonstrates top management's commitment and desire to adopt new management systems and policies towards the natural environment. More advanced environmental postures, such as commercial and environmental excellence or pragmatist and leading-edge or proactivist postures, are the most proactive and advanced environmental stances, whereby fully and actively adopting environmental management and policy entails being the leaders in the market.

Despite the outstanding and pioneering character of the multiple contributions from recent decades, much more effort is needed to gain a better understanding of environmental strategy typology (Potrich et al., 2019) and to adapt it to the current reality to go beyond the traditional (correction)/modern (prevention) dichotomy that has prevailed in the organisations and the natural environment literature debate. In this sense, it is remarkable that today we can observe pioneering companies going beyond previous environmental strategies (traditionally focused on the minimisation of negative environmental externalities) by creating positive environmental externalities instead, which we call 'regenerative strategies' and Hahn and Tampe define as 'business strategies that enhance, and drive through, the health of the socio-ecological system in a co-evolutionary process' (Hahn & Tampe, 2021:5).

Therefore, to shed light on the environmental behaviour of firms and adapt the theory to the current reality, in what follows we draw on Aragón-Correa's (1998) contribution and 'deconstruct' environmental strategy typologies using seminal works in the strategy tradition, such as Miles and Snow's (1978) generic strategy typologies, and in innovation studies, such as Levinthal and March's (1993) exploration–exploitation insights, linking in this way the strategy, environmental strategy and innovation management literature. The intellectual task of deconstructing complex environmental and social issues is necessary to discover the complex links among businesses, ethics and environmental and social issue responsiveness (Key, 1998). By deconstructing environmental strategies into their three main dimensions, we can identify their similarities, (in)consistencies and ultimate connections to environmental and social issues (Antolín-López & Montiel, 2016), contributing in this way to improving the understanding of what environmental strategies are while building bridges between strategy and environmental scholars and practitioners.

Firms adopting environmental postulates face multiple implications not only in their strategies at corporate, competitive and functional levels, but also in their structuring decisions and entrepreneurial and innovation orientations. In that sense, as Aragón-Correa (1998) indicates, the well-known typology of Miles and Snow (1978) serves as a landmark for classification purposes. Additionally, and due to the special significance of technology, innovation and entrepreneurial efforts in developing a new proactive environmental strategy, we conduct a more fine-grained analysis on the engineering dimension by incorporating the exploitation–exploration dilemma proposed by March (1991) and Levinthal and March (1993), which, as already mentioned, reinforces the logic and strategic implications of reactors', defenders', analysers' and prospectors' environmental strategic positioning.

3.3 Deconstructing Environmental Strategies

Although when Miles and Snow's contribution was first enunciated business strategy and the natural environment were two separate and distant areas, there is currently a consensus on the importance of the key role that a firm's concern for the environment plays in its business strategy. Therefore, as Aragón-Correa (1998) has posited, business and environmental strategies are interconnected. Thus, Miles and Snow's (1978) typology, one of the most popular and key conceptualisations of business strategy, is the right frame of reference for understanding how environmental strategies have been evolving since the emergence of the environmental management literature.

As Henriques and Sadorsky (1999) state, firms' approaches to the natural environment started to be analysed and catalogued in the corporate social responsibility literature with the typologies proposed by Carroll (1979) and Wartick and Cochran (1985). With the emergence of the environmental management literature during the 1990s, additional typologies of environmental strategies emerged, ranging from reactive/compliance postures to proactive/beyond compliance ones. These environmental postures show relevant parallelism with Miles and Snow's (1978) typology, and thus we dedicate Section 3.3.1 to the analysis of these common features.

3.3.1 Deconstruction Based on Miles and Snow's (1978) Strategy Tradition

Miles and Snow (1978) define four strategic types of organisations: reactors, defenders, analysers and prospectors. Each type of organisation has its own unique strategy that relates to its chosen market(s), and each has a particular configuration of technology, structure and process with regard to its market strategy. They also explain a fourth type of organisation named a reactor, which according to the authors is a 'strategic failure': there is 'no relationship between its strategy, technology, structure and process' (Miles & Snow, 1978:550).

Table 3.1 shows a deconstruction of environmental strategy typologies based on the strategy tradition of Miles and Snow (1978).

3.3.1.1 Defenders and Environmental Strategies

Defenders (Miles & Snow, 1978) search for an environment that is stable and appropriate for their organisation. Based on a literature review, we can state some of their main characteristics. They are usually large and established companies (Fiss, 2011) with a corporate strategic positioning focused on the production of only a limited and stable range of products to a narrow and secure market segment (Evans & Green, 2000; Hambric, 1981, 1982, 1983; Jennings & Seaman, 1994; McDaniel & Kolari, 1987; Rajaratman & Chonko, 1995; Snow & Hebriniak, 1980). Defenders aggressively prevent competitors from entering their domain, ignoring external developments and trends. They grow through market penetration and limited product development; in the long run, they maintain a small niche that is difficult for competitors to penetrate. At the competitive level, they mainly maintain a cost leadership advantage (Fiss, 2011), which is reached thanks to cost efficiency, their main priority at the functional level. This is attained through high ratios of capital intensity (Evans & Green, 2000; Maniora, 2018; Thomas & Ramaswamy, 1996) and low ratios of research and development (R&D) and advertising intensity (Liang et al., 2009; Maniora, 2018). Cost efficiency is also achieved by designing organisational structures characterised by high formalisation, high centralisation and high complexity (Fiss, 2011).

In the realm of environmental strategies, defenders demonstrate the adaptation of products and production processes to reduce pollution levels below legal requirements (Buysse & Verbeke, 2003). Belonging

Table 3.1 *Comparison of environmental strategies typologies according to the strategic positioning of Miles and Snow (1978)*

Author(s)	(Environmental) Strategies Typology			
	Reactor	Defender	Analyser	Prospector
Miles and Snow (1978)				
Hunt and Auster (1990)	Beginner Firefighting	Concerned citizen	Pragmatist	Proactivist
Roome (1992)	No compliance Compliance	Compliance-plus	Environmental marketing excellence	Leading edge/futurist
Hart (1995)	End-of-pipe	Pollution prevention	Product stewardship	Sustainable development
Aragón-Correa (1998)	Defender		Prospector	Entrepreneur
Sharma and Vredenburgh (1998)	Reactive		Proactive	
Henriques and Sadorsky (1999)	Reactive Defensive	Accommodative		Proactive
Buysse and Verbeke (2003)	Reactive	Pollution prevention	Environmental leaders	
Murillo-Luna et al. (2008)	Passive response Attention to legislation response	Attention to stakeholders response	Total environmental quality response	

Source: Authors' own elaboration

to this group are Hunt and Auster's (1990) concerned citizens and Roome's (1992) concerned compliance-plus firms. These are characterised by a proactive posture with regard to top management commitment and the desire to adopt new management systems and policies towards the natural environment, although the operational aspects of these policies are not fully developed. Defenders also show a strong environmental commitment in theory, coupled with a more moderated environmental approach in practice, allocating funds to environmental programmes but letting them run without thorough controls (Hunt & Auster, 1990).

Hart's (1995) and Buysse and Verbeke's (2003) pollution prevention firms can be classified as defenders as well, and the initial steps of Aragón-Correa's (1998) prospectors also fall under this category. Firms catalogued as accommodative by Henriques and Sadorsky (1999) and Murillo-Luna et al. (2008), who give the most proactive attention to legislation, can also be classified as defenders. One particular feature of firms belonging to this category is their short-term environmental business case conception, which is mostly restricted to collecting low-hanging fruit – the benefits of their environmental initiatives. They perform well via the traditional/regulated correction approach and very modestly via the voluntary/modern prevention approach (Aragón-Correa, 1998) and therefore cannot be considered proactive according to Sharma and Vredenburg's (1998) criteria. As a result, these environmental initiatives are also fairly limited in their development in terms of green organisational competencies, green employee skills and environmental issue integration (Buysse & Verbeke, 2003). This can be explained, since environmental initiatives are driven by environmental specialists who lack the necessary expertise in the business, legal and communication dimensions of environmental management (Hunt & Auster, 1990).

3.3.1.2 Prospectors and Environmental Strategies

According to Miles and Snow (1978) and based on a literature review, this type of small company (Fiss, 2011) usually searches for more dynamic environments, and its strategic positioning relies on finding and exploiting new products and market opportunities. In fact, its corporate strategy implies a broad and diversified product-market domain (Evans & Green, 2000; Jennings & Seaman, 1994; Rajaratman & Chonko, 1995; Shortell & Zajac, 1990; Snow & Hebriniak, 1980), although it does not maintain market strength in all the areas it enters. With a focus on their entrepreneurial function, prospectors are unstable with high changes in total revenues (Maniora, 2018). They are creators of change in their respective industries, value being first, and are pioneers in new products and markets (Hambrick, 1981, 1982). They show a rapid response to early opportunity signals (Jennings & Seaman, 1994; McDaniel & Kolari, 1987; Rajaratman & Chonko, 1995; Snow & Hebriniak, 1980) developing a reputation as innovators. At the competitive level, they mainly follow a differentiation strategy (Fiss, 2011) through continuous innovation, showing high ratios of R&D and marketing efforts (Evans & Green, 2000; Liang et al., 2009; Maniora, 2018; Thomas & Ramaswamy, 1996) and new product sales (Hambrick, 1983). To achieve innovation, they adopt flexible technology and administration structures, with a complex structure for pursuing innovation and creativity, low formalisation and low centralisation. The administrative challenge, then, is how to facilitate operations rather than how to control them (Fiss, 2011).

In the environmental arena, prospectors can be considered those with more proactive environmental strategies and have been catalogued as proactivist by Hunt and Auster (1990), as leading edge (Roome, 1992) and as sustainable development (Hart, 1995). Aragón-Correa's (1998) entrepreneurs also fall into this category, as do the most environmentally advanced proactive firms of Sharma and Vredenburg (1998) and Henriques and Sadorsky (1999), as well as Murillo- Luna et al.'s (2008) total environmental quality response firms. Most environmental leaders (Buysse & Verbeke, 2003) whose managers attach great importance to their stakeholders (Henriques & Sadorsky, 1999; Murillo-Luna et al., 2008) and are characterised by their high standards in green competencies and environmental reporting can also be considered prospectors.

Among firms that belong to this group, environmental management is a top priority, and their environmental actions and initiatives go beyond pure and simple competitive dynamics. Instead, environmental respect becomes a mission in itself, and such firms intensively and extensively share information with stakeholders (competitors, regulators and so on), working together to protect the natural environment (Hunt & Auster, 1990); they bring stakeholder integration, higher-order learning and continuous innovation capabilities (Sharma & Vredenburg, 1998) to their fullest extent. As creators of change, environmental prospectors perform well via any environmental approach, since they reach high environmental standards using the traditional/regulated correction approach when necessary and very high standards via the modern/voluntary prevention approach (Aragón-Correa, 1998; Murillo-Luna et al., 2008). Firms in this category also carry their environmental commitment to new markets, such as those in the developing world (Hart, 1995), where they can establish long-term positions for future competition.

3.3.1.3 Analysers and Environmental Strategies

Between the two extremes on this continuum are analysers. These are companies that try to minimise risks by maximising the opportunity for profitability. At a corporate level, they apply a balance between both previous types and try to exploit and find new market and product opportunities while simultaneously maintaining core traditional products and markets. Thus, they try to maintain a stable, limited line of products while moving quickly to follow a carefully selected set of more promising new developments in their industry (Jennings & Seaman, 1994; McDaniel & Kolari, 1987; Rajaratman & Chonko, 1995; Snow & Hebriniak, 1980). These organisations are seldom 'first in' with new products but carefully monitor the actions of their major competitors in a stable business. From an entrepreneurial perspective, they make new things only if the success of them has been previously demonstrated; they are usually 'second in', but offering a more cost-efficient product/service. At a competitive level, they pursue a dual advantage; that is, both differentiation and cost leadership competitive strategies (Fiss, 2011). In sum, they require a mix of technological and administrative flexibility and rigidity.

Under analysers can be catalogued the environmental pragmatists mentioned by Hunt and Auster (1990), as well as environmental excellence (Roome, 1992) and product stewardship firms (Hart, 1995). Aragón-Correa's (1998) most advanced prospectors and the less environmentally advanced proactive firms of Sharma and Vredenburg (1998) and Henriques and Sadorsky (1999), less environmentally advanced environmental leaders (Buysse & Verbeke, 2003) and firms that pay attention to stakeholders' responses (Murillo-Luna et al., 2008) can be considered analysers as well.

Firms that fall into this group have a particular focus on their environmental organisation and have established a solid set of systematic procedures for environmental protection (Aragón-Correa, 1998). Their environmental departments are stable and recognised, receive funding and drive environmental education and training programmes, giving way to the development of higher-order learning capabilities (Sharma & Vredenburg, 1998). Nevertheless, environmental management is not yet a top priority for them (Hunt & Auster, 1990). Since their stakeholders matter (Henriques & Sadorsky, 1999), their collaborations with external stakeholders on environmental issues are a priority regarding the development of their stakeholder integration capabilities (Sharma & Vredenburg, 1998), but are restricted to activities within the value chain of these firms' operations (Hart, 1995).

3.3.1.4 Reactors and Environmental Strategies

Following Miles and Snow (1978), reactors are characterised by a lack of strategic clarity. Their top managers may not clearly articulate their firm's strategic positioning, either at the corporate or competitive level, which implies a lack of clear and consistent product-market orientation (Hambrick, 1981, 1982; Jennings & Seaman, 1994; McDaniel & Kolari, 1987; Rajaratman & Chonko, 1995; Snow & Hebriniak, 1980), which is combined with a usually passive strategic attitude towards maintaining their established business positioning. From an entrepreneurial perspective, they do not take risks and usually take action only in those areas where they are forced to by environmental pressures. Additionally, they do not shape the formal structure and process of any strategy, maintaining their firm as it is despite any environmental changes. Consequently, they tend to have poor performance (Hambrick, 1981, 1982).

Miles and Snow's (1978) reactors' features can also be found in Hunt and Auster's (1990) beginners and firefighters and Roome's (1992) compliance and non-compliance firms. End-of-pipe firms (Hart, 1995), reactive firms (Buysse & Verbeke, 2003; Sharma & Vredenburg, 1998), reactive and defensive firms (Henriques & Sadorsky, 1999), Murillo-Luna et al.'s (2008) passive response firms and those giving less proactive attention to legislation can also be classified as reactors. Firms that fall into this category strongly believe that there is a clear trade-off between environmental protection and competitiveness (Hunt & Auster, 1990) and will not allocate resources to environmental management unless they are forced to do so by regulators. In this case, environmental reactors prefer to rely on expensive end-of-pipe devices instead of investing in the creation of new environmental capabilities. At best, then, firms in this category will show good performance using the traditional/regulated correction approach (Aragón-Correa, 1998). Moreover, apart from the media, these firms do not value any input from stakeholders (Henriques & Dadorsky, 1999). However, they attach great importance to environmental regulation (Buysse & Verbeke, 2003), as regulation represents the maximum threshold for their environmental efforts.

Continuing with this in-depth analysis of environmental strategies with regard to Miles and Snow's (1978) typology, following Aragón-Correa (1998), we add to the analysis three focal dimensions: (1) the engineering dimension, which refers to the technology a firm uses in producing its products, associated with the level of its innovation and R&D efforts; (2) the entrepreneurial dimension, distinguishing companies developing in the same core business from companies constantly involved in new business areas and ventures; and (3) the administrative dimension, focusing on how to organise a company to support its strategy. We therefore essentially separate organic (flexible, low formalisation, low centralisation) from mechanic (rigid, high formalisation and centralisation) firms, following Fiss (2011). Since Miles and Snow's typology includes the analyser as a mix between defender and prospector, we have split each dimension into three possible values (low, medium and high levels for the engineering and entrepreneurial dimensions; mechanic, mix and organic for the administrative dimension).

Thus, as Figure 3.1 shows, defenders are stable (only changing from year to year) in the different aspects related to the entrepreneurial (competitive age, attitude towards growth, market definition, environmental monitoring, product mix, etc.) and engineering (technological perspective, specificity of production employees' skills, philosophy towards production) dimensions (Smith et al., 1986, 1989). In turn, prospectors are top performers in the engineering, entrepreneurial and administrative dimensions, with high levels of internal R&D, willingness to enter new businesses and organic structures. Analysers fill the intermediate positions between defenders and prospectors, relying on the most stable defender structures and business conceptions to gain sufficient momentum to advance to more dynamic and flexible approaches in terms of the entrepreneurial, engineering and administrative dimensions. Finally, reactors are characterised by low levels of R&D, permanent ties to the same businesses and mechanical organisational structures.

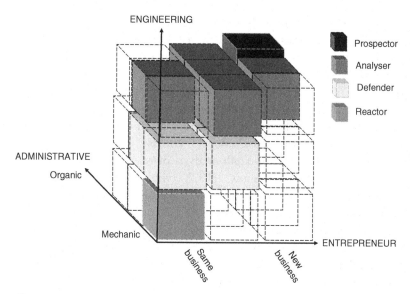

Figure 3.1 Deconstructing environmental strategies, based on Miles and Snow's (1978) typology
Source: Authors' own elaboration

3.3.2 Exploration–Exploitation Balance and Environmental Strategies

Certainly, if we assume that corporate environmentalism is one of the main currents and future challenges for academics, practitioners and policy-makers, we can frame companies developing environmental strategies as complex adaptive processes, where the significance of the engineering and entrepreneurial dimensions of Miles and Snow's typology in determining and understanding the inherent complexity of environmental strategies is crucial. In this vein, as March (1991:71) states, 'a central concern of studies of adaptive processes is the relation between the exploration of new possibilities and the exploitation of old certainties'.

In that sense, and to go a step beyond it in deconstructing processes through the engineering and entrepreneurial dimensions just presented, we incorporate the seminal works of March (1991) and Levinthal and March (1993) on the exploitation and exploration of organisational learning and innovation strategies. These works help extend our understanding and, as a new framing for environmental strategy typology, highlight the innovation efforts and entrepreneurial orientations among companies engaged in proactive corporate environmentalism (Hart, 1995). As March (1991) has stated, determining the balance and relation between the exploration of new possibilities and the exploitation of old certainties is a key issue in any firm's adaptive process. In that sense, companies, through their environmental strategic positioning, make choices between these due to the implications for variability, timing and risk.

3.3.2.1 Exploitation and Environmental Strategies

Originally, exploitation 'include[d] things [such] as refinement, choice, production, efficiency, selection, implementation, and execution' (March, 1991:71). Thus, refinement and/or repetition imply the modification and improvement of existing products and processes (Bierly et al., 2009; Jansen et al., 2006; Piao, 2014; Zi-Lin & Poh-Kam, 2004), maximising the contribution of organisational production capabilities – product exploitation – and encouraging market attendance frequency – market exploitation (Voss et al., 2008). Many empirical works have operationalised exploitation as patent citation (Cirilo et al., 2014; Russo & Vurro, 2010). Other works have divided it into internal exploitation, such as past efforts in product sales or resource utilisation, and external exploitation, such as alliances coded as manufacturing, licensing or supply chain or market utilisation (Conelly et al., 2018; Hoang & Rothaermel, 2010).

In the context of environmental strategies, exploitation fits Hart's (1995) pollution prevention strategic positioning, going beyond end-of-pipe solutions and just compliance (Roome, 1992) or focusing on legislation (Murillo-Luna et al., 2008). However, showing such reactive behaviour towards the natural environment (Buysee & Verbeke, 2003; Sharma & Vredenburgh, 1998) creates a defensive posture (Henriques & Sadorsky, 1999) in the market. In this case, a firm tries to reduce its negative impact on the natural environment through product and market exploitation, developing innovations on the basis of its existing knowledge trajectories.

3.3.2.2 Exploration and Environmental Strategies

Exploration 'includes things captured by terms such as search, variation, risk taking, experimentation, play, flexibility, discovery, [and] innovation' (March, 1991:71). Thus, any product that a firm has not previously released a prior version of (Stettner & Lavie, 2014), new product designs or the newness of projects developed by a firm (McGrath, 2001) show exploration. Exploration can be internal – for instance the proportion of previously unused citations (Russo & Vurro, 2010), past efforts in R&D (Hoang & Rothaermel, 2010) or the creation of revolutionary new conceptual approaches and boundaries (Voss et al., 2008) – or external – for example R&D strategic alliances (Piao, 2014) focused on discovering and developing new products (Conelly et al., 2018) or efforts to attract new audiences or find audiences in new markets (Jansen et al., 2006). In fact, exploration implies the introduction of a new generation of products, extending product range, opening up new markets and entering new technology fields (He & Wong, 2004); that is, experimenting with new products and services in local markets.

In terms of environmental strategic positioning, exploration implies the most radical and futurist (Roome, 1992) environmental postures, revealing the highest degree of environmental proactivity taken by firms (Henriques & Sadorsky, 1999; Sharma & Vredenburgh, 1998). Companies developing exploration thus assume the highest risks and longest-term returns by developing totally new green products and processes for new green markets, where external stakeholders' engagement plays a key role in these radical innovations, as Hart (1995) has described in his sustainable development strategy.

3.3.2.3 Exploitation: Exploration Balance and Environmental Strategies

As March (1991) has highlighted, both exploitation and exploration are important for firm adaptation, but they both compete for scarce resources, and managers should therefore find an appropriate balance between them for two main reasons: (1) if companies rely only on exploration strategies, they will surely suffer experimentation-associated costs without obtaining any benefits; (2) if companies rely solely on exploitation paths, they will probably be trapped in a suboptimal stable equilibrium.

Regarding organisational learning (Levinthal & March, 1993), the balance between exploitation, the refinement of an existing technology, and exploration, the invention of a new one (i.e. ambidexterity) is the central problem. Thus, exploratory behaviour correlates significantly with risk behaviour, while exploitative behaviour correlates

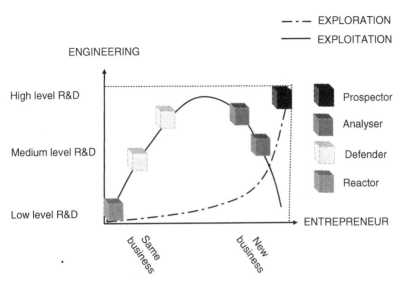

Figure 3.2 Deconstructing engineering and entrepreneurial environmental strategy dimensions via exploration and exploration balance
Source: Authors' own elaboration

with individual productivity (Mom et al., 2019). Exploratory innovation pursues radical innovations to serve emerging customers' needs or markets, whereas exploitative innovation pursues incremental improvements to meet the needs of existing consumers (Mom et al., 2019).

As Figure 3.2 shows, we can develop a better understanding of environmental strategies by focusing on exploitative, explorative or ambidexterity purposes. In this way, exploitation, understood as innovation that improves existing product quality, and production flexibility, reductions in operational costs and material consumption (He & Wong, 2004), encompass, for example, pollution prevention environmental strategies (Hart, 1995) and the well-known phenomenon of 'low-hanging fruit' (Hart, 1995; Judge & Douglas, 1998). In turn, exploration implies searching for new ideas, markets and relations that entail less certain outputs, longer time horizons and a greater degree of causal ambiguity between actions and expected results. Thus, exploration returns are less certain and more remote over time than exploitation returns (March, 1991). Hence, exploration encompasses highly proactive environmental strategic postures, such as Hart's (1995) sustainable development. Finally, ambidexterity or the exploitation–exploration balance fits Hart's (1995) product stewardship strategic posture, showing a more pragmatic environmental posture (Hunt & Auster, 1990) by pursuing environmental excellence (Roome, 1992) and a total quality environmental response (Murillo-Luna et al., 2008).

3.4 From Business as Usual to the Regenerative Strategy

As previously discussed, the traditional literature on organisations and the natural environment has focused on the reduction in negative environmental externalities via a business-as-usual logic (Nyberg & Wright, 2022), entailing a lack of exploration of the most proactive strategies that imply the creation of positive environmental externalities. As the United Nations (Independent Group of Scientists, 2019) has stated, a larger picture of climate change and pollution implies not only a reduction in current emissions into water, land or air. It implies regenerative postures for reducing the existing pollution on Earth. This is the real challenge for businesses and citizens.

In this way, as evidenced by Hepburn et al. (2019), carbon capture and utilisation (CCU) technologies offer new insights into the technical viability and economic possibilities of real, quick, scalable and generalised novel business models following a regenerative strategy. In this work, published in *Nature*, these authors, based on more than 11,000 published works, propose up to ten new applications of CO_2 directly captured from the atmosphere or industrial activities, ranging from CO_2-based chemical products to CO_2-based fuels, or concrete building materials, including land CO_2 sequestration.

Thus, as Table 3.1 shows, we propose a new environmental strategy typology where the creation of positive environmental externalities plays a key role in what we call the 'regenerative' strategy. Focused on environmental concerns, its roots can be found in Hart's (1995) sustainable development strategic positioning. Specifically, for a better understanding of environmental strategies, we have connected these to seminal works, Miles and Snow's (1978) four strategic positions/three strategic dimensions and Levinthal and March's (1993) exploitation and exploration strategies.

Hence, as the three dimensions of Figure 3.3 show, (1) pollution control fits with reactors with no or a minimum level of exploitation and exploration innovation efforts and a rigid organisational

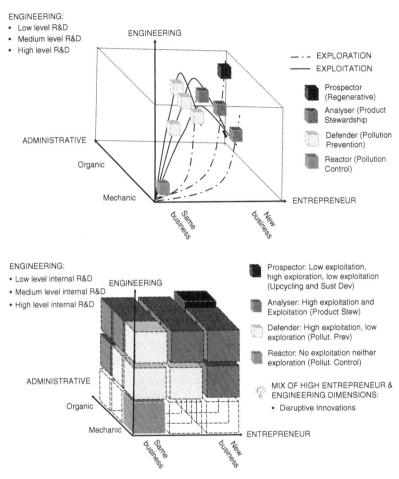

Figure 3.3(a, b) Environmental strategy typology, based on Miles and Snow's (1978) strategic dimensions and Levinthal and March's (1993) exploration–exploitation dilemma
Source: Authors' own elaboration

structure, acting in their traditional business; (2) pollution prevention fits with defenders with medium to high levels of exploitation and a mechanical structure, acting in their traditional business domains; (3) regenerative, as the most proactive positioning, fits with prospectors, characterised by high levels of exploration and a flexible and organic structure, constantly developing new ventures; and finally (4) product stewardship fits with analysers, understood as a mix of defender–prospector with balanced levels of exploitation and exploration and a structure that combines operational efficiency with flexibility, as well as a medium level of entrepreneurship.

Accordingly, as our proposal shows in Figure 3.3 and based on our previous reasoning, we propose the environmental strategy typology discussed in Sections 3.4.1–3.4.4.

3.4.1 Pollution Control Strategy

As a reactive environmental strategy, the aim of the pollution control strategy is law and stakeholder pressure compliance, usually via buying pollution control technology (as filters) and not changing products or production systems. Thus, the company pursues the aim of pollution reduction but adds pollution control costs to its cost structure without any benefits beyond those derived from environmental compliance. Then, this company gradually reduces its market position and competitiveness. According to institutional theory, the main aim of such a company is to maintain a certain legitimacy licence to operate and avoid the associated cost of environmental fines and penalties and stakeholders' monitoring.

This strategy fits the reactor typology proposed by Miles and Snow (1978), whereby a company simply catches up with the market as things change over time. As it lacks an environmental strategic vision and stable environmental strategy, it reacts only to ad hoc market and law changes. This reactive posture is the path of many large companies that lose market share over time. It is highly responsible for short-term environmental demands (Desarbo et al., 2005).

Following Levinthal and March (1993), pollution control positioning implies that a company does not pursue exploitation or exploration paths, or does so at a very low degree, which continually reduces competitiveness over time as markets and changes develop. Instead, it mainly and simply buys pollution control technology, achieving, in the best of circumstances, competitive parity by trying to match short-term results, with clear signals of learning failures, both exploitative and explorative.

Traditionally, large companies in the oil and gas industry such as ExxonMobil have followed this description. Its core business – energy and chemical products – as well as its organisational structure in four main divisions (upstream, downstream, chemical and natural gas) have remained quite stable over the past 135 years. From the 1980s to the mid-2000s, the company was a leader in climate change denial, opposing regulations to reduce climate change and funding organisations against the Kyoto Protocol. In fact, Farrell (2016) has highlighted the key role played by ExxonMobil – as a corporate benefactor – in the production and diffusion of disinformation on climate change. In the same vein, Supran et al. (2023), in a recent paper published in *Science*, highlight that although ExxonMobil's internal documents acknowledge that climate change is real and human caused, most of its public communications have promoted doubts on the matter. ExxonMobil is thus a clear example of Nyberg and Wright's (2022) literal denial. The company does not publicly acknowledge the existence of climate change, much less its anthropogenic nature.

As a reactor, then, this company fails to have a clear environmental vision and strategy, and has garnered several environmental fines and penalties, such as its recent payment of $2.5 million for pollution at Gulf Coast plants. In addition, as a pollution controller, among its end-of-pipe initiatives, it spent $300 million to install gas recovery and several monitoring devices and forms of pollution control technology at its petrochemical plants in Louisiana and Texas in response to normative and stakeholder pressures. In line with many other large actors in the energy sector, it has demonstrated a continued loss in competitiveness; regarding its main performance indicators during 2013–2017, its net income of $32.53 billion fell to $14.34 billion, its return on equity from 17.59 to 7.24 per cent, and its share value from $92.10 to $69.4.

Indeed, in the recent work of Supran et al. (2023) published in *Science*, a review of internal company reports by ExxonMobil's scientists on climate modelling projections between 1977 and 2003, they conclude that since the 1970s the company has been aware that its fossil fuel products could lead to global warming, with 'dramatic environmental effects before the year 2050' (Supran et al., 2023:1). Furthermore, their research extends similar projections and conclusions to other relevant organisations and companies, such as the largest trade association of oil and gas firms in the United States since the 1950s, the coal industry in the 1960s, energy companies such as Total Oil, and motor companies such as General Motors or Ford since at least the 1970s.

3.4.2 Pollution Prevention Strategy

As an environmental strategy going beyond compliance with the law that implies changes in a company's operational systems to reduce its negative environmental impact, this strategic positioning can be called a proactive strategy. Reductions in the materials and energy used and/or their change into less polluting ones, such as changes in a production system to reduce pollution, are common pollution prevention practices. As a result, 'low-hanging fruit' like reductions in cost structures as well as improvements in business efficiency, such as the prevention of potential penalties or the improvement of reputation and legitimacy in environmental affairs, reinforce this business model and competitiveness from the market side, but maintain a core business strategy of exploitation, reinforcing the current competitive position. As changes in production systems are needed, explicit team management support, internal communication and employee training in total environmental quality management are necessary.

Pollution prevention fits the defender typology (Miles & Snow, 1978): such a firm is satisfied with its current position in the market, and thus its innovation efforts are focused on modest improvements to retain its competitiveness, through manufacturing improvements, cost savings and so on, instead of developing new products for the market. It is engineering oriented, aims to maintain a secure niche in relatively stable market segments, and avoids looking outside its market, with a limited range of products and a high level of marketing capabilities and operational efficiency (Desarbo et al., 2005).

Following Levinthal and March (1993), pollution prevention focuses on exploitation as the main way of learning, an attempt to passively reap the rewards of what the company has already created, which allows production cost reduction as well as an increase in production efficiency while reducing environmental impact. As an experience-based organisational learning path, there are, however, some problems of myopia, such as (1) the tendency to ignore the long term; (2) the tendency to ignore the bigger picture; and (3) the tendency to overlook failures, with the consequent problems of adaptive intelligence.

Car manufacturer Volkswagen's environmental approach fits this description. After the Dieselgate scandal, the company began promoting its 'clean' diesel engines and one of its board members, Jürgen Stackmann, even declared that diesel engines 'will remain an important technology for years to come' (Kotassová, 2019). Volkswagen's attitude to this specific issue represented a clear example of Nyberg and Wright's (2022) implicatory denial. According to the multinational German carmaker, the existence of climate change is assumed, but it is not urgent.

3.4.3 Product Stewardship Strategy

Product stewardship is an advanced proactive environmental posture. It implies that a firm analyses and adopts all possible negative environmental impacts derived from its inputs, production system, product and product delivery process and utilisation by its end customers. In this way, environmental proactiveness starts with product and process eco-design, including all the stages in a product's life cycle, extending it to the value chain and its suppliers, distributors and end consumers. Following the postulates of the circular economy, the company aims to minimise the environmental impact of its products through its whole value chain. Its effective implementation therefore requires deep collaboration and engagement with external stakeholders.

Product stewardship could fit with an analyser (Miles & Snow, 1978), which in many cases is a blend of a prospector and defender. These tend to be among the largest companies, with the ability and capacity to develop new technologies and products, as well as to defend the market position of those they have already created. They are often market leaders with the innovation behaviour of a follower, building on others' innovations and developing new products. Usually they are not the first to create something new, but they may instead improve on the creation of another firm. They thus tend to prefer a 'second-but-better' strategy (Desarbo et al., 2005).

Following Levinthal and March's (1993) typology, a company pursuing a product stewardship positioning develops both exploitation and exploration learning paths equally to a medium-high degree. Its large scale allows it to innovate via new ventures with new radical products, often initially developed by other companies, to improve them and refine its technology, while improving its production systems and current products based on these wider and deeper knowledge domains and proven experiences and successes.

Tesla and its electric cars are a good example of an analyser, according to Miles and Snow's (1978) typology. Electric mobility had already been invented (Wakefield, 1994), but Elon Musk's company became a high environmental performer in the entrepreneurial and engineering dimensions and has been constantly involved in new ventures, putting into the spotlight innovative, radical products and relevant technological advances – second, but best. Additionally, to frame 'sustainable transportation', as its chief executive officer (CEO) declares, as a green product stewardship strategy is in development that includes the whole product life cycle, such as energy generation and storage. In this way, Tesla's declared future is a bet on clean technologies (Hart, 1997) and includes clean solar energy captured by a car and new durable and recyclable power batteries and car elements, among others. Thus, minimising CO_2 to reach zero emissions informs its concept of sustainable transportation.

Accordingly, Tesla is also a good example of Nyberg and Wright's (2022) interpretative denial, which frames climate change as a relevant issue and a new context to consider in business strategy via Porter's well-known slogan 'Green and Competitive' and business-as-usual logic.

3.4.4 Regenerative Strategy

Whereas the previous environmental strategies – from the more reactive postures to the more proactive ones – share the common aim of controlling (pollution control) and reducing (pollution prevention), to the minimum (product stewardship), a company's negative environmental impacts (or negative environmental externalities), the regenerative strategy goes a step further and maintains the environmental and social aim to create positive environmental impacts; that is, positive environmental and social externalities. These new business models are developed using disruptive technologies, creating completely novel products and production systems and, subsequently, new markets. Taking into account social issues and the corporate aim of creating positive social externalities, the regenerative strategy therefore draws on Hart's (1995) 'sustainable development' insights but incorporates a new, up-to-date technological point of view, which goes beyond sustainable development and 'green chemistry' and is characterised by 'the design of chemical products and processes that eliminate or reduce the use and generation of hazardous substances' (Glavic & Lukman, 2007:1880), whose main aim has been limited to reducing environmental impact.

Following Miles and Snow's (1978) typology, the regenerative posture fits the prospector type; usually such a company is the first in the market, stressing innovation and flexibility to quickly respond to changing and emergent market conditions. These firms are technologically innovative and seek new markets, being able to develop new technologies, products and markets rapidly, which requires strong R&D and solid market research (Desarbo et al., 2005). Framed by Levinthal and March's (1993) logic of organisational learning, a regenerative strategy perfectly fits exploration, where a company pursues new knowledge of things that might come to be known. To sustain exploration, the assignment of property rights – as patents – should be clearly stated, as well as the preference for risk-taking and avoiding rapid acculturation (no excessive socialisation).

Thus, companies developing regenerative environmental strategies can create positive environmental externalities in their daily business activities. Taking Nyberg and Wright's (2022) approach as a reference, regenerative businesses are not only 'green and competitive', but also maintain stakeholder embeddedness as both a top priority and an urgent necessity for addressing the climate emergency.

Hence, in the context of urgency and atmospheric decarbonisation, carbon capture technologies play a key role. As previously advanced, recent scientific and technological advances in CCU (Hepburn et al., 2019; MacDowell et al., 2017) have very promising economic and business applications, such as CO_2-based chemical products, including polymers, CO_2-based fuels, microalgae fuels and other products, concrete building materials, CO_2-enhanced oil recovery, bioenergy, enhanced weathering, forestry techniques, and land management via soil carbon sequestration techniques.

Enhancing oil recovery using CO_2 represents a significant regenerative strategy (Hepburn et al., 2019). Currently, liquid fuels, such as gasoline and diesel, are made by refining hydrocarbons drilled underground. However, these can be made with carbon from the atmosphere. Although traditionally carbon has been used to maximise the amount of oil recovered, currently representing over 5 per cent of the total US crude oil production, carbon-neutral liquid fuels are the largest potential market for CO_2. Carbon Engineering is a pioneering company in capturing CO_2 from the air. Its Canadian plant with its Direct Air Capture technology has been successfully operating for ten years. The company is working to build industrial-scale Direct Air

Capture facilities that will capture one million tons of carbon dioxide per year, the equivalent to the work of forty million trees capturing the average CO_2 emissions of 250,000 cars. As its former CEO Steve Oldham has declared, electric cars (with a price over \$40,000 per vehicle) can be a solution to climate change in developed countries, but they are not an option for most of the Earth's population. This is particularly true at the base of the pyramid (Hart, 1995) where most environmental and social challenges concentrate; that is, the 'countries of the South', as Oldham calls them. Instead of enhancing oil recovery, using CO_2 is a plausible solution that can be implemented at a planetary scale, is cheaper and is able to create positive environmental externalities through atmospheric decarbonisation in a virtuous cycle that ultimately produces synthetic fuels through Carbon Engineering's AIR TO FUELS technology. These have life-cycle carbon intensities lower than 30 gCO_2e/MJ (whereas typical fossil fuels are 95 gCO_2e/MJ). Direct Air Capture and AIR TO FUELS technologies can thus potentially achieve significant advances in decarbonisation by producing clean transportation synthetic fuels that have little or no carbon footprint on a large scale and by reusing current infrastructure and engines, which could ensure their direct implementation worldwide.

In other industries that are harder to decarbonise (Hepburn et al., 2019), such as construction, CO_2-based solutions can also be implemented. In the case of concrete building materials (Skocek et al., 2020), the key ingredient, cement, requires the use of lime, which is currently produced via the calcination of limestone in an emission-intensive process. In fact, concrete activity is the second most polluting industry in terms of CO_2 and is responsible for 7 per cent of CO_2 global emissions. Nevertheless, CO_2 – from the atmosphere or from the use of recycled concrete – can be transformed through a process of mineralisation in limestone and can then be utilised and sequestered over the long term in a concrete building. The case of Blue Planet illustrates this new regenerative business opportunity. It captures CO_2 from the atmosphere and converts it into limestone as the feedstock of concrete, asphalt and road base. This is a cheaper and more effective solution. Each tonne of limestone contains 440 kg of CO_2 that is sequestered, and each cubic metre of concrete can sequester a tonne of CO_2. This technology was applied in 2016 in Interim Boarding Area B of San Francisco International Airport.

Regarding other regenerative strategies related to soil and water habitat cleaning and restoration, the Spanish fashion company Ecoalf is relevant. This company is devoted to preserving the oceans by removing marine debris and trash from the bottom of them. Taking a step beyond recycling, Ecoalf applies cutting-edge technologies to transform marine debris into polymers and then synthetic fabrics to produce garments, in this way helping in the cleaning and restoration of the Mediterranean and portions of its habitats and biodiversity, such as the recovery of the endangered population of loggerhead turtles. With its Upcycling the Oceans programme, together with a zero emissions commitment and ecosystem embeddedness, the company has collaborated with more than 3,000 fishermen in fifty-one seaports and has removed from the Mediterranean more than 500 tonnes of plastic and fishing nets, transforming them into polymers and then fashionable clothes. As one of the first companies in this emergent regenerative market, Ecoalf is constantly pursuing new knowledge, paving the way for the next generation of sustainable businesses.

3.5 Concluding Remarks

The current general agreement on environmental strategic positioning typology, extending from reactive to more proactive postures, coexists with the emergence of different proposals for various typologies and labels for environmental strategies (Murillo-Luna et al., 2008).

As Key (1998) and Antolín-López and Montiel (2016) highlight, deconstruction is needed to obtain a deeper understanding of complex ethics and social and environmental issues, such as environmental strategies. Thus, we have developed a better understanding of environmental strategies, such as pollution prevention, pollution control and product stewardship, through a two-stage deconstruction. First, we deconstruct environmental strategies using the seminal work of Miles and Snow (1978) into their three main dimensions – engineering, administrative and entrepreneurial. Second, to reveal the complex links among strategy, innovation and cutting-edge, existing environmental technology (Hepburn et al., 2019), we have gone a step further, deconstructing the engineering and entrepreneurship environmental strategies' dimensions into exploitation, exploration and their balance, following the seminal work of Levinthal and March (1993) on innovation.

Accordingly, as previously remarked, pollution control can be catalogued as a reactor and non-innovative strategy. Pollution prevention fits the defender strategy and exploitation paths. Product stewardship fits the analyser and ambidexterity or exploitation–exploration balance postures. Whereas the initial environmental strategies shared the common aim of controlling (pollution control) and reducing (pollution prevention), to the minimum (product stewardship), a company's negative environmental impacts (or negative environmental externalities), our newly proposed environmental strategy typology, regenerative strategy, goes a step further and states that its environmental aim is to create positive environmental impacts – that is, the positive environmental externalities that are absolutely necessary to avoid imminent climate disaster (Lenton et al., 2019) – and ensures the preservation or enhancement of the health of systemic socioecological resilience in a coevolutionary process.

A regenerative strategy not only encompasses sustainable development strategy insights (Hart, 1995), but also incorporates a cutting-edge technological dimension in the environmental strategy portfolio that goes beyond the traditional (correction)/modern (prevention) approaches that have prevailed in the organisations and the natural environment literature. Thus, we propose a new 'regenerative' environmental strategy, whereby new business models are developed using cutting-edge technologies, such as CCU (Hepburn et al., 2019), which we have exemplified with three companies that are able to create positive environmental externalities in their daily business activities. In this way, the regenerative strategy fits the prospector strategy (Miles & Snow, 1978) and, mainly, the exploration pathway (Levinthal & March, 1993).

Today more than ever, the environmental science and management fields should face, together, the grand challenges of climate emergency, decarbonisation and environmental respect. As Mac Dowell et al. (2017) and Hepburn et al. (2019) highlight, like only a few other times in history, today cutting-edge technologies, such as CCU, are allowing, from both economic and technological points of view, the development of new business initiatives in many different industries, such as chemistry, food and beverages, fuels, construction and civil engineering, with real scalability and feasible planetary implementation. Management scholars and practitioners therefore have a unique opportunity to explore new sustainable business models that are capable of creating both profitability and positive environmental externalities in their daily productive activities, as the regenerative strategy demonstrates.

References

Antolín-López, D. C., and Montiel, I. (2016). Deconstructing corporate sustainability: A comparison of different stakeholder metrics. *Journal of Cleaner Production*, 136: 5–17.

Aragón-Correa, J. A. (1998). Strategic proactivity and firm approach to the natural environment. *Academy of Management Journal*, 41(5): 556–567.

Bansal, P., and Roth, K. (2000). Why companies go green: A model of ecological responsiveness. *Academy of Management Journal*, 43(4): 717–736.

Bierly, P. E., III, Damanpour, F., and Santoro, M. D. (2009). The application of external knowledge: Organizational conditions for exploration and exploitation. *Journal of Management Studies*, 46(3): 481–509.

Buysse, K., and Verbeke, A. (2003). Proactive environmental strategies: A stakeholder management perspective. *Strategic Management Journal*, 24(5): 453–470.

Carrol, A. B. (1979). A three-dimensional conceptual model of corporate social performance. *Academy of Management Review*, 4(4): 497–505.

Cirillo, B., Brusoni, S., and Valentini, G. (2014). The rejuvenation of inventors through corporate spinouts. *Organization Science*, 25(6): 1764–1784.

Conelly, B. L., Shi, W., Hoskisson, R. E., and Koka, B. R. (2018). Shareholder influence of joint venture exploration. *Journal of Management*, 45(8): 3178–3203.

Delmas, M. A., and Toffel, M. W. (2008). Organizational responses to environmental demands: Opening the black box. *Strategic Management Journal*, 29(10): 1027–1055.

Demirel, P., and Kesidou, E. (2019). Sustainability-oriented capabilities for eco-innovation: Meeting the regulatory, technology, and market demands. *Business Strategy and the Environment*, 28(5): 847–857.

DeSarbo, W. S., Di Benedetto, C. A., Song, M., and Sinha, I. (2005). Revisiting the Miles and Snow strategic framework: Uncovering interrelationships between strategic types, capabilities, environmental uncertainty, and firm performance. *Strategic Management Journal*, 26(1): 47–74.

Evans, J. D., and Green, C. L. (2000). Marketing strategy, constituent influence, and resource allocation: An application of the Miles and Snow typology to closely held firms in Chapter 11 bankruptcy. *Journal of Business Research*, 50(2): 225–231.

Farrell, J. (2016). Network structure and influence of the climate change counter-mover. *Nature Climate Change*, 6: 370–374.

Fiss, P. (2011). Building better causal theories: A fuzzy set approach to typologies in organization research. *Academy of Management Journal*, 54(2): 393–420.

Glavic, P., and Lukman, R. (2007). Review of sustainability terms and their definitions. *Journal of Cleaner Production*, 15(18): 1875–1885.

Hahn, T., and Tampe, M. (2021). Strategies for regenerative business. *Strategic Organization*, 19(3): 456–477.

Hambrick, D. C. (1981). Strategic awareness within top management teams. *Strategic Management Journal*, 2(3): 263–279.

Hambrick, D. C. (1982). Environmental scanning and organizational strategy. *Strategic Management Journal*, 3(2): 159–174.

Hambrick, D. C. (1983). Some tests of the effectiveness and functional attributes of Miles and Snow's strategic types. *Academy of Management Journal*, 26(1): 5–26.

Hart, S. (1995). A natural resource-based view of the firm. *Academy of Management Review*, 20(4): 986–1014.

Hart, S. (1997). Beyond greening: Strategies for a sustainable world. *Harvard Business Review*, 75: 66–76.

He, Z.-L., and Wong, P.-K. (2004). Exploration vs. exploitation: An empirical test of the ambidexterity hypothesis. *Organization Science*, 15(4): 481–494.

Henriques, I., and Sadorsky, P. (1999). The relationships between environmental commitment and managerial perceptions of stakeholder importance. *Academy of Management Journal*, 42(1): 87–99.

Hepburn, C., Adlen, E., Beddington, J. et al. (2019). The technological and economic prospects for CO_2 utilization and removal. *Nature*, 575: 87–97.

Hoang, H. A., and Rothaermel, F. T. (2010). Leveraging internal and external experience: Exploration, exploitation, and R&D project performance. *Strategic Management Journal*, 31(7): 734–758.

Hunt, C. B., and Auster, E. R. (1990). Proactive environmental management: Avoiding the toxic trap. *Sloan Management Review*, 31(2): 7–18.

Independent Group of Scientists appointed by the Secretary-General. (2019). *Global Sustainable Development Report 2019: The Future Is Now – Science for Achieving Sustainable Development*. New York: United Nations.

Jansen, J. J., Van den Bosch, F. A., and Volberda, H. W. (2006). Exploratory innovation, exploitative innovation, and performance: Effects of organizational antecedents and environmental moderators. *Management Science*, 52(11): 1661–1674.

Jennings, D. F., and Seaman, S. L. (1994). High and low levels of organizational adaptation: An empirical analysis of strategy, structure, and performance. *Strategic Management Journal*, 15(6): 459–475.

Judge, W. Q., and Douglas, T. J. (1998). Performance implications of incorporating natural environmental issues into the strategic planning process: An empirical test. *Journal of Management Studies*, 35(2): 241–262.

Key, S. (1998). Deconstruct social issues for business. *Business and Society*, 37(1), 109–110.

Kotassová, I. (2019, 30 January). Volkswagen nearly killed diesel cars. Now it says they're back. *CNN*. https://edition.cnn.com/2019/01/30/business/diesel-volkswagen-sales/index.html.

Lenton, T. M., Rockström, J., Gaffney, O. et al. (2019). Climate tipping points. Too risky to bet against. *Nature*, 575: 592–595.

Levinthal, D., and March, J. G. (1993). The myopia of learning. *Strategic Management Journal*, 14(52): 95–112.

Liang, X., Musteen, M., and Deepak, K. D. (2009). Strategic orientation and the choice of foreign entry mode: An empirical examination. *Management International Review*, 49(3): 269–290.

Lin, L. H., and Ho, Y. L. (2016). Institutional pressures and environmental performance in the global automotive industry: The mediating role of organizational ambidexterity. *Long Range Planning*, 49(6): 764–775.

Mac Dowell, N., Fennel, P., Shah, N., and Maitland, G. (2017). The role of CO_2 capture and utilization in mitigating climate change. *Nature Climate Change*, 7(4): 243–249.

Malen, J., and Marcus, A. A. (2019). Environmental externalities and weak appropriability: Influences on firm pollution reduction technology development. *Business and Society*, 58(8): 1599–1633.

Maniora, J. (2018). Mismanagement of sustainability: What business strategy makes the difference? Empirical evidence from the USA. *Journal of Business Ethics*, 152(4): 931–947.

March, J. G. (1991). Exploration and exploitation in organizational learning. *Organization Science*, 2(1): 71–87.

McDaniel, S. W., and Kolari, J. W. (1987). Marketing strategy implications of the Miles and Snow strategic typology. *Journal of Marketing*, 51(4): 19–30.

McGrath, R. G. (2001). Exploratory learning, innovative capacity, and managerial oversight. *Academy of Management Journal*, 44(1): 118–131.

Miles, R. E., and Snow, C. C. (1978). *Organizational Strategy, Structure and Process*. New York: McGraw-Hill.

Mom, T. J., Chang, Y., Cholakova, M., and Jansen, J. (2019). A multilevel integrated framework of firm HR practices, individual ambidexterity, and organizational ambidexterity. *Journal of Management*, 4(7): 3009–3034.

Murillo-Luna, J. L., Garcés-Ayerbe, C., and Rivera-Torres, P. (2008). Why do patterns of environmental response differ? A stakeholder pressure approach. *Strategic Management Journal*, 29(11): 1225–1240.

Nyberg, D., and Wright, C. (2022). Climate-proofing management research. *Academy of Management Perspectives*, 36(2): 713–728.

Orsatti, G., Quatraro, F., and Pezzoni, M. (2020). The antecedents of green technologies: The role of team-level recombinant capabilities. *Research Policy*, 49(3): 103919.

Piao, M. (2014). A long life after exploitation and exploration. *European Journal of Innovation Management*, 17(2): 209–228.

Porter, M., and van der Linde, C. (1995). Green and competitive: Ending the stalemate. *Harvard Business Review*, 73(5): 120–134.

Potrich, L., Nogueira Cortimiglia, M., and Fleith de Medeiros, J. (2019). A systematic literature review on firm level proactive environmental management. *Journal of Environmental Management*, 243(2): 273–286.

Rajaratnam, D., and Chonko, L. B. (1995). The effect of business strategy type on marketing organization design, product-market growth strategy, relative marketing effort, and organization performance. *Journal of Marketing Theory and Practice*, 3(3): 60–75.

Rivera, J., and Clement, V. (2018). Business adaptation to climate change: American ski resorts and warmer temperatures. *Business Strategy and the Environment*, 28: 1285–1301.

Roome, N. (1992). Developing environmental management systems. *Business, Strategy and the Environment*, 1(1): 11–24.

Russo, A., and Vurro, C. (2010). Cross-boundary ambidexterity: Balancing exploration and exploitation in the fuel cell industry. *European Management Review*, 7(1): 30–45.

Sharma, S., and Vredenburgh, H. (1998). Proactive corporate environmental strategy and the development of competitively valuable organizational capabilities. *Strategic Management Journal*, 19(8): 729–753.

Shortell, S. M., and Zajac, E. J. (1990). Perceptual and archival measures of Miles and Snow's strategic types: A comprehensive assessment of reliability and validity. *Academy of Management Journal*, 33(4): 817–832.

Skocek, J., Zajac, M., and Haha, M. (2020). Carbon capture and utilization by mineralization of cement pastes derived from recycled concrete. *Scientific Reports*, 10: 5614.

Smith, K. G., Guthrie, J. P., and Chen, M. J. (1986). Miles and Snow's typology of strategy, organizational size and organizational performance. *Academy of Management Annual Meeting Proceedings*, 1: 45–49.

Smith, K. G., Guthrie, J. P., and Chen, M. J. (1989). Strategy, size and performance. *Organization Studies*, 10(1): 63–81.

Snow, C. C., and Hrebiniak, L. G. (1980). Strategy, distinctive competence, and organizational performance. *Administrative Science Quarterly*, 25(2): 317–336.

Stettner, U., and Lavie, D. (2014). Ambidexterity under scrutiny: Exploration and exploitation via internal organization, alliances, and acquisitions. *Strategic Management Journal*, 35(13): 1903–1929.

Supran, G., Rahmstorf, S., and Oreskes, N. (2023). Assessing ExxonMobil's global warming projections. *Science*, 379(6628): eabk0063.

Tashman, P., and Rivera, J. (2016). Ecological uncertainty, adaptation, and mitigation in the U.S. ski resort industry: Managing resource dependence and institutional pressures. *Strategic Management Journal*, 37: 1507–1525.

Thomas, A. S., and Ramaswamy, K. (1996). Matching managers to strategy: Further tests of the Miles and Snow typology. *British Journal of Management*, 7(3): 247–261.

Voss, G. B., Sirdeshmukh, D., and Voss, Z. G. (2008). The effects of slack resources and environmental threat on product exploration and exploitation. *Academy of Management Journal*, 51(1): 147–164.

Wakefield, E. (1994). *History of the Electric Automobile*. Warrendale, PA: Society of Automotive Engineers.

Wartick, S. L., and Cochran, P. L. (1985). The evolution of the corporate social performance model. *Academy of Management Review*, 10(4): 758–769.

Zi-Lin, H., and Wong, P. K. (2004). Exploration vs. exploitation: An empirical test of the ambidexterity hypothesis. *Organization Science*, 15(4): 481–494.

4 | *Sustainable Business Models*

The best way to predict the future is to create it.

Peter Drucker

Sustainable development is more than a goal. It is our responsibility to our planet and future generations.

António Guterres, Secretary-General of the United Nations

4.1 Business Models

The term 'business model' has been widely applied during the last three decades by managers, consultants and scholars; often, it has been misunderstood and used interchangeably with other rather similar terms, such as strategy or business (Magretta, 2002; DaSilva & Trkman, 2014).

According to DaSilva and Trkman (2014), the term 'business model' was mentioned for the first time in academia in a paper on business games for training, proposed in 1957 by Bellman et al. Nevertheless, not until the 1990s did the term and its related research flourish – primarily due to the conjoint effect of several driving forces, such as the development of information and telecommunications technologies (IT), the emergence of internet or dot.com companies and the Nasdaq index, the increasing deregulation and globalisation of economies, and new low-cost competitors (Magretta, 2002; Casadesus-Masanell & Ricart, 2011; Teece, 2010; Zott & Amit, 2007, 2010) – to understand the radically new competitive parameters of e-business. In fact, IT and internet advances have increased the opportunities to design new organisational forms and business models (Zott & Amit, 2007), changing the ways in which economic activities and organisations interact and reshaping industries. The business model's origins in and relevance to consultancy and business practice materialised in the prominence of

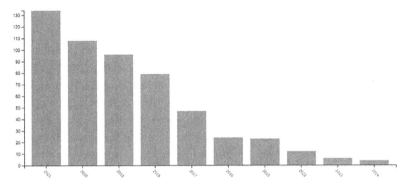

Figure 4.1 Published academic papers on business models
Source: Web of Science, Journal Citation Report (Clarivate, 2022)

key pieces of literature published during the first years of the twenty-first century in leading academic-practitioner journals such as *Harvard Business Review, Long Range Planning* and *MIT Sloan Management Review*; a special issue of *Long Range Planning* devoted to business models in April 2010 was even guest edited by Charles Baden-Fuller, Benoit Demil, Xavier Lecoq and Ian MacMillan. Figure 4.1 shows the increase in academic papers published in the leading academic journals included in the Journal Citation Report.

One of the earliest and vaguest definitions of the business model was established by Michael Lewis in his 1999 book *The New, New Thing: A Silicon Valley Story* (Ovans, 2015): 'all it really meant was how you planned to make money'. Peter Drucker also gave an approximate definition of the term as the 'assumptions about which a company gets paid' as part of his theory of the business: assumptions about the market – identifying customers and competitors – about technology and its dynamics, and about a firm's strengths, weaknesses, opportunities and threats (SWOT) analysis (Drucker, 1995). Magretta (2002) then complemented Drucker's questions as follows: Who is the customer? What does the customer value? How do we make money in the business? How can we deliver value to customers at an appropriate cost? For Magretta, a business model has two parts: (1) a set of activities associated with producing or delivering something; and (2) a set of activities devoted to selling something, in what he calls a 'story' (or stories) that explains how companies actually work.

Another seminal work on business model design was carried out by Casadesus-Manasell and Ricart (2011). For them, only a certain type of business model effectiveness can be tested in comparison with competing ones. They define a business model, based on Magretta's (2002) concept, as a story that explains how a company works, highlighting three main characteristics of an effective business model: (1) aligned with the firm's goals; (2) self-reinforcing; and (3) robust. Such a model also comprises two main elements: choices and consequences. Overall, these features should trigger virtuous cycles that are self-reinforcing.

Zott and Amit (2010:216) later introduced a novel, key issue that was transcendent for the design of sustainable business models (SBMs). They conceptualised a firm's model as 'a system of interdependent activities that transcends the focal firm and spans its boundaries', highlighting cooperation with partners, suppliers or customers on the basis of innovation. Business model design is a key decision in entrepreneurial activity, whether creating a totally new firm or when firms rethink their extant business models. Thus, Zott and Amit (2010) differentiate between the activities in a focal firm's business model – combining different resources and capabilities inside the organisation to perform different activities – and its activity system, the set of activities and their interdependencies, both inside and outside among partners, customers and so on, transcending the focal firm's organisational boundaries in terms of the design of its revenue model and appropriation of generated value. In brief, Zott and Amit (2010:219) define a business model as 'the content, structure, and governance of transactions designed to create value through the exploitation of business opportunities'.

Amit and Zott (2012) thus infer, from business practices, different business model innovation pathways, such as adding new activities – content; linking activities in novel ways – structure; or changing one or more parties that perform any of these activities – governance.

According to Linder and Williander (2017), the conceptual logic of a business model is determined by how it creates and appropriates economic value, which is facilitated when a solution to a customer's problem is at a lower cost than the value of the solved problem.

While these proposals focus on the internal and engineering activities performed by a firm, Teece (2010) highlights the essence of a business model from the market perspective: the way a firm delivers value to customers, entices them to pay for that value, and converts their payments into profits. In fact, for him, many innovators fail to capture value with the innovative business model.

Finally, for established firms there are notable additional difficulties in or barriers to innovating with business models, which are fundamental for firm adaptation to continuous technological and environmental change. Based on Chesbrough (2010), there are two types of barriers: (1) those due to disruptive technologies; and (2) those due to cognitive barriers. The first emerge because of a conflict between the business model already established for an existing technology and the necessary changes and risks in modifying it to instil value in a new disruptive technology. The second derive from the existing dominant logic of well-established and successful business models, which limits and filters key information for corporate decision processes, ignoring the potentially valuable use of technologies that do not fit these models.

4.1.1 Strategic Management and Business Models

Although business models have been widely adopted by business consultants and practitioners, their logic and roots are at the core of the strategic management tradition and the term strategy (Magretta, 2002; Casadesus-Manasell & Ricart, 2011; DaSilva & Trkman, 2014). Nevertheless, prominent researchers, such as Teece (2010), note that the concept of business models lacks theoretical grounding in economic and management studies. Among the possible reasons for an economic tradition, he highlights how in the oversimplified world of economic theory, business models are redundant because producers can create and capture value simply by offering their products at competitive market prices. However, market equilibrium and perfect competition are far removed from the inherent complexities and dilemmas in the real world. Thus, business models play a key role in management, strategy and marketing science.

A possible explanation for this in the field of strategic management is provided by Zott and Amit (2007), who state that according to contingency theory, there is not a unique and optimal strategy for all firms and environmental conditions. Instead, the most appropriate strategy depends on a set of contingent circumstances. Thus, any set of managerial choices and their consequences has many different contingencies. Under this logic, business models can enrich and empower the traditional concept of strategy; that is, form a relevant topic of study for strategic management research.

Moreover, in this book we add two contingency-based, complementary perspectives to address how firms and businesses aim to manage the climate emergency grand challenge in their strategy: Chapter 3 concerns environmental strategies and greening businesses; and the current chapter discusses sustainable business models. These are two complementary points of view for understanding this complex and most challenging phenomenon of climate emergency and firm strategy.

Several theoretical frameworks have been used to explain how business models emerge, are configured and function: the resource-based view (RBV; Barney, 1991), the dynamic capabilities perspective (Teece et al., 1997), transaction cost economics (TCE; Williamson, 1975) and the stakeholder perspective (Freeman, 1984).

The RBV, the currently dominant paradigm in strategic management (Newbert, 2008), plays a key role in explaining business models. Successful business models can be understood as unique bundles of resources and capabilities, which are rare, valuable and difficult to imitate and substitute (Barney, 1991); these lead firms to sustainable competitive advantages. Additionally, a business model's dynamic nature and complexity extend beyond the static nature of the RBV and fit the main arguments proposed by the dynamic capabilities perspective (Teece et al., 1997).

Applying this framework, Brennan and Tennant (2018) explore business models of sustainability, where value creation is the output of multiple interactions of a firm's resources, both structural and cultural. Sustainability cultural resources include relevant concepts such as net positive benefits – positive sustainability externalities – and the creation of value for the 'common good'.

The rise of business models during the internet and e-business era has placed focus on how they can drastically decrease transaction costs (DaSilva & Trkman, 2014), triggering the virtualisation of industries and transactions. In this way, placing value in organisational resources requires a combination of the RBV and TCE, producing a unique combination of resources for transaction innovation and efficiency, generating value both for customers and the firm. In fact, one of the most widespread definitions of business models, created by Zott and Amit (2010), explicitly includes 'the content, structure, and governance of transactions' between the focal firm and its exchange partners, confirming the utility of TCE in explaining how companies function. Zott and Amit (2007) suggested that a business model is a structural template of how a firm transacts with its customers, partners and vendors.

Currently, new stakeholder theory (Barney, 2018; Gibson et al., 2021; McGahan, 2021) is gaining momentum and placing a new emphasis on explaining business models and sustainable development, whereby new modes of stakeholder interaction, engagement and forms of governance open innovation practices for sustainability and even the redefinition of a firm's purpose, beyond shareholder and manager primacy and simple economic profit (World Economic Forum, 2022), towards the 'common good' and a wider and more inclusive stakeholder perspective, both internally and externally. These comprise the key pieces in this new socioenvironmental value creation logic. In this sense, Evans et al. (2017) and Geissdoerfer et al. (2018) apply stakeholder theory to highlight one of the core features of SBMs: jointly with process, product or service innovations, SBMs imply changes in a firm's government systems and influence of stakeholders, transforming stakeholder relationships via a wider perspective and longer view of time, passing from a transactional mindset towards trust-based, mutually beneficial and enduring relationships with key internal and external stakeholders. Similarly, Brozovic (2020) remarks that an SBM involves a wider set of stakeholders than a traditional business model.

Paradox theory has been widely adopted (Van der Byl & Slawinski, 2015; Hahn et al., 2018) in recent, novel SBM definitions to highlight the increasing tensions among contradictory forms of sustainable value creation (Stal et al., 2022) in long- versus short-term orientations; narrow manager and shareholder primacy versus wider stakeholder perspectives – including the natural environment, society and even future generations, and the internal conception of value creation; and narrow economic profit versus wider organisational resilience and shared value, co-created by firms and their internal and external stakeholders.

Finally, it is necessary to distinguish business models from the key term 'strategy', although several researchers have used them interchangeably. In an attempt to clarify and distinguish these two terms, Casadesus-Masanell and Ricart (2011:9) state that business models are the reflections of a realised strategy: a business model 'refers to the logic of the company, describing how it operates, creates, and captures value for the company's stakeholders in the competitive arena, whereas a strategy refers to the plan created for a unique and valuable position involving a distinctive set of activities'. Thus, we can understand a business model as the set of managerial strategic and tactical choices for and consequences of a certain higher plan or strategy or plan of action for contingencies. In a similar way, Magretta (2002) distinguishes business models from strategy. Business models describe how the different pieces of a business fit together, as a system, whereas a competitive strategy explains how a company performs better than its rivals.

4.1.2 Main Aspects and Elements of a Business Model

The main functions of a business model, according to Chesbrough (2010), are the following: (1) articulation of the value proposition for users, based on technology; (2) identification of a market segment and revenue generation; (3) structure definition and value chain; (4) delineation of revenue mechanism; (5) determination of cost structure and profit potential; (6) description of the position of the firm within the supplier–customer network; and (7) formulation of competitive strategy to hold a sustained competitive advantage.

Casadesus-Masanell and Ricart (2011) have proposed three main characteristics of an effective business model: alignment with company goals, self-reinforcement and robustness. Hence, decisions or choices made by management should deliver consequences that facilitate the achievement of a firm's goals. Additionally, these choices are interrelated in a synergistic way, reinforcing the business model and its internal consistency and capability to be sustained over time amid external threats, such as environmental dynamism or competitors' imitation or substitution attempts. Overall, they propose that the main components of a business model are (1) managerial actions or choices; and (2) their consequences. For instance:

- A firm makes three types of choices: (1) policy choices determine the actions taken by the firm across all its operations, such as plant location or the use of an unskilled workforce; (2) asset choices concern the tangible resources a firm deploys, such as manufacturing facilities and storage; and (3) governance choices, which include how a firm decides what to make or buy.

- These choices have consequences that can be flexible or rigid: flexible consequences respond quickly amid choice changes, such as price policy and sales volume, whereas rigid consequences take time to adapt to changes in choices, such as brand image, as they are the bases for firm competitiveness and business model robustness and are responsible for competitive advantage maintenance due to imperfections in their imitability by competitors. In fact, when a firm competes with other business model rivals, it should quickly build rigid consequences to create and capture more value than its rivals.

In one of the first quantitative empirical studies on business models, Zott and Amit (2007) analysed their design, as configurations or constellations of design elements including two main mechanisms, efficiency and novelty, which are necessarily associated with firm performance and value creation. Business models can create value in two ways: by enhancing customers' willingness to pay or by decreasing suppliers' and partners' opportunity costs. In this way, the value created by a business model should be its power relative to that of rival business models when subjected to environmental conditions, such as munificence or dynamism.

According to Zott and Amit (2007), the first mechanism in a business model's design is its novelty, the conceptualisation and adoption of new modes of economic exchange that can be achieved. Thus, business model innovation can complement the firm in terms of products, production systems, delivery, marketing and so on, generating entrepreneurial rents. There are numerous examples of pioneering companies developing novelty business models in the hospitality industry, such as Airbnb, or in car mobility, such as Uber.

Another key aspect of business model design is efficiency (Zott and Amit, 2007). That is, entrepreneurs can create wealth by imitating or being inspired by other existing and successful business models, which they can improve through transaction efficiency. In fact, the essence of the alternative mechanism is a reduction in transaction costs (Williamson, 1975) by attenuating uncertainty, complexity or information asymmetry, as well as by reducing coordination costs and transaction risks. Amazon's business model, aimed at enhancing transaction cost patency, is an effective example of an efficiency-centred business model. It reduces the cost of providing information for logistics firms, increases the reliability and simplicity of transactions, accelerates them and reduces inventory levels.

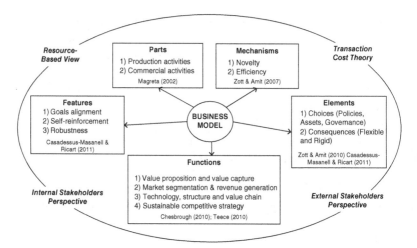

Figure 4.2 Business models
Source: Authors' own elaboration

Zott and Amit (2010) updated the design elements of a business model and activity systems, adding design terms including the degree of novelty, lock-in, complementarity and efficiency of business models, first described in their 2007 proposal. Briefly, the design elements they describe are the following:

• Activity system content refers to the choice of activities to be carried out.
• Activity system structure describes the relationships among activities in terms of core–periphery relationships.
• Activity system governance refers to who performs the activities and is related to make/buy decisions.

For Teece (2010), the five elements of a business model interrelate in a virtuous cycle: (1) the selection of technologies and features embedded in a product; (2) the determination of benefit in the eyes of customers; (3) the identification of market segments; (4) the confirmation of available revenue streams; and (5) the design of a capture value mechanism.

Figure 4.2 thus presents the main elements, features, functions, parts and elements of a general business model, as well as the main related theoretical frameworks.

4.2 Sustainable Business Models

Current business practitioners' points of view and priorities reflect relevant claims in academia: a real form of sustainable strategy, a focus on sustainable performance (Bansal, 2019; Sharma, 2022; Montiel et al., 2020) and wide stakeholder engagement; that is, approaching sustainability as a business opportunity.

In an SBM literature review carried out by Brozovic (2020), he found several commonalities in the definitions of an SBM: the most important are (1) referral to the balance of economic, social and environmental sustainability; (2) a wider stakeholder perspective, beyond customers and shareholders; and (3) a longer-term perspective. Thus, Brozovic (2020:766) proposes an integrative definition of an SBM: 'it helps to describe, analyse, manage, and communicate (a) a company's sustainable value proposition to customers and all stakeholders, (b) how it creates and delivers this value, and (c) how it captures economic value while maintaining or regenerating natural, social, and economic capital beyond its organisational boundaries'. In this way, the meaning of a value proposition extends beyond its traditional definition by including environmental, social and economic value.

In fact, value as a key concept in a business model definition should be modified for sustainability. Thus, Geissdoerfer et al. (2018) and Evans et al. (2017) propose several challenges that any SBM must face:

- Value proposition: The triple bottom line, through the balanced and holistic co-creation of economic profits, social and environmental values, while considering the needs of all stakeholders (Stal et al., 2022). Some examples of environmental value include renewable resources, low emissions, limited waste, protection of biodiversity and pollution prevention. Forms of social value include equality and diversity management, well-being, secure livelihood, labour standards, and health and safety. Last, economic value examples are profitability, return on assets or investments, financial resilience, long-term viability and market-to-book ratio.
- Mindset: New business rules, values, behaviour and performance metrics reflecting the new value proposition. In fact, the SBM requires a new metric for sustainability including multiple stakeholders and highlighting the natural environment and society as primary stakeholders. As Sharma (2022) proposes, firms should pass from environmental management to environmental performance

via the logic suggesting that 'what you cannot measure, you cannot manage effectively'. As a clear and unified metric of the triple bottom line, its disclosure, through reporting, is a key activity to include in an effective SBM.

- Technological innovation, both social and environmental: An SBM should manage the usually negative social and environmental impacts or externalities of daily business activities to minimise them (such as zero emissions) or even, as we propose in Chapter 5, convert them into positive environmental and social externalities, as the regenerative strategy proposes. This also implies a firm's resource and capability orchestration for sustainability. Possibly effective pathways for this include taxes and permits or monetising environmental externalities, such as a product stewardship strategy including the cost of products' end-of-life recovery, reuse, treatment or disposal or improving their ecodesign for recyclability.
- Value networks and stakeholders, mutually reinforcing: An SBM requires extensive firm stakeholder engagement, both internal and external and both in the external market and beyond it, as Figure 4.3 shows, from a systemic and global perspective. An SBM should introduce the concept of a value network and a new network governance model, integrating sustainability in a way that ensures value co-creation both for the firm and for all stakeholders in the very long term. Accordingly, we propose that networks, through deliberate interaction, partnering, networking and learning, are a key driver in a modified firm's implementation of an SBM, such as organisational resilience.

In fact, as Stal et al. (2022) highlight, business model innovation for sustainability requires additional efforts in intersectoral collaboration among firms and other actors, such as other firms and governmental and civil society actors, to address the major challenge of sustainability. Multigovernance structures, including public and private initiatives, are especially suited to managing systemic thinking for sustainability, which involves interdependent biophysical complexities, tensions and paradoxes that extend beyond the business sphere.

Nevertheless, as Brennan and Tennant (2018) highlight, one of the first issues that SBMs must resolve is the trade-off of economic, environmental and social value through the prioritisation of sustainability-related 'cultural' resources. To overcome such a trade-off, they

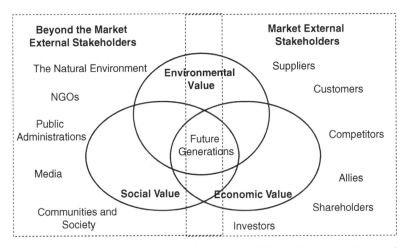

Figure 4.3 Sustainable business models: the amplified value proposition and the new emphasis on external stakeholders
Source: Authors' own elaboration

propose the concept of a sustainable value chain, integrating the supply chain into SBMs.

Brennan and Tennant (2018) characterise business models for sustainability as a mechanism for firms to address the root causes of unsustainability, creating synergies among economic, social and ecological value; that is, delivering 'common good' value. Trade-offs in sustainable value creation occur when firms promote only their own economic prosperity at the expense of environmental and social goals. Accordingly, Brennan and Tennant (2018) propose a solution to this: changing governance structures in the supply chain, by reconfiguring firm resources and the supply chain, creating multiple relationships among partners, activating multiple interrelated power relations, exploring new logics, resolving trade-offs and creating value for the common good, in line with the postulates of industrial symbiosis and ecology (Lüdeke-Freund et al., 2018). Table 4.1 shows some of the most relevant definitions of sustainable business models.

From a practitioner-consultancy point of view, the latest McKinsey global survey (McKinsey, 2021) of 2,475 managers worldwide sheds light on how companies can capture the value of sustainability. A key distinctive aspect of value-creating companies is their optimistic

Table 4.1 *Sustainable business model definitions*

Author(s)	Label	Definition/characterisation
Evans et al. (2017:600)	Business model innovation for sustainability	Not necessarily achieved through technology, products or service innovation alone but also through the innovation of the business model itself. It implies changes in the relationships with stakeholders and the way a firm is governed, a wider and longer-term view, from a transactional mindset towards trust-based, mutually beneficial and enduring relationships with key internal and external stakeholders
Linder and Williander (2017:183)	Circular business model	The conceptual logic for value creation is based on utilising economic value retained in products after use in the production of new offerings. It implies a return flow to the producer from users, although there can be intermediaries between these two parties. It overlaps with the concept of closed-loop supply chain and always involves recycling, remanufacturing, reuse or one of their sibling activities (e.g. refurbishment, renovation, repair)
Brennan and Tennant (2018:2)	Business model for sustainability	Mechanisms for firms to address the root causes of unsustainability, creating synergies between economic, environmental, and social value or delivering 'common good' value
Geissdoerfer et al. (2018:403–404)	Sustainable business model	Incorporate proactive multistakeholder management and the creation of monetary and nonmonetary value for a broad range of stakeholders and hold a long-term perspective
Lüdeke-Freund et al. (2018:37)	Circular economy business model	A means for redefining how companies create value while adhering to CE [circular economy] principles … It builds on industrial ecology concepts such as closed-loop material systems, industrial symbiosis, or cascading

Source	Concept	Description
Brozovic (2020:766)	Sustainable (strong) business model	Helps describe, analyse, manage, and communicate (a) a company's sustainable value proposition to customers and all stakeholders, (b) how it creates and delivers this value, and (c) how it captures economic value while maintaining or regenerating natural, social, and economic capital beyond its organisational boundaries
Frishammar and Parida (2019:8)	Circular business model	A focal company, together with partners, uses innovation to create, capture, and deliver value to improve resource efficiency by extending the lifespan of products and parts, thereby realising environmental, social, and economic benefits
Reim et al. (2021:2745–2746)	Circular business model	Features a conceptual logic in which value creation is based on utilising economic value retained in products after use … Needs to be designed to create and capture value while helping achieve the ideal state of resource usage … Its logic entails that firms can reduce their negative impact on the environment by using this alternative value proposition to deliver and capture value
Hofmann and Jaeger-Erben (2019:272)	Circular business model	Connects business configurations focusing on results- and performance-oriented product-service-systems: manufacturing and offering durable, reliable, recyclable, modular, and repairable products; and/or practising conscious sales on the consumption side of the business that involves (non)consumer decisions such as repairing, maintaining, or upgrading instead of buying new products
Young and Reeves (2020:3)	Sustainable business model innovation	Innovation of business models and ecosystems to co-optimise for business and societal benefits
Stal et al. (2022:445–446)	Business model innovation for sustainability	Integrates environmental, social, and economic value creation, and appropriation … This triple-bottom-line integrates sustainability as a core concern of the business model

Source: Authors' own elaboration

outlook – nearly double that of current positions – on sustainability and value generation in the next five years. Increasing sustainable optimism has been detected in certain industrial contexts such as electric power and natural gas, oil and gas, the social sector, automotive and assembly, and telecom. More interestingly, certain distinctive management practices are followed by the companies that generate value from their sustainability programmes.

The first step is to make sustainability a strategic priority for the whole company. Thus, more than half of respondents from value creators indicate that their chief executive officer (CEO) makes sustainability a priority for strategy. Here, it is relevant to understand which sustainable practices are more linked to financial performance. In this sense, the most relevant ones highlighted in the survey fit the main theoretical frameworks analysed in this work:

• The natural resource-based view includes alignment with the firm's mission, goal and values; attracting, motivating and retaining talented employees; improving operational efficiency; building an effective corporate reputation; or responding to competitive pressure.
• Institutional theory and the stakeholder perspective concern meeting the expectations of customers, investors, industry norms and standards, non-governmental organisations (NGOs), supply chains and regulatory requirements.
• The microfoundations of strategy concern the internal relevance of CEO expectations of and beliefs in sustainability, as well as the orientation towards organisational resilience issues (Ortiz-de Mandojana & Bansal, 2016), such a promoting the ability to grow, develop new growth opportunities or focus on sustainability performance (Sharma, 2022) by making a tangible, positive impact on an environmental issue.

Additionally, aligning with the latest academic claims (Bansal, 2019; Sharma, 2022; Montiel et al., 2020; Aguilera et al., 2022), leading and value creator companies are translating sustainable strategy into sustainable performance, as the survey results show in definitive terms. Companies should have a sharp focus with clear priorities, targets and goals based on key sustainability indicators.

The second practice detected is to make sustainability a key element in organisational culture and employee training programmes. As the natural resource-based view (Hart, 1995; Hart & Dowell,

2011) suggests, a proactive sustainability and environmental strategic posture implies the real engagement of organisational employees. In this sense, nearly three-fifths of respondents said that sustainability is part of their organisational culture. Additionally, employee training in value creators is focused on integrating sustainability practices in work and understanding how sustainability aligns with strategy.

Third, value-creating companies, in terms of sustainability, are more apt to engage external stakeholders and be in value chain collaboration with customers and suppliers as well as business partners in their sustainability programmes, in coherence with the advanced postulates of product stewardship and sustainable development in the natural resource-based view (Hart, 1995) and from the new stakeholder perspective (Barney, 2018; Gibson et al., 2021). Thus, value creators put more effort into understanding new customers' expectations and engaging customers with the sustainability attributes of sustainable products. Additionally, value creators collaborate with their suppliers, contract manufacturers, distributors and other value chain partners on sustainability issues to reduce energy, water use and waste generation along their whole value chain.

Exploring why managers fail when they develop and implement SBMs, Bhattacharya and Polman (2017) focus on identifying the six thorny challenges of an SBM, linking academic research with their long-term experience as business practitioners and consultants in multinational corporations and public institutions. In fact, many of their identified challenges have appeared in recent business practitioners' surveys, such as that by McKinsey. These are as follows:

- Sustainability should be the firm's priority, not another change initiative. It requires a wider engagement with the entire organisation and multiple external stakeholders, both market stakeholders and beyond-market stakeholders, which modifies the firm's purpose. Only the CEO can lead this transformative change.
- Looking at the entire value chain is critical to reduce the footprint beyond organisational boundaries, from cradle to grave. An SBM requires an integrated perspective including marketing and supply chain aspects, as industrial symbiosis proclaims.
- Sustainability should be a priority for the company's board. Changes in a firm's purpose towards sustainability imply many changes in its

board of directors' perspectives, led by managers, such as a change in focus from short to long term or on stakeholder management, leaving the primacy of shareholder value creation for a wider conception of stakeholder engagement and organisational resilience.

- Gaining buy-in from any undecideds. All transformative changes inside corporations have many forms of resistance to change and undecideds. Managers should act as true leaders and agents of change, giving information and facilitating change.
- Employee engagement, making sustainability part of every employee's task. Most advanced environmental and sustainability practices require employee commitment and training, as well as flexible organisational structures and additional necessary resources supporting change.
- Redefining the competitive space by collaborating. The sustainability challenge is too great for a single company. Alliances allow firms to access expert, diverse knowledge and relationships to solve and approach complex problems.

Additionally, from a managerial perspective, a recent report, written by Young and Reeves for the Henderson Institute at the Boston Consulting Group in 2020, discusses how companies are making significant advances in sustainability management in coherence with the recommendations of several global institutions, such as the Independent Group of Scientists (2019) on sustainable development and the World Economic Forum (2020) on rethinking capitalism towards a more sustainable firm purpose and environmental, social and governance (ESG) commitment. Accordingly, they show an increasing commitment path towards corporate social responsibility, which implies minor changes in core business models and value drivers; towards compliance-driven and reactive changes for a sustainability stage mainly driven by regulatory and stakeholder pressures for sustainability; and finally towards a sustainable business model innovation stage, where the innovation of business models inside ecosystems or industrial symbioses co-optimises business, social and environmental issues.

In this report, Young and Reeves (2020) consider strategy and sustainability as mutually reinforcing, and define the following main features of a successful SBM:

- Offers efficient scalability without diminishing returns or increasing failure risk.

- Promotes differentiation and reinforces competitiveness.
- Reduces the potential for commoditisation.
- Creates environmental and societal surpluses.
- Remains durable amid emerging socioenvironmental trends.
- Provides network and value chain added value.
- Harnesses or reshapes business ecosystems and industrial symbiosis for sustainability and competitive advantage.
- Generates returns for shareholders and net positives for socioenvironmental external stakeholders.
- Redefines firm purpose towards wider stakeholder engagement with employees, customers, investors and other stakeholders.

To implement such an SBM, Young and Reeves (2020) articulate specific methodological steps:

- First, it is mandatory to expand the business context in terms of the firm's boundaries, resources and time horizons, covering the whole supply chain – from cradle to grave – and product life cycles.
- Second, it is useful to develop a series of stress tests of the business model against externalities, such as emerging socioenvironmental trends, and to develop several strategic materiality scenarios. The aim is to develop a business envisioned in very different operations to assess its limits, risks, main challenges and potential economic and sustainability opportunities. Additionally, it is important to assess business scalability, to discover any possibly hidden constraints and breakpoints.
- Third, it is useful to apply modular transformations to remove fracture points and create new competitive advantages, moving the company towards organisational resilience and sustainability. This is possible with a vertical integration strategy across all stages in the supply chain, from product creation to end of life, which minimises environmental damage. The principles of the circular economy or industrial symbiosis (Walls & Paquin, 2015) are useful for this purpose. Jointly, the business model should expand the societal context, inserting the value-sustainable efforts made by the company in the market through product differentiation, brand and reputation building, and by collaborating in the creation of new businesses with public-private initiatives, especially in developing and fast-growing economies.
- Finally, SBMs should create an environmental and societal surplus, in line with the main proposal of this book exploring the

regenerative strategy and positive environmental externalities. Following Aguilera et al. (2022) and Sharma (2022), sustainability performance should be an organisational aim in itself, moving from traditional 'business-as-usual' strategies and a compliance logic to proactive action and competitive advantage in a sustainable and shared way (Porter & Kramer, 2011).

Nevertheless, SBMs have been subject to several criticisms. For example, Brozovic (2020) highlights how SBMs merely update traditional aims (focus on the short term and customer primacy) with sustainable principles, failing to capture the interdependencies of businesses and natural ecosystems. Hence, he introduces the term 'strong sustainable business model' (SSBM), where a complete integration of environmental sustainability within the core business is performed. Following this logic, the natural environment is the primary stakeholder. In summary, SBMs suffer from the lack of a whole systems viewpoint. Table 4.2 lists the main differences among the traditional, sustainable and strong sustainable business models.

Finally, for managing an SBM several authors have proposed different SBM typologies. For instance, Hofmann and Jaeger-Erben (2019) distinguish the circular-ecological, base-of-the-pyramid poverty and other social reality business models. Geissdoerfer et al. (2018), in their literature review on SBMs, describe several typologies or archetypes of SBM types and strategies:

- SBM innovation types such as a sustainable start-up, creating a new firm to support it, or an SBM carried out inside an existing firm, e.g. SBM transformation, SBM diversification and SBM acquisition.
- SBM types including circular business models that are closing, slowing, intensifying, dematerialising or narrowing resource loops; social enterprises, which generate profits via business activity or reinvest them; base-of-the-pyramid solutions that meet the needs of poverty; and product–service systems that integrate products and services into customer offerings that provide a product or functionality.
- SBM strategies including those that maximise material and energy efficiency, close resource loops, substitute renewables and natural processes, deliver functionality rather than ownership, or repurpose tasks for society or the environment, inclusive value creation, etc.

Table 4.2 *Traditional, sustainable and strong sustainable principles*

Overarching business model themes	Traditional business model elements	Sustainable business model commonalities	Strong sustainable business model principles
Value proposition	Market offering	Economic, social and environmental proposition	Preservation and regeneration of the natural environment
Stakeholders	Customers, relationships	Multistakeholder perspective	The natural environment as a primary constraining factor
Value creation	Resources, infrastructure, process and activities, management, strategy	Infused with innovation to incorporate sustainability	Systemic and ecosystem perspective
Value capture and market conditions	Revenue model, financial model, market conditions	Long-term perspective	Transformation of the economic and business systems to encompass value types other than financial value

Source: Brozovic (2020:768)

Accordingly, in Sections 4.3 and 4.4, we introduce two types of SBMs based mainly on the value proposition and innovation systems: environmental and social models.

4.3 Environmentally Sustainable Business Models

A recent but growing literature on environmental business models has shifted the principles and postulates of industrial symbiosis and the circular economy to the microeconomic perspective of businesses (Geissdoerfer et al., 2018). Thus, most papers label these 'circular business models'. In comparison to the more general SBMs, environmental or circular business models focus on the compatibility of economic and environmental value propositions and the prominence of ecological or environmental innovations while maintaining the other main features: multistakeholder and holistic stakeholder perspectives and long-term orientation. Some of the key definitions and the related labels of environmental business models are listed in Table 4.2 concerning a more general perspective on SBM.

Circular business models can be catalogued and are diametrically opposed to the dominant linear business models in previous decades, which mostly incorporate principles of acceleration, such as raising the frequency of product innovation and boosting the number of products sold within a period to increase business competitiveness. Circular business models differ from linear models in several key points (Hofmann & Jaeger-Erben, 2019). Circular business models close and slow resource flows. Thus, the flows of materials are organised, closing resource flows and the speeds at which they circle within the prevailing economic order, for instance, slowing these resource flows. In this way, they connect post-use and process waste with production through processes such as recycling and repurposing by-products, and attempt to preserve the inherent value of products and product components by increasing their maximum number of use phases and times through repair, maintenance, upcycle, resale, refurbishment or remanufacture.

Overall, then, circular business models could fit the imperative of continuous economic growth by decoupling expansion from ecological damage. Nevertheless, as Hofmann and Zu Knyphausen-Ausefß (2022) remark, most studies have explored circular business models in niches in the premium segment, avoiding large markets in developed and developing economies that deal with the basic necessities of the world population. Accordingly, paradoxically, although circular and social business models appear to be a great challenge in approaching sustainable development, existing theory and empirical evidence seem to focus on the narrow context of rich countries and premium segments.

A circular business model can be defined as 'a representation of a certain complex system focused on sets of activities and resources that explain how an organisation creates, captures, and delivers value while using and offering preexisting products, components, or materials that pass through multiple use cycles' (Hofmann & Zu Knyphausen-Ausefß, 2022:2470). Thus, organisations strive to produce minimal adverse effects on the natural environment and to increase product life cycles, from ecodesign and material extraction to disposal (Araujo-Galvao et al., 2022), following a product stewardship logic (Hart, 1995).

According to a literature review on sustainable and circular business models by Geissdoerfer et al. (2018), circular business models are part of a more sustainable business model, which incorporates, jointly, the more general features of an SBM – sustainable value, proactive multistakeholder management and long-term perspective – and the following key features: closing, slowing, intensifying, dematerialising and narrowing resource loops, in coherence with circular economy and industrial symbiosis postulates.

The transition to circular business models requires defining the organisational business model jointly with ecosystem innovation by highlighting the role of stakeholder engagement in a self-sufficient ecosystem (Moggi & Dameri, 2021), following a new stakeholder perspective (Gibson et al., 2021; McGahan, 2021) to frame them. Indeed, Moggi and Dameri (2021) suggest that most circular business models depend on cooperation and partnership between firms and beyond-market stakeholders, such as local communities, non-profit organisations, local administrations and governments and citizens. These are the sources for new and radical knowledge and expertise (Gibson et al., 2021), for pooling concrete resources into a network, and for co-creating value in a business ecosystem where a set of actors – producers, suppliers, service providers, end-users, regulators and civil society organisations – contribute to a collective outcome. Thus, collaboration is mandatory, and the traditional boundaries of a business model must be reshaped. As Moggi and Dameri (2021) remark, it is particularly relevant for circular business models to engage with a broad range of knowledge and expertise from different individuals and entities from very different industries and backgrounds, just as we propose when we state that the regenerative strategy for facing climate and planetary emergencies must overcome the existing gaps in science and management.

For Brozovic (2020), strong sustainability considers natural capital a non-substitutable form of capital that contributes to human health and wider welfare. In that sense, profound changes in global economic and social systems are mandatory to preserve natural capital and human civilisation. When defining their business value proposition, firms should maintain and can even benefit from biogeochemical cycles in the natural ecosystem; when framing stakeholders, nature should be considered the primary constraining factor.

In his exploratory qualitative research on eight business ventures in permaculture farms in Sweden, Brozovic (2020) lists several principles for an SSBM, which Table 4.3 shows.

Table 4.3 *Strong sustainable business model framework*

Main issues	SSBM framework	Main findings
Value proposition	Value proposition aimed at nature	The main functions of this kind of business are to preserve, regenerate and benefit nature
	Value proposition beyond financial	Enriched with e.g. well-being, happiness, health and care for other living beings
Stakeholders	Nature is the primary stakeholder	Among various stakeholders, the needs of nature are always put at the front
	Strong local anchorage	Businesses are an integral part of their local communities and aim for resilience at the local community level
	Solidarity and cooperation	Businesses share their ideas and insights in an inclusive manner and are organised cooperatively
Practical apparatus	Infused with systemic and ecosystem perspectives	Understanding the role of the firm in the natural ecosystem, and how the firm creates value via its practical apparatus
Value capture and market conditions	Deliberately limited growth	Growth is not an end in itself: it is more important to develop a business that contributes to the well-being of employees, the local community and nature
	Diversity of income sources	Just as biological diversity contributes to ecosystem resilience, a diversity of income sources enhances economic resilience
	Value capture beyond financial	Stakeholders contribute to the firm not only with financial resources but with other forms of value created through sharing and meetings

Source: Brozovic (2020:771–772)

Adopting an RBV spin-off called the 'dynamic capabilities approach' (Teece, 2010), Hofmann and Zu Knyphausen-Ausefβ (2022) carry out qualitative research on circular business models, identifying three main organisational capabilities – or tasks – necessary to adopt and manage a circular business model:

- Contextualising involves research efforts that forecast and imagine trends for a business model portfolio and includes overcoming the narrow scanning radius of a linear business model. Thus, the organisation must harmonise its strategy with circular economy-oriented investments.
- Dynamic costructuring addresses questions such as how much seed capital is needed to invest in circular innovation systems or which employees are suited to constituting that system while considering contextual conditions. Additionally, it concerns the ability to measure and actualise the circular innovation system. Iteratively practising and learning circular value creation activities lead to preparing and realising the final market launch of the circular business model experiment.
- Governing intangible assets refers to the development and refinement of the knowledge governance approach to handle and reprocess the knowledge stocks and intellectual assets elicited by the circular innovation system.

Finally, the importance of the transition from linear to circular business models is underscored to overcome circular economy barriers. Putting disruptive business models into practice as circular ones implies breaking down certain barriers. In their empirical study in the developing economy context of Brazil, Araujo-Galvao et al. (2022) identify several barriers to circular business models, organised around three main categories:

- Organisational environment, which includes the existing organisational culture, managerial capabilities and business model conception.
- External environments, such as barriers related to circular economy chain complexity and collaboration and availability of infrastructure or consumption-related barriers, such as the lack of awareness, owner perception or rejection of remanufactured products.
- Technological, including the lack of appropriate and cutting-edge technological innovations and of techno-scientific knowledge among managers and employees.

4.4 Social Business Models

The capitalist system is being scrutinised, as it is responsible for most social, environmental and economic problems (Porter & Kramer, 2011). Traditional business models that do not consider social and environmental negative externalities and continue to focus on a narrow conception of short-term shareholder value creation are losing social legitimacy. The suggested solution, then, is a revolutionary concept of value: 'the principle of shared value, which involves creating economic value in a way that also creates value for society by addressing its needs and challenges' (Porter & Kramer, 2011:4).

Innovative business models, as strategic pedagogic tools for understanding new business and competitive realities, have also been used to highlight the social dimension of the grand challenge of sustainable development. Exploring social businesses to differentiate them from regular ones in the capitalist system, Yunus et al. (2010) state that in contrast to regular firms that seek profit maximisation for shareholders, a social business aims for social profit maximisation. However, in contrast to non-profit organisations, a social business shares with regular firms the need to repay invested capital as a self-sustainability business model. Figure 4.4 illustrates this dichotomy.

One of the first studies analysing SBMs was 'The fortune at the bottom of the pyramid' by Prahalad and Hart (2002). This work revolutionised the concept of business models, opening the door to business opportunities inside the largest markets, impoverished or low-income markets, and bringing prosperity to aspiring impoverished populations.

The first wave of the bottom of the pyramid (BoP; Lashitew et al., 2022) was the time for multinational companies (MNCs) to take advantage of a globalised world through a new lens, 'inclusive capitalism'. The BoP was introduced as a win-win strategy for MNCs capable of competing at the bottom of the world economic pyramid with the promise of firm growth, profitability and improvement for the majority of the global population and humankind, lifting billions of people out of poverty and desperation. As Seelos and Mair (2007) have highlighted, firms could design profitable business models and create markets in this new competitive arena of deep poverty.

The grand social challenge for capitalist businesses has been to reinvent business models to attend to the necessities of the BoP in a

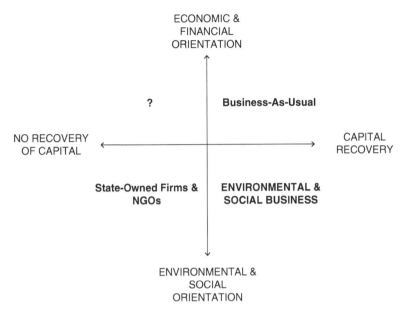

Figure 4.4 Social businesses, non-profit organisations and profit-maximising businesses
Source: Authors' own elaboration based on Yunus et al. (2010:310)

profitable way. At the beginning of the twenty-first century, the BoP represented the world's four billion poorest people – approximately two-thirds of the global population. Two main features characterise the BoP: (1) it is by far the largest market, representing a multitrillion-dollar market; and (2) it is growing. Recent estimates, such as those by Guillén (2020), show that more than 400 million people will be born in sub-Saharan Africa in the world's latest baby boom.

By 2002 the majority of the top 200 MNCs in the world were based in developed countries, with business models designed for wealthy people. In fact, as Prahalad and Hart (2002) remark, the BoP has been an unattractive market for MNCs due to several generalised beliefs and misunderstandings: (1) impoverished people are not the target because current production costs cannot be recovered through low prices; (2) they do not use the same products and services as sold in the developed world; (3) they cannot pay for cutting-edge technology; (4) governments and NGOs should cover impoverished people's necessities; and (5) managers are not excited by the social dimensions of these businesses. Nevertheless, Prahalad and Hart (2002) underline some drivers of innovation at the BoP, such as the increased access to TV and the internet, economic deregulation, overcompetition in the developed world, and the need to discourage migration, both from rural areas to cities and from the developing to the developed world. Indeed, according to Kim and Mauborgne (2004), the BoP could be framed as the biggest new 'blue ocean' strategy, with almost infinite business opportunities for pioneering companies acting there.

Contrary to the common considerations at the beginning of the twenty-first century, Prahalad and Hart (2002) showed that impoverished populations could be a very profitable market if MNCs changed their business models. For them, four main elements of a BoP business model are thus key to a thriving BoP market:

- Creating buyer power. Several problems affect minimum buying power to create a market economy. For example, by 2001 nearly a billion people were either underemployed or had low-paying jobs. Additionally, commercial credit has historically been unavailable to very poor people. In that sense, one of the very well-known and successful cases of social business models was the experience in Bangladesh (Yunus et al., 2010) of the revolutionary social business model of Grameen Bank and microcredit.
- Shaping aspirations. Sustainable product innovations initiated at the BoP and promoted through education not only benefit BoP consumers but also reshape consumer behaviours in developed countries, constituting a market pull for disruptive innovations.
- Improving access. Because BoP communities are often physically and economically isolated, novel delivery systems and communication channels are needed for doing business there, such as alliances with creative local communities.
- Tailoring local solutions. Finally, MNCs should play a more active role in narrowing the gap between rich and poor populations. Product development for the BoP should combine MNCs' advanced technology with deep local insights in an effective combination of local cultural values and preferences and global knowledge and technology, highlighting the strategic role of the entire value chain in the BoP. MNCs must work together with local NGOs, communities and governments to establish business solutions.

Overall, then, Prahalad and Hart (2002) advance some key elements of a sustainable business model acting at the BoP: (1) build a local base of social and political support; (2) carry out R&D and market research focused on the impoverished population's characteristics and needs in each region, while adapting foreign solutions to local needs and identifying useful local principles and applications; (3) enhance collaboration and alliances with a wider typology of local stakeholders to co-create value, learn, apply and improve social legitimacy; (4) create value locally by increasing employment intensity; and finally (5) reinvent cost structures, caring for the whole value chain.

The most recognised and successful business model at the base of the pyramid is the Grameen Bank (Yunus et al., 2010). Indeed, in 2006 Professor Muhammad Yunus and his Grameen Bank initiative won the Nobel Peace Prize. Grameen's network of approximately thirty sister organisations pioneered microcredit, revolutionising microfinance while providing loans to over 7.5 million impoverished people, 97% of whom were women, helping them lift themselves out of poverty. Alleviating poverty was this revolutionary company's aim, creating the first explicit social value of the new social business models.

A social business model can be defined as underpinning 'a self-sustaining company that sells goods or services and repays its owners' investments, but whose primary purpose is to serve society and improve the lot of the poor' (Yunus et al., 2010:309). In developing a social business model based on the Grameen experience in Bangladesh, Yunus et al. (2010) propose several similarities with conventional innovation business models, such as challenging conventional wisdom, finding complementary partners or undertaking continuous improvement, and new social-specific ones, such as favouring social profit-oriented stakeholders and the clear specification of social profit objectives.

The creation and appropriation of social value are key elements in any social business model. As Lashitew et al. (2022) remark, the literature on BoP strategies emphasises that social value-creating firms require a new collaborative, multistakeholder business approach. They signal BoP literature as one of the pioneering research streams in the field of social business models and divide it into two waves: (1) the first tried to show developed-world MNCs the market potential of low-income consumers at the BoP via a logic of 'blue ocean strategies'

(Kim & Mauborgne, 2004), to create social value by combining a firm's financial profitability for shareholders and positive social and environmental outcomes; and (2) the 'second generation' of BoP strategies, focusing on creating social value with and for local stakeholders through business collaboration with civil society organisations and governmental institutions; that is, highlighting two main features of a social business model – the collaborative and multistakeholder approach, and cross-sectoral collaboration among firms, governmental and civil society actors for social business innovation (Stal et al., 2022). These comprise the only pathway to reconfiguring organisational resources and capabilities in an open and learning innovation paradigm.

4.4.1 Main Components of a Social Business Model

Yunus et al. (2010) have developed the four elements of a social business model, distinguishing value proposition, value constellation, social profit equation and economic profit equation. The value proposition includes the products and services as well as a clear specification of stakeholders and their needs to be covered. The value constellation establishes the set of both internal and external value chains in a new collaborative paradigm while jointly, with the necessary and traditional economic profit equation, considering sales revenues, cost structure and capital employed, fulfilling the 'no economic loss' shift to make a self-sustained business model. Thus, a challenging new social profit equation is stated, including explicit social and environmental profits.

Considering social value, or shared value (Porter & Kramer, 2011), as the cornerstone of a social business model, as Figure 4.5 shows, Lashitew et al. (2022) suggest that social value includes three main components: (1) consumer value, defined in the value offering – the value proposition; (2) producer value, the firm and its partners – the value constellation; and (3) stakeholder value – or the economic and social profit equation – which includes shareholder value as well as other values created for diverse stakeholders: tax benefits for governments, social benefits for workers and local communities, positive externalities and so on. Social value can be split into three activities: value offering, value creation and value capture (Lashitew et al., 2022):

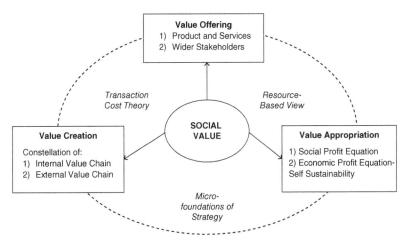

Figure 4.5 The main elements of a social business model
Source: Authors' own elaboration based on Yunus et al. (2010) and Lashitew et al. (2022)

- The social value offer aims to increase customers' social value by offering them goods or services that are affordable (with tailored prices to low-income consumers), essential (by covering essential needs such as sanitation, food, health, education, etc.) and/or universal (trying to cover those needs for the majority of the population). Overall, society's needs, in a wide sense, are met in the firm's reconceived products and markets (Porter & Kramer, 2011).
- Value creation concerns the design of the activities, resources and processes needed to create the social value offering, both internal to the firm and external, through interlinks with its partners. The RBV and transaction cost logics determine the content, structure and governance of the firm's activities. The redefinition of value chain productivity should consider social and environmental externalities, even when their internalisation may inflict internal costs on the firm (Porter & Kramer, 2011).
- Value capture and appropriation refer to how the firm captures the economic value created by different stakeholders. Contrary to the classical shareholders' rent appropriation scheme, a new resource-based view (Barney, 2018) incorporates into this logic a wider stakeholder perspective, including members of the business ecosystem, the government and even local communities (Gibson et al., 2021).

Creating social value implies identifying the key societal segments for whom value is created, as well as the governance mechanism (Lashitew et al., 2022).

In conclusion, a social business model pivots around a concept of social value that distinguishes this type of business from regular ones, expanding the total pool of economic and social value. Furthermore, societal needs define the markets and social harms create internal costs for firms (Porter & Kramer, 2011). In terms of a frame, the traditional business and management theories of the transaction cost economy and the RBV delineate value creation and the constellation of the firm's internal and external activities in the value chain under a new, reinforced collaborative logic among the firm and its stakeholders. The importance and embeddedness of context and environment for a social business drive the key role of its stakeholders, moving beyond their collaboration towards competitive advantage co-creation and rent appropriation (Barney, 2018), constituting, under this competitive logic, traditional fringe stakeholders (Hart & Sharma, 2004) such as local communities as strategic elements for firms (Gibson et al., 2021) that radically transforms the firms' purpose into economic but social profit equations, showing the relevance of a wider stakeholder conception in social business models and social values.

Furthermore, social businesses are intrinsic to social entrepreneurship (Diaz-Sarachaga & Ariza-Montes, 2022) and the role played by individuals – that is, the role of key organisational members, usually the CEO and top management team – in explaining the firm's strategy and performance on a microfoundation of strategy logic. As Yunus et al. (2010) highlight, humans have the instinctive, natural desire to make life better for their fellow humans if they can, the same 'sympathy' and natural human desire that limit selfish individualism, as stated several centuries ago by Adam Smith in his *Theory of the Moral Sentiments* (1790).

4.5 Concluding Remarks

Finally, although we have distinguished between social and environmental business models in this chapter, both are interrelated in a regenerative strategy logic (Hahn & Tampe, 2021). As Scarpellini (2022) remarks, there are several social impacts of circular business models on social equity and future generations. Circular business models have high potential for job creation across the whole value chain, as well as for employee participation and empowerment, as social actors. Additionally, local communities benefit from circular business and industrial symbiosis; from better community living standards, education and training, environmental taxes and local gross domestic product contributions; and from enhanced bilateral communication in future issues and decision-making processes. Overall, we bring together different categories of social impacts: jobs, new profiles and skills, tax revenues and other fees, awareness, transparency and stakeholders, public health, education, partnership and collaboration, employee participation, patents and innovations, and investments and gross value-added activities.

In sum, as Porter and Kramer first advanced in 2011, 'not all profit is equal. Profits involving a social purpose represent a higher form of capitalism, one that creates a positive cycle of company and community prosperity' (Porter & Kramer, 2011:15).

References

Aguilera, R., Aragón-Correa, J. A., and Marano, V. (2022). Rethinking corporate power to tackle grand societal challenges: Lessons from political philosophy. *Academy of Management Review*, 47(4): 456.

Amit, R., and Zott, C. (2012). Creating value through business model innovation. *MIT Sloan Management Review*, 53(3): 40–49.

Araujo-Galvao, G., Evans, S., Scoleze-Ferrer, P., and Monteiro-de Carvalho, M. (2022). Circular business model: Breaking down barriers towards sustainable development. *Business Strategy and the Environment*, 31(4): 1504–1524.

Bansal, P. (2019). Sustainable development in an age of disruption. *Academy of Management Discoveries*, 5(1): 8–12.

Barney, J. (1991). Firm resources and sustained competitive advantage. *Journal of Management*, 17(1): 99–120.

Barney, J. (2018). Why resource-based theory's model of profit appropriation must incorporate a stakeholder perspective. *Strategic Management Journal*, 39(13): 3305–3325.

Bhattacharya, C. B., and Polman, P. (2017). Sustainability lessons from the front lines. *MIT Sloan Management Review*, 58(2): 71–78.

Brennan, G., and Tennant, M. (2018). Sustainable value and trade-offs: Exploring situational logics and power relations in a UK brewery's malt network business model. *Business Strategy and the Environment*, 27(5): 621–630.

Brozovic, D. (2020). Business model based on strong sustainability: Insights from an empirical study. *Business Strategy and the Environment*, 29(2): 763–778.

Casadesus-Masanell, R., and Ricart, J. E. (2011). How to design a winning business model. *Harvard Business Review*, 89(1–2): 100–107.

Chesbrough, H. (2010). Business model innovation: Opportunities and barriers. *Long Range Planning*, 43(2–3): 354–363.

Clarivate. (2022). Web of Science/Social Sciences Citation Index. https://clarivate.com/products/scientific-and-academic-research/research-discovery-and-workflow-solutions/webofscience-platform/web-of-science-core-collection/social-sciences-citation-index.

DaSilva, C. M., and Trkman, P. (2014). Business model: What it is and what it is not. *Long Range Planning*, 47(6): 379–389.

Diaz-Sarachaga, J., and Ariza-Montes, A. (2022). The role of social entrepreneurship in the attainment of the sustainable development goals. *Journal of Business Research*, 152: 242–250.

Drucker, P. (1995). *People and Performance: The Best of Peter Drucker on Management*. London: Routledge.

Evans, S., Vladimirova, D., Holgado, M. et al. (2017). Business model innovation for sustainability: Towards a unified perspective for creation of sustainable business models. *Business Strategy and the Environment*, 26(5): 597–608.

Freeman, R. (1984). *Strategic Management: A Stakeholder Approach*. Boston, MA: Pitman Press.

Frishammar, J., and Parida, V. (2019). Circular business model transformation: A roadmap for incumbent firms. *California Management Review*, 61(2): 5–29.

Geissdoerfer, M., Vladimirova, D., and Evans, S. (2018). Sustainable business model innovation: A review. *Journal of Cleaner Production*, 198: 401–416.

Gibson, C., Gibson, S., and Webster, Q. (2021). Expanding our resources: Including community in the resource-based view of the firm. *Journal of Management*, 47(7): 1878–1898.

Guillen, M. (2020). *2030: How Today's Biggest Trends Will Collide and Reshape the Future of Everything*. New York: History Press.

Hahn, T., Figge, F., Pinkse, J. et al. (2018). A paradox perspective on corporate sustainability: Descriptive, instrumental, and normative aspects. *Journal of Business Ethics*, 148: 235–248.

Hahn, T., and Tampe, M. (2021). Strategies for regenerative business. *Strategic Organization*, 19(3): 456–477.

Hart, S. (1995). A natural-resource-based view of the firm. *Academy of Management Review*, 20(4): 986–1014.

Hart, S., and Dowell, G. (2011). A natural-resource-based view of the firm: Fifteen years after. *Journal of Management*, 37(5): 1464–1479.

Hart, S. L., and Sharma, S. (2004). Engaging fringe stakeholders for competitive imagination. *Academy of Management Perspectives*, 18(1): 7–18.

Hofmann, F., and Jaeger-Erben, M. (2019). Organizational transition management of circular business model innovations. *Business Strategy and the Environment*, 29(6): 2770–2788.

Hofmann, F., and Zu Knyphausen-Auseſβ, D. (2022). Circular business model experimentation capabilities: A case study approach. *Business Strategy and the Environment*, 31(4): 2469–2488.

Independent Group of Scientists appointed by the Secretary-General. (2019). *Global Sustainable Development Report 2019: The Future Is Now – Science for Achieving Sustainable Development*. New York: United Nations.

Kim, W., and Mauborgne, R. (2004). Blue ocean strategy. *Harvard Business Review*, 2004(October): 76–84.

Lambert, S. C., and Davidson, R. A. (2013). Applications of the business models in studies of enterprise success, innovation and classification: An analysis of empirical research from 1996 to 2010. *European Management Journal*, 31(6): 668–681.

Lashitew, A., van Tulder, R., and Muche, L. (2022). Social value creation in institutional voids: A model perspective. *Business & Society*, 61(8): 1992–2037.

Linder, M., and Williander, M. (2017). Circular business model innovation: Inherent uncertainties. *Business Strategy and the Environment*, 26(2): 182–196.

Lubik, S., and Garnsey, E. (2016). Early business model evolution in science-based ventures: The case of advanced materials. *Long Range Planning*, 49(3): 393–408.

Lüdeke-Freund, F., Gold, S., and Bocken, N. (2018). A review and typology of circular economy business models patterns. *Journal of Industrial Ecology*, 23(1): 36–61.

Magretta, J. (2002). Why business models matter. *Harvard Business Review*, 80(5): 96–92.

McGahan, A. (2021). Integrating insights from the resource-based view into the new stakeholder theory. *Journal of Management*, 47(7): 1734–1756.

McKinsey (2021, April). How companies capture the value of sustainability: Survey findings. *McKinsey & Company*. www.mckinsey.com/~/media/mckinsey/business%20functions/sustainability/our%20insights/how%20companies%20capture%20the%20value%20of%20sustainability%20survey%20findings/how-companies-capture-the-value-of-sustainability-survey-findings-vf.pdf.

Moggi, S., and Dameri, R. (2021). Circular business model evolution: Stakeholder matters for a self-sufficient ecosystem. *Business Strategy and the Environment*, 30(3): 2830–2843.

Montiel, I., Gallo, P. J., and Antolin-Lopez, R. (2020). What on earth should managers learn about corporate sustainability? A threshold concept approach. *Journal of Business Ethics*, 162(4): 857–880.

Newbert, S. (2008). Value, rareness, competitive advantage, and performance: A conceptual-level empirical investigation of the resource-based view of the firm. *Strategic Management Journal*, 29(7): 745–768.

Ortiz-de-Mandojana, N., and Bansal, P. (2016). The long-term benefits of organizational resilience through sustainable business practices. *Strategic Management Journal*, 37(8): 1615–1631.

Ovans, A. (2015, 23 January). What is a business model? *Harvard Business Review*. https://hbr.org/2015/01/what-is-a-business-model.

Porter, M., and Kramer, M. (2011). Creating shared value. *Harvard Business Review*, 89(1): 2–17.

Prahalad, C., and Hart, S. (2002). The fortune at the bottom of the pyramid. *Strategy+Business*, 26(1): 1–16.

Reim, W., Sjödin, D., and Parida, V. (2021). Circular business model implementation: A capability development case study from the manufacturing industry. *Business Strategy and the Environment*, 30(6): 2745–2757.

Scarpellini, S. (2022). Social impacts of a circular business model: An approach from a sustainability accounting and reporting perspective. *Corporate Social Responsibility & Environmental Management*, 29(3): 646–656.

Seelos, C., and Mair, J. (2007). Profitable business models and market creation in the context of deep poverty: A strategic view. *Academy of Management Perspectives*, 21(4): 49–63.

Sharma, S. (2022). From environmental strategy to environmental impact. *Academy of Management Discoveries*, 8(1): 1–6.

Smith, A. (1790). *The Theory of Moral Sentiments*. London: A. Millar. (6th ed. 2006. São Paulo: Metalibri.)

Stal, H. I., Bengtsson, M, and Mazhynski, S. (2022). Cross-sectoral collaboration in business model innovation for sustainable development: Tensions and compromises. *Business Strategy and the Environment*, 31(1): 445–463.

Teece, D. J. (2010). Business models, business strategy and innovation. *Long Range Planning*, 43(2–3): 172–194.

Teece, D. J., Pisano, G., and Shuen, A. (1997). Dynamic capabilities and strategic management. *Strategic Management Journal*, 18(7): 509–533.

Van der Byl, C. A., and Slawinski, N. (2015). Embracing tensions in corporate sustainability: A review of research from win-wins and trade-offs to paradoxes and beyond. *Organization & Environment*, 28(1): 54–79.

Walls, J. L., and Paquin, R. L. (2015). Organizational perspectives of industrial symbiosis: A review and synthesis. *Organization & Environment*, 28(1): 32–53.

Williamson, O. E. (1975). Markets and hierarchies: Analysis and antitrust implications: A study in the economics of internal organization. University of Illinois at Urbana-Champaign's Academy for Entrepreneurial Leadership Historical Research Reference in Entrepreneurship. https://ssrn.com/abstract=1496220.

World Economic Forum. (2020). *The Global Risks Report 2020*. Geneva: World Economic Forum. www.weforum.org/reports/the-global-risks-report-2020.

World Economic Forum. (2022). *The Global Risks Report 2022*. Geneva: World Economic Forum. www.weforum.org/reports/global-risks-report-2022.

Young, D., and Reeves, M. (2020). The quest for sustainable business model innovation. Boston, MA: Boston Consulting Group. www.bcg.com/publications/2020/quest-sustainable-business-model-innovation.

Yunus, M., Moingeon, B., and Lehmann-Ortega, L. (2010). Building social business models: Lessons from the Grameen experience. *Long Range Planning*, 43(2–3): 308–325.

Zott, C., and Amit, R. (2007). Business model design and the performance of entrepreneurial firms. *Organization Science*, 18(2): 181–199.

Zott, C., and Amit, R. (2010). Business model design: An activity system perspective. *Long Range Planning*, 43(2–3): 216–226.

5 | Climate Emergency in the Anthropocentric Era

The 59th minute: David Suzuki, a Canadian naturalist, tells a story of bacteria in a test tube. To explain geometric growth in a closed system, he asks us to imagine a test tube in which the bacteria double each minute. At the 60th minute, the test tube is full. At the 59th minute, the test tube is only half full. At the 56th minute, the test tube is only 6.25 percent full at which point the bacteria look around and say to each other, 'oh, there's lots of room to grow. But, in only 2 minutes, the bacteria will see the limits to growth, and in just one more minute, the bacteria will start to expire as they fill the test tube.'

> David Suzuki, Scientist, in the film *Force of Nature*
> (2010), National Film Board of Canada, www.nfb.ca/
> interactive/the_test_tube_with_david_suzuki. Advising
> us that at no other time in history has research on
> sustainable development been more important

The world is reaching the tipping point beyond which climate change may become irreversible. If this happens, we risk denying present and future generations the right to a healthy and sustainable planet – the whole of humanity stands to lose.

> Kofi Annan, former Secretary-General of the United Nations

5.1 Introduction

This chapter delves into the relationship between humans and the natural environment. It focuses on three key aspects: (1) the context, which provides an idea of the importance of humans in relation to the natural environment on which they depend; (2) the reasons why human intervention in the natural environment is considered to have led to the so-called anthropocentric era; and (3) the ways in which intensive human intervention has fundamentally altered the balances in the biosphere and the effects of that.

First, this chapter invites the reader to reflect on the role played by humans in the evolution of the planet and life on Earth (Richter-Boix, 2022). Thus, it shows how *Homo sapiens* has outlived other human species and explains how, despite its recent (in geological terms) presence on the planet, its impact has been of such a magnitude that it has altered the basic balances in the biosphere to the point of endangering its own survival.

It also provides evidence for why the period in which humans have intensified their impact on the natural environment is commonly referred to as the Anthropocene. To delimit the limits of the anthropocentric era as objectively as possible, following Smil (2018), we opt for an energy perspective that shows how the ways of generating energy and the intensity of energy generation are key factors in quantifying and determining the time frame in which the Anthropocene takes place, emphasising that the transition to the Anthropocene has not occurred abruptly and disruptively, but is the product of a trajectory in which different energy-generation technologies have overlapped over time.

Finally, following Rockström et al. (2009), we discuss the effects of the Anthropocene on the nine planetary subsystems (climate change, ocean acidification, ozone depletion, atmospheric aerosol loading, phosphorous and nitrogen cycles, global freshwater use, land system change, biodiversity loss and chemical pollution) and on the balance among them, placing special emphasis on the relationship among the increase in the concentration of greenhouse gases in the atmosphere and climate change and rising temperatures. Following Kemp et al. (2022), this analysis goes a step further, as it not only analyses the conventional temperature increase thresholds established by international institutions, but also takes into consideration the possible effects on potentially catastrophic scenarios, which, although they have not been analysed in depth and have often been ignored (we shall see why), may occur. We argue that these other unpleasant scenarios must be considered if we want to undertake adequate and consistent management of environmental risks.

The chapter concludes with a final reflection on how we should approach the environmental challenge from a balanced perspective that effectively accounts for the risks we face without being catastrophic or supposing that technology will save us and that *Homo sapiens* will succeed, as it has always done, in overcoming difficulties via the almost magical advent of new inventions that will radically change our way of relating to the natural environment within a short time. From a historical perspective, such changes have rarely occurred (as discussed later) and require several generations to be properly deployed on the scale that the environmental challenge requires. Recognising this, business and management scholars must begin, as soon as possible, to put in place regenerative strategies that will enable us to transition to more environmentally beneficial energy sources in the shortest possible time. The degree of penetration of such strategies will determine the pace of the transition and therefore the likelihood of success in meeting the environmental grand challenge.

5.2 The Human Being and the Natural Environment

5.2.1 The Origins

López-Otín and Kroemer (2020) explain simply and in a few lines how it all began. Thus, an estimated 14 billion years ago, a whole universe was born out of nothing, and light and matter were created. The universe expanded and then cooled sufficiently for elementary particles to give rise to the first atoms, molecules and organised matter. Approximately 4.5 billion years ago, the Sun was formed, the planets of the solar system were formed, and with them the planet Earth. After a collision with a Mars-sized protoplanet called Tea, the Moon was formed. Subsequently, two fundamental events occurred: on the one hand, the Great Oxygenation, which led to the beginning of the oxygenated atmosphere we enjoy today (via the release of oxygen from cyanobacteria); and on the other, the division of primitive cells, generating ever more complex and surprising forms of life.

Therefore, if we analyse the role of *Homo sapiens* from a temporal point of view, we can say that our species is a newcomer. Moreover, in terms of biomass – the total amount of living matter – we remain small, despite having exceeded 8 billion persons. Plants account for 82 per cent of biomass, bacteria account for 13 per cent, and the remaining 5 per cent is divided between fungi, protists (simple unicellular organisms that do not form tissues), viruses and animals. Among the latter, we represent only 0.01 per cent of the total. Nevertheless, we are a successful species and have a great capacity to alter the planet.

The oldest remains of *Homo sapiens* ever found were discovered in 2017 at the Jebel Irhoud archaeological site in western Morocco. According to this scientific evidence, the origin of our species dates back 300,000 years, when our ancestors began to spread across the African continent. We can therefore consider that 300,000 years ago, there were populations in Africa with traits very similar to ours.

To assess the impact of human beings on the natural environment throughout history, it is useful to have a perspective from which to approach the subject. Hence, the work of Richter-Boix (2022), which we follow, provides interesting clues for understanding how we got to where we are today.

First, it is worth noting that *Homo sapiens* has outlived all other human species, which gives an idea of its importance and ability to adapt. It coincided over time with other *Homo* groups, whom we were sure to have met at some point. *Homo neanderthalensis, Homo denisova, Homo floresiensis* and *Homo luzoniensis* or *Homo naledi* also inhabited our planet in Europe, Southeast Asia and Africa, yet we are now alone. None of these *Homo* groups has survived, and their respective disappearances took place a few thousand years after the arrival of *Homo sapiens* in their regions.

It is not possible to pinpoint with any great accuracy what our longevity as a species is due to, although our ability to cooperate and our supposed technological capacity are often mentioned as the more plausible explanations. In any case, whatever the explanation, the bottom line is that *Homo sapiens* has survived and has had an unprecedented impact on life on the planet.

As mentioned, *Homo sapiens* emerged approximately 300,000 years ago and since then has always depended on the natural environment and made use of it for survival, shelter, food or to improve its well-being in one way or another. In other words, human beings as we know them today have always had a very close relationship with the natural environment and have utilised it. From the time of hunter-gatherers to the present day, *Homo sapiens* has made more or less intensive use of the natural environment in which it lives. Without seeking to be exhaustive, some data reveal the intensity with which human beings have related to the natural environment.

For example, at the height of the Roman Empire, approximately 26,000 kilometres of forest were cut down to produce more than 80,000 tonnes of iron for fuel, causing levels of pollution that did not recur until the so-called Industrial Revolution, as attested by ice cores – cylindrical samples of ice obtained by drilling – collected from glaciers in the Alps or Greenland.

In mining and metallurgical areas trees were scarce, and some of the timber used in Rome's buildings did not come from their immediate vicinity, as the surrounding valleys had been deforested. Thus, in the fourth century CE, Rome needed to import timber from North Africa both for life in the city and for the upkeep of its fleet and war efforts. Its incessant activity in the Mediterranean caused havoc in many orders and the deterioration of forest resources, as shown by pollen records. Mediterranean forests were replaced by crops or pastures.

As if time has stood still and nothing has changed since these remote times, during them the most powerful areas bought resources from other regions that in return exploited their natural environment. Whereas in antiquity Rome depended on timber found at the source of the Tiber and Athens on wood from Macedonia and Thrace to build its ships, today the jungles of Indonesia and Malaysia are being plundered for palm oil, and the Amazon loses hundreds of thousands of hectares every year to pasture. As the height of irony, one of the largest multinational companies whose name refers to the Amazon is responsible for supplying us with goods and services that leave behind an indigestible carbon footprint.

All this activity, the endless desire for growth and the increasing commodification of biodiversity that we are currently witnessing have had devastating effects on the living beings that still accompany *Homo sapiens* on its journey. Thus, according to the International Union for Conservation of Nature, in 2022 more than 42,100 species were in danger of extinction (41 per cent of amphibians and 27 per cent of mammals, to name but a few) and could soon join the list of extinct species that already includes sea cows, the dodo and Icelandic walruses. As Richter-Boix (2022) argues, while it is true that sooner or later all organisms disappear and are replaced by others in an evolutionary process, the process by which an evolutionary line changes and gives rise to new forms before disappearing over time cannot effectively explain its radical disappearance without any continuity. At best, we are concerned with the survival of the species to which we attribute some practical utility; hence, in a display of ecological short-sightedness, we ignore the others.

There is no doubt that humankind today has reached levels of well-being that were unimaginable only a couple of centuries ago. However, it has done so at the expense of the planet and biodiversity. Since the sixteenth century, 690 vertebrate animal species have become extinct, 77 per cent of the Earth's land surface and 87 per cent of the oceans have been modified by our activities, and we have destroyed half of all plant biomass (Richter-Boix, 2022).

While it is true that the impact of *Homo sapiens* on the natural environment has been significant throughout the ages, we have not always been so voracious; we have not always impacted the natural environment with such intensity. There is a period in which humans' impact on nature has been particularly intense and problematic in environmental terms. This period is commonly referred to as the Anthropocene, and Section 5.2.2 is devoted to its analysis.

5.2.2 The Anthropocentric Era

The term 'Anthropocene' became very popular after it was first mentioned by Crutzen in 2002 in the journal *Nature* (Crutzen, 2002); it refers to the era in history when humans began (and continue) to play a major role in climate change. In geological terms, the Anthropocene complements the Holocene, the temperate period of the last ten to twelve millennia in which we now find ourselves. According to Crutzen (2002), the Holocene alone cannot explain the intense modifications that the planet is undergoing, as these are a consequence of human action. For him, the beginning of the Anthropocene dates to the end of the eighteenth century amid the onset of increasing concentrations of carbon dioxide (CO_2) and methane.

This date coincides with the design of Watt's steam engine (1769) and the start of what some call the Industrial Revolution, which could be considered a turning point in human beings' relationship with nature in terms of energy. In this respect, as Smil (2018) suggests, although the invention of the steam engine is usually credited to Watt, before him other inventors worked on previous and similar models, such as Papin in 1690, Savery shortly afterwards and Newcomen in 1712, revealing how inventions progress gradually and are improved over time.

In relation to the Industrial Revolution, as Smil points out there are some authors who consider it a myth and argue that it has little to do with revolution. That is, the supposed revolutionary economic and social changes were not in fact revolutionary and, in any case, they were restricted to certain industries (cotton, iron or transport), leaving other sectors completely on the margins of the salient advances.

Therefore, and as Fueyo (2022) remarks, the consensus regarding the beginning of the Anthropocene is not total; other authors even suggest that it truly began at the moment when humans were able to generate nuclear energy and created the atomic bomb – much more recently, in approximately 1945.

Perhaps the most objective way to determine when human activity began to impact the planet's climate is to take a strictly energetic approach, as detailed by Smil (2018). The energetic approach is essential if one seeks to determine how human activity began to alter the planet's climate. In this regard, Smil points out that changes in the ways and forms in which societies create and use energy are rarely disruptive and that the shift from one energy source to another occurs in a progressive, uneven way, with different forms of energy production coexisting in certain periods of time.

This progressive character of energy transitions is clearly seen in relation to the steam engine, whose peak occurred more than a century after Watt's patent, in approximately 1840 due to its importance in the manufacturing industry and the construction of railways and steamships. Even so, the importance of human labour and animal traction continued to grow throughout the nineteenth century. Moreover, just when steam engines had become most efficient and powerful, and despite their constant presence in industry, railways and shipping, steam turbines and internal combustion engines – the spread of which was made possible by the availability of abundant fuels from oil – undermined their privileged position in power generation.

Therefore, ruling out disruptive changes, the energy foundations of civilisation in 1800 were very similar to those existing in 1700 or even 1300. During these periods, wood, coal, human labour and draught animals were the basis of energy production. In contrast, the energy fundamentals in 1900 were very different from those prevailing in 1800 and quite similar to our energy fundamentals today. The shift from plant biomass fuels to fossil fuels, the generation of electricity and the shift from animated to mechanical energy sources led to unprecedented changes in the way humans lived and the ways they used energy. Whereas in the mid-nineteenth century more than 80 per cent of all power generated came from human labour, by the beginning of the twentieth century steam engines provided approximately one-third of it; by the beginning of the twenty-first century, virtually all but a fraction of all available power came from internal combustion engines and electricity generators.

In 1800, 98 per cent of the energy consumed came from plant biomass (wood and charcoal); by 1900, the energy supply had doubled and already half of it came from fossil fuels, mainly coal. Whereas in 1800 the most powerful inanimate engine – the improved Watt steam engine – had a capacity of just over 100 kW, by 1900 the largest steam engines were thirty times more powerful. However, although in 1900 the United States and France, for example, were fossil societies, the rest of the world still obtained half its energy from wood, charcoal and crop residues (Smil, 2018).

In short, although human beings have undoubtedly had an impact on the planet and this impact has been intensifying – giving rise to the more or less accepted denomination of the Anthropocene – to maintain that the beginning of this period occurred in a disruptive way at a specific moment in time is very attractive and interesting from a didactic point of view. However, there is very little here that is concrete; it is more appropriate to speak of transitions. Thus, in the first of these, the main prime mover for energy production was human labour; in the second, the steam engine took centre stage; and the third was dominated – and still is – by internal combustion engines and electricity generators, with fossil fuel use playing a very prominent role in the latter two transitions.

Some rather illuminating data may help us to locate in time the moment from which the pace of transition has accelerated and the intensity and impact of human activity on the natural environment have begun to occur on an unprecedented scale. For example, the global expansion of coal mining and hydrocarbon production increased annual fossil carbon extraction by a factor of twenty between 1900 and 2015, while global CO_2 emissions from burning fossil fuels increased from 534 metric tonnes in 1900 to 1.63 gigatonnes in 1950, 6.77 gigatonnes in 2000 and 9.14 gigatonnes in 2010.

As Smil (2018) shows, there has been exponential growth in the production of fossil fuels since large-scale extraction began in the nineteenth century. Such fuels were first used to power steam engines, then in internal combustion engines and steam and gas turbines, and subsequently in electricity production. Again, as noted already, the shift from one primary engine to another for power generation was not a disruptive process. In the 1860s, when oil extraction began to expand, there would not be any commercial internal combustion engines capable of powering vehicles until twenty-five years later. On the other hand, it took the latter part of the eighteenth century and six decades of the nineteenth to understand the basic principles of electricity, reaffirming that it takes at least three generations for a new energy resource to become globally dominant, as Smil (2018) argues.

However, the pace of transition has undoubtedly accelerated. The change that in prehistoric times involved the control of fire and the creation of better hunting tools took tens of thousands of years. Subsequently, sedentary agriculture took millennia to develop, but today's fossil-fuel-based societies have intensified the speed of change to unimaginable and planetarily unsustainable limits.

Thus, coal mining increased 100-fold between 1810 and 1910, oil extraction increased 300-fold between 1880 and 2015, and natural gas production increased 1000-fold in the same period. All this has been accompanied by an increase in the efficiency of energy supply that allows three times as much useful energy to be obtained compared to a century ago. As a result, the global supply of useful energy has increased more than eightfold.

We have become *energivorous* societies (Smil, 2018) that compulsively transform and consume unprecedented amounts of energy. Moreover, this amount of energy is mostly not used to satisfy vital needs. Mass consumer goods and leisure activities and services of all kinds, along with transport, account for most of the energy consumed in the most developed societies, which stand out for using energy in an increasingly irrational way.

For example, the United States increased its per capita energy consumption sixfold between 1900 and 2000, China increased this almost tenfold between 1900 and 2015, and Japan increased it fifteenfold. As Smil (2018) points out, this problem is compounded by the degree of technical uniformity behind these energy consumption figures. Thus, the number of companies that provide us with such a rate of unbridled fossil fuel-based energy consumption is decreasing, making it more difficult to obtain viable alternatives for a new transition.

While all this energy capacity has allowed us to achieve the important advances (agricultural productivity, industrialisation and urbanisation, transport and communications, among others) that have improved our average quality of life and the level of well-being we enjoy, it has also had negative consequences that threaten our civilisation. This rate of unbridled energy consumption is not acceptable and is not environmentally sustainable. The environmental deterioration that has occurred has destabilised the biosphere, with undesirable consequences such as those discussed in Section 5.3.

5.3 Climate and Planetary Emergency

The Anthropocene, understood as 'a geological period characterised by a dominant human influence on the functioning of the ecosystem' (Ergene et al., 2021:4), implies a new geological epoch in which humans have exerted a long-term and documentable impact on terrestrial ecosystems: the hydrosphere, cryosphere, biosphere and lithosphere (Hoffman & Jennings, 2021).

The Anthropocene constitutes an unprecedented phase in the evolution of life on Earth, with one species, humans, exerting extensive control. As shown previously, the still increasing intensity of anthropogenic forces in the twenty-first century has widespread implications that jeopardise the foundations of our civilisation.

In short, as Revelle and Suess (1957:19) point out, 'human beings are now carrying out a large-scale geophysical experiment of a kind that could not have happened in the past nor be reproduced in the future. Within a few centuries, we are returning to the atmosphere and oceans the concentrated organic carbon stored in sedimentary rocks over hundreds of millions of years.'

Faced with this worrying scenario, in 2019 more than 11,000 scientists from 153 countries declared a climate emergency (Ripple et al., 2020), highlighting through figures and graphs very troubling trends in vital signs on a planetary scale. They declared an ethical obligation to warn humanity about catastrophic threats. Parallel to this declaration, the climate emergency declaration movement has been growing. Since 2016, it has seen an increasing number of local, national and supranational entities sign climate emergency declarations, with the final impetus coming from the IPCC (2018) Special Report, which constituted a major wake-up call.

As reported by Climate Emergency Declaration and Mobilisation in Action (CEDAMIA, 2023), the first climate emergency declaration

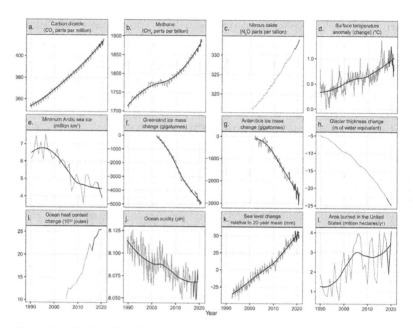

Figure 5.1 Carbon dioxide, methane, nitrous oxide and surface temperature anomaly levels
Source: Ripple et al. (2021:895)

at the local level took place in 2016, and the first at the national level was made by the Republic of Ireland in 2019, followed in the same year by the European Parliament. As of 2023, a total of 2,320 declarations had been made at an aggregated (national plus local) level worldwide, a clear indication of the widespread concern that the climate is a global issue that crosses all levels.

Thus, the climate emergency is a present reality on a planetary scale with a continuous upward trend. Indeed, according to Ripple et al. (2021), there are recent scientific signs of change on a planetary scale. In fact, among thirty-one tracked variables, eighteen have reached new all-time records, such as greenhouse gas emissions and temperatures, ocean changes, melting ice in poles and glaciers, the deforestation of the Amazon rainforest, and detrimental food policies. Figure 5.1 graphically depicts this evolution.

According to the IPCC's fourth assessment report (IPCC, 2007), abrupt changes are large-scale changes that occur much faster than a normal change in terms of their relevant force, such as rising atmospheric CO_2 concentrations.

As Ripple et al. (2021) remark, currently climate temperature is warming at approximately 1.25°C; hence, in combination with other feedback loops and the reaching of several tipping points, a massive-scale climate response is mandatory. Jointly with this declaration, they note that due to the limited time available, immediate and drastic reductions in greenhouse gases are essential. In the same vein, Brovkin et al. (2021) use geological records to show that abrupt changes in the Earth's system can occur on timescales short enough to challenge the capacity of humanity to adequately address and mitigate environmental threats. Many abrupt changes arise from slow changes in one component of the Earth's system and eventually pass a critical threshold, after which impacts cascade through coupled climate-ecological-social systems, similar to the beginning of this chapter and the well-known 59th minute story. Therefore, not only is a reduction in current emissions of greenhouse gases mandatory, but humanity also needs to decarbonise the atmosphere, as well as address other gases.

Therefore, in light of the data and warnings of science, there are strong reasons to believe that the relative stability of the current geological period – the Holocene – is in danger (Rockström et al., 2009). According to such analyses, this is due to human intervention in the basic balances in the biosphere during the period that is more or less generally referred to as the Anthropocene, which, as we have analysed, is characterised by an increase in the use of fossil fuels on a heretofore unseen scale in all areas and by unbridled energy consumption. That is, without human intervention, the stability of the Holocene would have continued for at least several thousand more years.

To clearly show the planetary changes that could make it impossible for our planet to sustain itself in the Holocene, relevant authors have identified nine planetary subsystems to which special attention must be given to prevent them from exceeding certain maximum thresholds or critical levels, as Figure 5.2 shows. Exceeding these thresholds could have devastating effects of unimaginable magnitude on the planet and our civilisation. These nine planetary subsystems with particular relevance are (Smil, 2022): climate change; ocean acidification (which, in addition to destroying marine ecosystems and interfering with marine photosynthesis, endangers marine organisms responsible for building the calcium carbonate structures that act as carbon sinks); stratospheric ozone depletion (ozone protects us from ultraviolet radiation); atmospheric aerosols (pollutants that reduce visibility and cause lung disorders); interference with nitrogen and phosphorus

PLANETARY BOUNDARIES		
Earth-system process	Parameters	Proposed boundary
Climate change	(i) Atmospheric carbon dioxide concentration (parts per million by volume)	350
	(ii) Change in radiative forcing (watts per metre squared)	1
Rate of biodiversity loss	Extinction rate (number of species per million species per year)	10
Nitrogen cycle (part of a boundary with the phosphorus cycle)	Amount of N_2 removed from the atmosphere for human use (millions of tonnes per year)	35
Phosphorus cycle (part of a boundary with the nitrogen cycle)	Quantity of P flowing into the oceans (millions of tonnes per year)	11
Stratospheric ozone depletion	Concentration of ozone (Dobson unit)	276
Ocean acidification	Global mean saturation state of aragonite in surface sea water	2.75
Global freshwater use	Consumption of freshwater by humans (km^3 per year)	4,000
Change in land use	Percentage of global land cover converted to cropland	15
Atmospheric aerosol loading	Overall particulate concentration in the atmosphere. on a regional basis	
Chemical pollution	For example, amount emitted to, or concentration of persistent organic pollutants, plastics, endocrine disrupters, heavy metals and nuclear waste in, the global environment, or the effects on ecosystem and functioning of Earth system thereof	

Figure 5.2 Earth system process and planetary boundaries
Source: Rockström et al. (2009:473)

cycles (mainly the release of these nutrients into freshwater and coastal waters); freshwater consumption (overextraction and misuse of aquifers); changes in land use (deforestation, agriculture, urban and industrial expansion); biodiversity loss; and chemical pollution.

Although traditionally climate tipping points have been associated with singular and independent catastrophes with very important negative impacts of a low occurrence probability, the increasing probability of high-impact ocean tipping points is due to several factors, such as warming, ocean acidification or deoxygenation. These tipping points are interconnected and should be combined with other gradual environmental changes, as they work together in serious singular catastrophic events that have cumulative and often compounding negative societal and Earth system impacts (Heinzea et al., 2021).

Thus, individual catastrophic events with an extraordinarily negative impact, such as the collapse of ocean overturning circulations or the rapid and partial disintegration of the West Antarctic Ice Sheet, are of a low probability before 2100 (Heinzea et al., 2021). Nevertheless, as these examples highlight, the focus should be placed on current and imminent ocean changes. The oceans can be considered a grand reservoir of heat and dissolved carbon. Since the Industrial Revolution, the oceans have sequestered between 30 and 40 per cent of total CO_2 and 93 per cent of the heat added by human activity.

Tipping points occur in very different systems in different disciplines, such as ecology, economy or engineering. Tipping elements are Earth's subsystems that pass a critical threshold or tipping point at which a small perturbation can qualitatively alter their state of development (Kröne et al., 2020). Often tipping elements are interconnected, implying that if one tipping element crosses its tipping point, it can produce a cascade of interconnected tipping elements via the domino effect of a significant impact on the system.

For environmental subsystems, tipping points can be understood as fold bifurcations, such as global ocean circulation, the Greenland Ice Sheet or tropical rainforests, among others. Coupled cusp catastrophes have been studied in detail in regard to two or three subsystems or in combination with Hopf bifurcations; that is, critical points. Figure 5.3 shows a model of a tipping network.

Thus, as Rockström et al. (2009) point out, all these subsystems are interrelated, whereby exceeding the safety zone in one or more of them can lead to unpredictable cascading effects that profoundly and irreversibly alter life on the planet. At least four of these safety thresholds have already been exceeded: climate change, biodiversity loss, interference with nitrogen and phosphorus cycles, and land use changes. Two others (ocean acidification and freshwater use) are on track to reach the established safety thresholds, while stratospheric ozone depletion is the only one that appears to be under control thus far. In this regard, it is estimated that oceans will notably be 150 per cent more acidic in 2050 than they were in the early nineteenth century (Fueyo, 2022).

In relation to chemical pollution and atmospheric aerosols, the data collected do not allow robust conclusions to be drawn (Hickel, 2018). We are therefore facing an emergency scenario, as corroborated by Lenton et al. (2022), who note that current scientific evidence on the threat of tipping points such as global warming, ice collapse and biosphere limits indicates that we are approaching an interconnected global cascade of tipping points. As Figure 5.4 shows, we are in a state

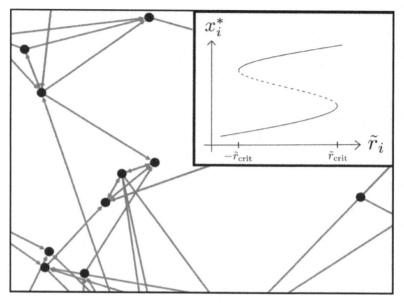

Figure 5.3 A conceptual model of interconnected tipping points
Source: Krönke et al. (2020:2)
Illustration of a tipping network. Each node represents a tipping element with a corresponding state variable x_i. A directed link corresponds to a positive linear coupling with strength d. The effective control parameter $\tilde{r}_i$ of a node depends on the state of the nodes it is coupled to. The equilibria with respect to the effective control parameter are qualitatively illustrated in the box.

of planetary emergency: both the risk and the urgency of the situation are acute.

Moreover, some data illustrate the interconnections between relevant subsystems and their severity. Thus, as MacDowell et al. (2017) have quantified, anthropogenic CO_2 emissions in 2000–2014 grew at a rate of 2.5 per cent each year, each a percentage point more than in 1970–2000, an approximate increase of 31.9–35.5 Gt CO_2 emissions. In the same vein, Jambeck et al. (2015) estimate that 275 million metric tonnes of plastic waste were generated in 192 coastal countries – 93 per cent of the global population – in 2010, with 4.8–12.7 million metric tonnes of plastic entering the oceans. Thus, Lebreton et al. (2019) call for a rapid reduction in plastic emissions and the active removal of plastic waste from the oceans. As Rockström et al. (2009) point out, this is a delicate balance in which, for example, changes in

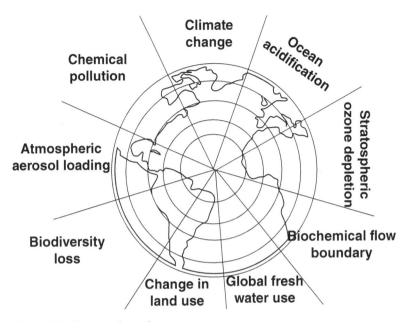

Figure 5.4 Planetary boundaries
Source: Authors' own elaboration based on Rockström et al. (2009:472)

land use in the Amazon can alter the availability of water resources in Tibet, or sandstorms from the Sahara can carry minerals to the Amazon and help fertilise it.

Thus, according to Ripple et al. (2021), the Brazilian Amazon's destruction increased in 2009–2020, reaching 1.11 million hectares destroyed in a twelve-year period. Indeed, as Qin et al. (2021) highlight, the Amazon region is transitioning from being a carbon sink to a carbon source. In addition, and as Krönke et al. (2020) point out, networks with a limited spatial organisation such as the Amazon rainforest's networks are the most vulnerable. Such studies suggest that the Amazon forest-climate system is especially vulnerable to the occurrence of tipping point cascades.

An excellent example of interaction and cascading effects is provided by Wunderling et al. (2021) regarding the connection between the Greenland Ice Sheet, the Atlantic Meridional Overturning Circulation (AMOC), the West Antarctic Ice Sheet and the Amazon rainforest. According to these authors, when considering the interactions among the respective wetlands, the aggregate effect is destabilising and causes non-linear responses in these different planetary subsystems. Thus, the cascading effects will be mainly initiated by the polar ice sheets and will use the AMOC as a transmitter element. Thus, if Greenland transgresses its threshold, the probability that the AMOC will as well is increased by a factor of ten. This can be seen among the rest of the interconnections. In addition to that already mentioned, the connection between the wetlands in Greenland and sea level rise stands out.

However, analysis of each of the nine planetary subsystems and their respective connections with one another is a task far beyond the scope of this book. Accordingly, we focus specifically on climate change because of its strong and evident connections with the intensity of the CO_2 emissions (Rockström et al., 2009) of the energivorous societies referred to earlier.

5.4 Critical Climate Change Scenarios: An Uneasy Look

We have already crossed the boundary limit for atmospheric CO_2 that was fixed at 350 parts per million (ppm): we are over 400 ppm, and climbing. More specifically, the global average atmospheric CO_2 was 409.8 ppm in 2019, 416.19 ppm in April 2021, and almost 421 ppm in May 2022, a level higher than at any point in at least the past 800,000 years.

The year 2020 was the second hottest on record and, as scientific monitoring highlights, three of the most important greenhouse gases – CO_2, methane and nitrous oxide – showed new year-to-date records in the atmosphere in 2020 and 2022. Specifically, CO_2 reached almost 421 ppm in May 2022 (Fountain, 2022). Although the COVID-19 pandemic reduced fossil fuel investment and energy consumption, greenhouse gas emissions continued to increase.

Oceans also offer clear signs of climate emergency. As Figure 5.1 shows (Ripple et al., 2021), ocean warming trends and sea levels have set new records, and acidification continues to increase. Thus, due to the high concentrations of CO_2 in the oceans and the large amount of CO_2 they are forced to absorb, seawater is becoming acidic (lowering its pH) and endangering both its capacity to absorb CO_2 and the marine ecosystems that inhabit it. As illustrated in Figure 5.5, the pH of the ocean is following a constant downward trend.

However, despite the worrying trends shown among some of the most relevant parameters, the potentially catastrophic scenarios that

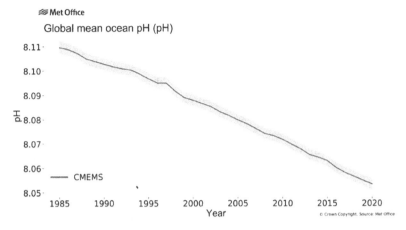

Global mean surface pH from E.U. Copernicus Marine Service Information (blue) covering the period 1985-2020. The shaded area indicates the estimated uncertainty in each estimate. Data from Copernicus Marine Environment Monitoring Service.

Figure 5.5 Global mean ocean pH
Source: https://gcos.wmo.int/en/global-climate-indicators

could occur have been little studied. As mentioned by the IPCC (2007), the situations that could occur in scenarios where global warming reaches 3°C or more have barely been analysed. This is evidence of the deficient management of the risks associated with a complex problem that we do not fully understand (Kemp et al., 2022).

There are several reasons that have prevented or delayed in-depth analysis of these other critical scenarios that civilisation could potentially face. As mentioned by relevant authors, one of the main reasons concerns the targets set in international agreements, which, for example, focus on limiting the increase in global warming to 1.5°C (best-case scenario) or 2°C (worst-case scenario). Another reason concerns climate scientists' fear of being seen as preachers of disaster, and yet another the fact that none of us wants to even imagine what would happen if the complex interactions of planetary systems were to cause consequences totally beyond our control and understanding. In short, our civilisation has too much at stake not to perform a proper risk analysis of this complex situation.

The truth is that taking these critical scenarios into account is a necessary exercise of prudence in view of the evidence. As has been indicated, greenhouse gas emissions continue to grow; if this trajectory continues, the planet will be within the critical range (2.1–3.9°C) of temperature increase by the year 2100. Even if all the targets and commitments established at the international level are met (which is unlikely), we will still be in the critical range at 1.7–2.6°C. Given that temperature increases of more than 2°C have not occurred on the planet's surface since the Pleistocene epoch (Kemp et al., 2022), it would be wise to be as cautious and forward-looking as possible.

Even if greenhouse gas emissions begin to decline, many uncertainties have not been properly modelled, such as methane emissions due to the thawing of Arctic permafrost or the apparent loss in capacity of the planet's carbon sinks. Thus, as Smil (2022) notes, the biosphere lost 14 per cent of its trees between 1900 and 2015 due to logging, and as the planet's forests are becoming younger and lower in height, they cannot store as much carbon as in the past. In other words, even if we were to suddenly stop emitting greenhouse gases, the capacity of the planet's carbon sinks has already been depleted by our past activities. The same applies to the effect that high concentrations of CO_2 can have on certain types of cloud formations, which could disappear, leading to an even greater increase in temperature. In short, the deeper the analysis goes, the more novel variables that have to be taken into consideration appear and the greater the uncertainty.

The same reasoning can be applied regarding Antarctic ice trends, which could reverse even if the temperature were to return to current levels. Moreover, the disappearance of glaciers reduces the surface area reflecting solar radiation (more sunlight is absorbed by the Earth's surface), which in turn leads to a rise in temperatures.

Furthermore, temperature increases beyond 2°C can have devastating effects on food supplies and the economy in general. In terms of food supplies, for instance regarding maize, if we fall in the range between 3°C and 4°C, the main producing regions will experience unsustainable production losses. In terms of the more global economic impacts, the Swiss Re Institute states that global gross domestic product will be altered by any rise in temperature. It estimates that this will fall by 4 per cent if the objectives of the Paris Agreement are met – that is, if the 2°C increase is reached; there will be a fall of 14 per cent if we reach the 2.6°C mark and a catastrophic fall of 18 per cent if we reach a 3.2°C increase (Fueyo, 2022).

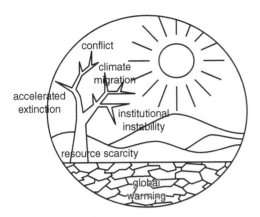

Figure 5.6 Global warming's cascading effects
Source: Authors' own elaboration

Hence, there are several reasons to take a serious look at other potential critical scenarios and to be aware of the full extent of the climate emergency (Kemp et al., 2022).

As already discussed, the link between climate change and greenhouse gas emissions is well known, as Figure 5.6 shows. However, the rate of greenhouse gas emissions has not slowed but rather increased. In view of the evidence, then, we are not using energy rationally, and the foundations of our civilisation are still based on the use of fossil fuels. If we continue at this rate, by the end of the twenty-first century we will have passed the thresholds that have led to mass extinctions in the past.

Climate change has the potential to trigger a wide range of conflicts, from making life impossible in certain regions (causing mass migration) to increasing the likelihood of future pandemics. Regarding the lack of minimum living conditions in the places most affected by climate change, currently more than 2.5 billion people do not have access to clean water and only have access to 5 litres per day, yet in Europe more than 150 litres per person per day are wasted (Araujo, 2022). Therefore, it is estimated that by 2070 nearly 2 billion people will live in extremely hot areas, with all that this implies in terms of political instability, economic inequality and government fragility.

On the other hand, and in relation to the increased likelihood of future pandemics, it is worth recalling what Richter-Boix (2022) has mentioned regarding the relationship between deforestation and zoonosis. That is, as *Homo sapiens* has increasingly colonised previously inaccessible wilderness, the risk of infectious diseases passing from animals to humans has grown considerably.

In short, temperature increases beyond the thresholds generally considered could lead to cascading effects and consequences that we are not yet able to foresee, but that nevertheless need to be considered if we are to carry out a proper risk analysis that explores a wide range of potentially critical possibilities.

5.5 Concluding Remarks

As the scientific evidence shows, the anthropocentric era requires transformational changes in business and the economy and in how humans relate to the natural world. It implies regenerative postures to reduce the existing pollution on Earth. As Ergene et al. (2021) point out, humanity is facing a new ecological responsibility; in its translation to the business sphere, past and current solutions for managing an organisation and the environment via a 'business-as-usual' approach must be shifted to regenerative approaches adopting a systemic socio-ecological well-being rationale. As Whiteman et al. (2013) and Sharma (2022) claim, it is time to reconsider the ecological and systemic foundations for sustainability and to integrate management studies more closely with the natural sciences. New transdisciplinary management theories can explain the existence and behaviour of companies and effectively bridge the existing divide between management and organisational research and natural climate science concerning the current climate emergency. Now is the time to build a new paradigm within which science and business research and practitioners can take common action (Hoffman & Jennings, 2021).

As Alvarez et al. (2020) claim, society increasingly expects companies to take the lead in helping resolve problems of environmental and social sustainability. The existing gap between climate change science and management research (Nyberg & Wright, 2022) must be overcome. Current levels of atmospheric, soil and water pollution and degradation demand new, disruptive innovations and business solutions that extend beyond the traditional reduction in negative environmental externalities and are able to reduce current levels of pollution by creating positive environmental externalities and, more importantly, reversing climate and environmental emergencies.

As Bansal (2019) and Sharma (2022) advocate, amid this grand challenge, corporate environmentalism requires integrating social, organisational and management theories with energy and biophysical systems to enrich the theoretical perspectives and empirical approaches framing this complex phenomenon.

As Ergene et al. (2021) point out, the management field has failed to pay attention to the root issues of the current climate emergency. Even the most advanced product stewardship and industrial symbiosis/ ecosystems postulates, which commonly argue for the maintenance of environmental integrity by minimising the industrial system's ecological footprint through the productive use of waste, high resource intensity and accelerated biological degrading processes, are not sufficient to reverse the climate emergency. In this vein, Nyberg and Wright (2022) underscore the need to refocus research and engage with new and emerging concepts – such as regenerative strategies – that better address the grand challenge of climate mitigation. Although current management theories, models and concepts legitimise 'business-as-usual' tactics amid a clear lack of attention to natural environment problems, the growing climate emergency demands new solutions beyond 'greening the business' or 'sustainability' postures. These include, for example, the reversion of current environmental degradation with carbon capture technologies or business models that pay attention to the broader nature and long-term benefits of corporate sustainability (Ortiz-de Mandojana & Bansal, 2016).

However, we must also be cautious. Despite the degree of progress in climate science and the sophisticated models that warn us of the catastrophic effects as analysed in this chapter, the complexity of the phenomena associated with the climate emergency is tremendous, and we are still far from understanding them in all their magnitude. According to the latest analyses, we may have surpassed the indicated thresholds, and we are currently hovering around a temperature increase of approximately 2.3°C. On the other hand, the scenarios put forward by the IPCC in which global emissions are halved by 2030 and eliminated by 2050 seem clearly unrealistic, given the energy fundamentals of our societies (Smil, 2022).

This in no way suggests that we do not take seriously all the warnings of the catastrophic consequences of rising temperatures. On the contrary, no single technology is going to save us, nor (unfortunately) are we going to abandon our dependence on fossil fuels in the short or medium term (in fact, as we write this, the German government is rethinking its planned ban on petrol and diesel engines in 2035). What needs to be accomplished, then, is to prepare for the transition now. As mentioned, management scholars and businesses have a major responsibility in this task.

Thus, the implementation of regenerative strategies for an energy transition is urgent and cannot wait, as we discuss in Chapter 6.

References

Alvarez, S. A., Zander, U., Barney, J. B., and Afuah, A. (2020). Developing a theory of the firm for the 21st century. *Academy of Management Review*, 45(4): 711–716.

Araujo, J. (2022). *Somos agua que piensa*. Barcelona: Editorial Crítica.

Bansal, P. (2019). Sustainable development in an age of disruption. *Academy of Management Discoveries*, 5(1): 8–12.

Brovkin, V., Brook, E., Williams, J. W. et al. (2021). Past abrupt changes, tipping points and cascading impacts in the Earth system. *Nature Geoscience*, 14: 550–558.

Climate Emergency Declaration and Mobilisation in Action. (2023, 6 May). Climate Emergency Declaration fact sheet: Sheet 1. www.cedamia.org/fact-sheets.

Crutzen, P. J. (2002). Geology of mankind: The Anthropocene. *Nature*, 415: 23.

Ergene, S., Banerjee, S. B., and Hoffman, A. J. (2021). (Un)sustainability and organization studies: Towards a radical engagement. *Organization Studies*, 42(8): 1319–1335.

Fountain, H. (2022, 3 June). Carbon dioxide levels are highest in human history. *New York Times*. www.nytimes.com/2022/06/03/climate/carbon-dioxide-record.html.

Fueyo, J. (2022). *Blues para un planeta azul: El último desafío de la civilización para evitar el abismo del cambio climático*. Barcelona: Ediciones B.

Heinzea, C., Blencknerc, H., Rusieckaa, D. et al. (2021). The quiet crossing of ocean tipping points. *PNAS*, 118(9): e20084781181-9.

Hickel, J. (2018). Is it possible to achieve a good life for all within planetary boundaries? *Third World Quarterly*, 40(1): 18–35.

Hoffman, A. J., and Jennings, P. D. (2021). Institutional-political scenarios for Anthropocene society. *Business & Society*, 60(1): 57–94.

International Union for Conservation of Nature. (2023, 6 May). More than 42,100 species are threatened with extinction. www.iucnredlist.org/about/citationinfo.

IPCC. (2007). Fourth Assessment Report. www.ipcc.ch/assessment-report/ar4.

IPCC. (2018). Special report: Global warming of 1.5°C. www.ipcc.ch/sr15.

Jambeck, J. R., Geyer, R., Wilcox, C. et al. (2015). Plastic waste inputs from land into the ocean. *Science*, 347(6223): 768–771.

Kemp, L., Xu, C., Depledge, J. et al. (2022). Climate endgame: Exploring catastrophic climate change scenarios. *Proceedings of the National Academy of Sciences*, 119(34): e2108146119.

Krönke, J., Wunderling, N., Winkelman, R. et al. (2020). Dynamics of tipping points on complex networks. *Physical Review E*, 1010(4): 0423111–0423119.

Lebreton, L., Egger, M., and Slat, B. (2019). A global mass budget for positively buoyant macroplastic debris in the ocean. *Scientific Reports*, 9(1): 12922.

Lenton, T. M., Benson, S., Smith, T. et al. (2022). Operationalising positive tipping points towards global sustainability. *Global Sustainability*, 5(e1): 1–16.

López Otín, C., and Kroemer, G. (2020). *El sueño del tiempo*. Barcelona: Paidós.

Mac Dowell, N., Fenell, P. S., Shah, N., and Maitland, G. C. (2017). The role of CO_2 capture and utilization in mitigating climate change. *Nature Climate Change*, 7: 243–249.

Nyberg, D., and Wright, C. (2022). Climate-proofing management research. *Academy of Management Perspectives*, 36(2): 713–728.

Ortiz-de-Mandojana, N., and Bansal, P. (2016). The long-term benefits of organizational resilience through sustainable business practices. *Strategic Management Journal*, 37(8): 1615–1631.

Qin, Y., Xiao, X., Wigneron, J. P. et al. (2021). Carbon loss from forest degradation exceeds that from deforestation in the Brazilian Amazon. *Nature Climate Change*, 11(5): 442–448.

Revelle, R., and Suess, H. E. (1957). Carbon dioxide exchange between atmosphere and ocean and the question of an increase of atmospheric CO_2 during the past decades. *Tellus*, 9(1): 18–27.

Richter-Boix, A. (2022). *El primate que cambió el mundo: nuestra relación con la naturaleza desde las cavernas hasta hoy*. Barcelona: GeoPlaneta.

Ripple, W. J., Wolf, C., Newsome, T. M., Barnard, P., and Moomaw, W. R. (2020). World scientists' warming of a climate emergency. *BioScience*, 70(1): 8–12.

Ripple, W. J., Wolf, C., Newsome, T. et al. (2021). World scientists' warming of a climate emergency 2021. *BioScience*, 71(9): 894–898.

Rockstrom, J., Steffen, W., Noone, K. et al. (2009). A safe operating space for humanity: Identifying and quantifying planetary boundaries that must not be transgressed could help prevent human activities from causing unacceptable environmental change, argue Johan Rockstrom and colleagues. *Nature*, 461(7263): 472–476.

Sharma, S. (2022). From environmental strategy to environmental impact. *Academy of Management Discoveries*, 8(1): 1–6.

Smil, V. (2018). *Energy and Civilization: A History*. Cambridge, MA: MIT Press.

Smil, V. (2022). *How the World Really Works: A Scientist's Guide to Our Past, Present and Future*. London: Penguin.

Whiteman, G., Walker, B., and Perego, P. (2013). Planetary boundaries: Ecological foundations for corporate sustainability. *Journal of Management Studies*, 50(2): 307–336.

Wunderling, N., Donges, J. F., Kurths, J., and Windelmann, R. (2021). Interacting tipping elements increase risk of climate domino effects under global warming. *Earth System Dynamics*, 12(2): 601–619.

6 | *The Regenerative Strategy*

To feel much for others and little for ourselves, that to restrain our selfish, and to indulge our benevolent affections, constitutes the perfection of human nature; and can alone produce among mankind that harmony of sentiments and passions in which consists of their whole grace and propriety.

Adam Smith, The Theory of Moral Sentiments, 1790

Without action, climate catastrophe is coming for all of us.

António Guterres, Secretary-General of the
United Nations, January 2023

6.1 Exploring Disruptive Businesses: Defining the Regenerative Strategy

In the capitalist tradition, wealth creation for corporate shareholders – with its associated societal and environmental externalities – has been the essential aim of a firm's mission (Friedman, 1970; Jensen & Meckling, 1976). Although the grand environmental challenges we face have led management scholars to claim that businesses must have a sustainable relationship with the natural environment on which they depend (Aguilera et al., 2022), business activity represents perhaps the greatest threat to the integrity of the biosphere today. As Gladwin et al. (1995:974) remind us, 'modern management theory is constricted by a fractured epistemology, which separates humanity from nature and truth from morality. Reintegration is necessary if organisational science is to support ecologically and socially sustainable development.'

In 2020, for the first time in the history of the Global Risk Survey carried out by the World Economic Forum, environmental concerns dominated the top long-term risks by likelihood, constituting three of the top five risks by impact of an environmental nature. A recent report on the global risks by the World Economic Forum (2022)

Table 6.1 *Most severe risks on a global scale over the next ten years*

Rank	Severe risk	Nature
1	Climate action failure	Environmental
2	Extreme weather	Environmental
3	Biodiversity loss	Environmental
4	Social cohesion erosion	Societal
5	Livelihood crises	Societal
6	Infectious diseases	Societal
7	Human environmental damage	Environmental
8	Natural resource crisis	Environmental
9	Debt crises	Economic
10	Geo-economic confrontation	Geopolitical

Source: World Economic Forum Global Risks Perception Survey 2021–2022 (2022:14)

presented three environmental concerns as the most critical to address in the next ten years. As Table 6.1 shows, sustainable development is a major challenge: among the ten more severe risks, eight are of a social-environmental nature. According to this survey, climate change continues to be perceived as the gravest threat to humanity, with failure in climate action the most important risk. Thus, the planet cannot wait: 'extreme weather' and 'climate action failure' are among the top five short-term risks to the world, but the five most menacing long-term threats are all environmental. 'Climate action failure', 'extreme weather' and 'biodiversity loss' also rank as the three most potentially severe risks in the next decade.

Indeed, in this report, the World Economic Forum (2022:31) suggests that 'without stronger action, global capacity to mitigate and adapt will be diminished, eventually leading to a "too little, too late" situation and ultimately a "hothouse world scenario" with runaway climate change that makes the world all but uninhabitable. The world will face high costs if we collectively fail to achieve the net-zero goal by 2050. Complete climate inaction will lead to losses projected to be between 4% and 18% of global GDP with different impacts across regions.'

As we have stated in several parts of this book, and as Alvarez et al. (2020) remark, society's increasing expectations for the leading role of business in facing the climate emergency call for strong action. In this regard, our disruptive proposal is the regenerative strategy.

All extant 'business-as-usual' common environmental positioning logic fails to pay attention to the root issues and the big picture of the current climate emergency (Bansal, 2019; Ergene et al., 2021; Sharma, 2022; Aguilera et al., 2022). Even the most advanced product stewardship and industrial symbiosis/ecosystems and circular economy postulates, which commonly concern the maintenance of environmental integrity by minimising the industrial system's ecological footprint through sustainable business model implementation and the productive use of waste, high resource intensity and accelerated biological degradation processes, are not enough to reverse the climate emergency.

Accordingly, the current Anthropocene era requires transformational changes in the relationship between business and the natural environment. As Bansal (2019) notes, in no other time in history has research on sustainability been more important. According to Whiteman et al. (2013), the planet's boundaries rest on nine critical earth-system thresholds: (1) climate change; (2) biodiversity loss; (3) interference with the nitrogen and phosphorus cycles; (4) stratospheric ozone depletion; (5) ocean acidification; (6) global freshwater use; (7) change in land use; (8) chemical pollution; and (9) atmospheric aerosol loading. In fact, three of these boundaries – the rate of biodiversity loss, the nitrogen cycle and climate change – have already been crossed.

To address this, we propose a new business–natural environment relationship based on a disruptive environmental regenerative strategy aimed at guiding the energy transition of tomorrow's businesses. This regenerative strategy can be considered disruptive because it extends beyond the zero-pollution logic and seeks, as an environmental aim, the reversion of current environmental degradation and the creation of positive environmental externalities, which implies fundamental changes in the logic of doing business that affect firms' organisation, purpose, time scope and technology. New regenerative business models will be developed using disruptive technologies that draw on new technological paradigms, creating completely new products and production systems and subsequent new markets in a climate-proofed environmental strategy.

The current climate emergency requires radical and disruptive changes in business model conception, production, market, structure and entrepreneurial dimensions to carry out the new regenerative strategy. These new, radically climate-proofed proactive business models are developed by linking cutting-edge technologies from science with new theoretical postulates from management and strategy (Barney, 2018; Alvarez et al., 2020). This is the most proactive strategic posture; it implies the potential reversion of the current climate emergency and natural environment degradation and the creation of positive environmental externalities, a disruptive approach that leaves the business-as-usual logic behind (Wright & Nyberg, 2017).

Thus, as Figure 6.1 shows, we propose an enhanced environmental strategy typology – pollution control, pollution prevention, product stewardship and regeneration – where the reversion of current environmental degradation and the creation of environmental externalities play a key role in the last process, not only contributing to the end of global warming and natural environment degradation, but also reducing the current levels of pollution in the atmosphere, water and land, reversing the climate emergency and related land and water environmental degradation. This represents the initial steps in real climate-proofing management research (Nyberg & Wright, 2022; Sharma, 2022). Jointly with the main four environmental strategic positionings, non-compliance refers to companies with a passive attitude towards environmental demands.

As shown in Chapter 5, the current Anthropocene era requires transformational changes in the business–natural environment relationship. Regarding the nine critical earth-system thresholds (Whiteman et al., 2013), as already mentioned three of these boundaries – the rate of biodiversity loss, the nitrogen cycle and climate change – have already been crossed. As Bansal (2019) highlights, as business activities breach planetary boundaries, sustainable development becomes more critical and urgent than ever. To properly address these planetary boundaries, we propose the regenerative strategy, which extends beyond the zero-pollution logic and seeks, as the main environmental aim, the reversion of current environmental degradation and the creation of positive environmental externalities. As mentioned, new regenerative business models will be developed using disruptive technologies that draw on new technological paradigms, creating completely new products and production systems and subsequent new markets in a climate-proofed environmental strategy. This implies a disruptive change in the conception of a new climate-proof corporate environmentalism (Nyberg & Wright, 2022) with the following main new features: (1) prospection; (2)

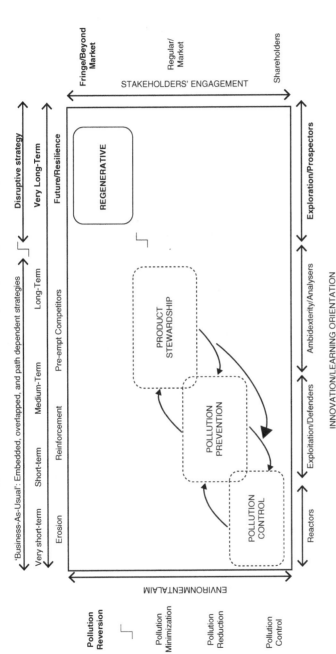

Figure 6.1 Business-as-usual and regenerative environmental strategies
Source: Authors' own elaboration

learning path exploration; (3) very long-term orientation; (4) systemic resilience; (5) fringe stakeholders' engagement; and (6) reversion of environmental damage and creation of positive environmental externalities.

According to Miles and Snow's (1978) corporate strategy typology, regenerative firms are prospectors; they are usually the first in the market, stressing innovation and flexibility to quickly respond to changing and emergent market conditions. They are technically innovative and seek new products and markets, able to develop new cutting-edge environmental technologies, products and markets rapidly, thereby requiring strong research and development (R&D) and engineering efforts and solid market research (Desarbo et al., 2005). Framed in the Levinthal and March (1993) logic of organisational learning paths, the regenerative strategy perfectly fits exploration, where a company pursues the new knowledge of things that might come to be known.

In contrast to the 'business-as-usual', traditional environmental thinking, whereby management academics and practitioners tend to ignore the temporality in the causal relationship between corporate environmentalism and organisational performance, companies following the regenerative strategy should take into account that their most strategic and relevant benefits will be achieved in the long and very long term in the form of organisational resilience (Ortiz-de Mandojana & Bansal, 2016:1617), defined as 'the incremental capacity of an organisation to anticipate and adjust to the environment'. Therefore, the regenerative strategy extends beyond current competitive advantage reinforcement and/or competitors' pre-emption towards future positioning (Hart, 1995) to embrace a long-term resiliency approach to sustainability (Ortiz-de Mandojana & Bansal, 2016). Specifically, resilience as an interdisciplinary concept describes one of the main purposes of organisations described by Miles and Snow (1978) and Levinthal and March (1993), operating dynamically as complex adaptative systems. Thus, beyond the well-known short-term focus on 'low-hanging fruit', Ortiz-de Mandojana and Bansal (2016) have tested among North American companies how social and environmental practices achieve resilience-related benefits in the following fifteen years in the form of higher survival rates, reduced financial volatility and additional business growth opportunities.

Finally, companies developing regenerative environmental strategies should manage the three main climate emergency thresholds by creating positive environmental externalities in their daily business activities. Regenerative firms will be key players in the transition to the sustainable economy of the future and, more specifically, in the fight against climate emergencies – first by decarbonizing the atmosphere, then by integrating themselves into the natural and social ecosystem where they operate to protect natural habitats and prevent biodiversity loss. According to the three main environmental challenges mentioned by Whiteman et al. (2013) and a literature review on natural science, the most recent scientific and technological advances in carbon capture and utilisation (Hepburn et al., 2019; MacDowell et al., 2017) have very promising economic and business applications, such as carbon dioxide (CO_2)-based chemical products, including polymers, CO_2-based fuels, microalgae fuels and other products; concrete building materials; CO_2-enhanced oil recovery; bioenergy; enhanced weathering; forestry techniques; and land management via soil carbon sequestration techniques.

Thus, jointly with the exploratory and prospective characterisation of regenerative firms, the basic principles of the regenerative strategy that we propose are summarised in the following main features:

- Going beyond zero emissions, through the creation of positive environmental externalities that can be carried out in different environmental areas such as atmospheric decarbonisation, natural habitat restoration, biodiversity conservation, etc. This strategic behaviour fits with prospectors according to Miles and Snow (1978) and learning path exploration (Levinthal & March, 1993), i.e. being the first in the market and developing cutting-edge technologies (Hepburn et al., 2019; MacDowell et al., 2017), such as CO_2-based synthetic ultra-low carbon fuels, concrete building materials and CO_2-based chemical products, including polymers.

- The new firm purpose passes from eco-financial performance to environmental performance (Sharma, 2022) and systemic socioecological resilience (Ortiz-de Mandojana & Bansal, 2016; Williams et al., 2021). Organisational resilience refers to companies' ability to anticipate and adjust to the environment, resulting in improved survival rates, reduced financial volatility or better business growth opportunities. This wider conception of the value proposition rests at the heart of sustainable development. In fact, as Bansal (2019) declares, sustainable development in an age of disruption requires intergenerational equity, implying that business models' value proposition should meet everyone's current basic needs within the constraints of the Earth's production capacity limits to ensure the needs of the next generations.

- Wider stakeholder engagement and integration. Recent developments in the most widely used theories on organisations and the environment, such as the resource-based view (RBV) and institutional theory, call for a wider conception of a company's stakeholders and their integration and engagement in the company's activities and aim. That is, following the RBV, a new profit-generation logic considering market and beyond-market stakeholders is needed (Barney, 2018) to avoid shareholders' and managers' primacy and take into account non-traditional business stakeholders beyond the market such as the natural environment, governments and communities. Hence, Gibson et al. (2021) extend the RBV by including the community as a strategic resource considered in business models. In a similar way but from an institutional perspective, Hoffman and Jennings (2021) compose new institutional-political scenarios for Anthropocene societies, such as the incorporation of political and institutional power more explicitly in designing and developing paths for change in all spheres – cultural, economic, business, political, educational and so on. Thus, the neglected 'voice' of non-humans – the natural environment – as well as future generations – the unborn – should be taken into account in the social construction of institutions in our societies, economies and businesses.
- Very long-term orientation. Extant sustainable business models are subject to temporal tensions between the traditional short-termism of business-as-usual logic and the long- and very long-term logic of regenerative strategies. As Slawinski and Bansal (2012) remark, time plays a central role in organisational responses to climate change in two ways: (1) in organisational responses to climate change; and (2) in organisational time perspectives or the time horizon of investments.

Therefore, this book refines the existing environmental business models and develops the theory on environmental strategies by conveniently addressing the grand challenge of climate emergency through the regenerative strategy where companies not only reduce their negative environmental externalities and create positive environmental externalities, but also, for the first time, reverse current environmental degradation.

The regenerative strategy extends beyond zero pollution and seeks as its environmental aim not only the creation of positive environmental externalities, but also, more importantly, the reversion of current environmental degradation. Companies following the regenerative strategy should take into account that their most strategic and relevant benefits will be achieved in the long and very long term, moving beyond current competitive advantage reinforcement and/or competitor pre-emption towards a long-term resiliency approach to sustainability in which adaptation to the dynamics of the local socioecological systems where they operate constitutes one of their main objectives (Hahn & Tampe, 2021).

6.2 The Regenerative Strategy: Technological Prospection

As Figure 6.2 shows, the regenerative strategy implies a disruptive change, the conception of a new climate-proof corporate environmentalism (Nyberg & Wright, 2022) with the following main new features:

- According to strategy and innovation/learning research traditions, it fits with the prospection and exploration learning path of cutting-edge climate technologies, allowing a firm to create positive environmental externalities by reversing current air, soil and water pollution and working together with the natural and management sciences to overcome traditional, reductionist and fragmented disciplinary knowledge silos (Chen & Hitt, 2021).
- It redefines the firm's purpose, avoiding the just-profit logic via the firm's aim of systemic social and ecological resilience and its future positioning.
- It considers holistic stakeholder engagement and orientation, highlighting the role of fringe or beyond-market stakeholders.
- It adopts a new time perspective on the tension between the traditional short-termism and the necessary long-termism and very long-termism of a disruptive regenerative strategy.

Accordingly, the regenerative strategy stresses, more than ever, the sustainability paradox by accommodating conflicting economic, social and environmental aims while developing a novel spatial-temporality approach, leading to a disruptive conception of sustainable development (Hart, 1995; Montiel et al., 2020).

First, following the strategy tradition, regenerative businesses fit Miles and Snow's (1978) prospectors' strategic posture. Usually the first in the market, they stress innovation and flexibility to quickly respond to changing and emergent market conditions. They are technically innovative and seek new products and markets, and are capable of developing new cutting-edge environmental technologies, products and markets rapidly, which requires strong R&D and engineering efforts from different

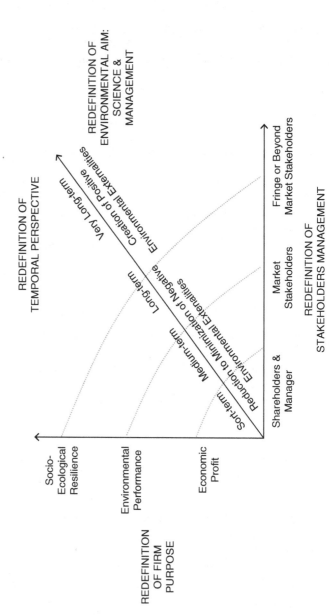

Figure 6.2 The regenerative strategy's disruptive features
Source: Authors' own elaboration

spheres of science (Sharma, 2022) and solid market research (Desarbo et al., 2005). Framed in Levinthal and March's (1993) logic, the regenerative strategy perfectly fits exploration; that is, when a company pursues the new knowledge of things that might come to be known. As in the regenerative pursuit of pollution reversion and sustainable development postulates, it is only possible to work across transdisciplinary knowledge silos from the natural and management studies in this new paradigm for sustainable development (Bansal, 2019).

To realise this new sustainable development paradigm, management science must overcome its anthropocentric focus. The traditional disassociation between organisational studies and the natural environment – for instance the lack of attention to non-human nature and biophysical foundations, whereby natural, organic or earth system limits have not been considered – must change (Gladwin et al., 1995). Those authors proposed a definition of sustainable development highlighting its main components as a process of achieving human development in an inclusive, connected, equitable, prudent and secure manner:

- Inclusiveness implies that sustainability embraces both environmental and human systems, both near and far, in both the present and the future.
- As shown previously, connectivity implies that world problems, i.e. natural, societal and economic systems, demand a holistic understanding of their interconnectedness and interdependencies.
- Equity, understood as the fair distribution of resources and property rights, both intra- and intergenerational, is at the heart of sustainable development.
- Due to the great uncertainty and unpredictability of climate emergency dimensions, interconnectedness, tipping points, etc., as the most recent Intergovernmental Panel on Climate Change reports state (IPCC, 2014, 2023), prudence and humility in pursuing sustainable development should be a guiding point. This demands precaution, pre-emptive safeguards, safety margins, etc.
- Finally, sustainable development should ensure a safe, healthy and high quality of life for the current and future generations on the Earth.

Pioneering companies developing regenerative environmental strategies should address the previously mentioned planetary emergency thresholds by reversing environmental damage and creating positive environmental externalities in their daily business activities – cutting-edge atmosphere decarbonisation technology is a good example. As Bansal (2019) and Sharma (2022) advocate, corporate environmentalism in the age of disruption requires integrating social, organisational and management theories with energy and biophysical systems to enrich the theoretical perspectives and empirical approaches framing this complex phenomenon.

At this stage, then, we aim to blend the most advanced environmental management expertise, postulates and practices that imply the redefinition of firm purpose. McGahan (2021), Bansal (2019) and Aguilera et al. (2022) demand – both in the long and very long term and regarding systemic resilience issues – the engagement of all types of stakeholders, both market and beyond the market or at the fringe. Barney (2018) and Gibson et al. (2021) highlight that the available cutting-edge technologies provided by natural sciences are crucial in effectively developing new exploration innovation and learning pathways via the prospector strategic positioning of a firm.

Hence, regenerative businesses must adapt to evolving conditions through stakeholder collaboration (Hahn & Tampe, 2021). As Dentoni et al. (2021) remark, the role of cross-sector partnerships is crucial to achieve socioecological resilience in disruptive sustainable business models. They highlight three main elements of cross-sector partnership – strategic, institutional and learning – as follows:

- Strategic elements are the processes of value creation and appropriation among multiple stakeholders, including their impacts on socioecological systems. Through in-depth interdependencies, cross-sector partners mitigate uncertainty and potential consequences for the environment jointly, with a deep understanding of each business model.
- Institutional elements refer to organisational arrangements for managing the interplay of heterogeneous and conflicting perspectives among the agents trying to collaborate. These include both formal and informal structures for regulating interactions among partners.
- Learning elements refer to the processes of experimentation and sensemaking that create and develop knowledge and capabilities among multiple stakeholders. Learning in cross-sector partnerships can shape outcomes via more collaborative practices and stronger alignments.

To illustrate the creation of positive environmental externalities by putting into action cutting-edge climate science advancements, as a new source of disruptive business models, we introduce the latest decarbonisation initiative: creating synthetic CO_2-based fuel from atmospheric water and CO_2.

This technology provides a suitable basis for the development of regenerative strategies, and its technological foundations rest on the entire thermochemical solar fuel production chain – from water (H_2O) and CO_2 captured directly from the air to the synthesis of drop-in transportation fuels, such as methanol and kerosene, which currently represent approximately 8 per cent of anthropogenic CO_2 emissions. This was recently evaluated by Schäppi et al. (2022), with their findings published in *Nature* (Figure 6.3 briefly shows the whole chain). This study was carried out on the roof of ETH's machine laboratory building in Zurich. Moving beyond previously small-scale evidence, they worked with a modular 5 kW thermal pilot-scale solar system, operated in field conditions.

As Figure 6.3 shows, there are three main units: (1) the Direct Air Capture (DAC) unit, which extracts CO_2 and H_2O directly from the air; (2) the solar redox unit, which converts CO_2 and H_2O into the desired mixture of carbon monoxide (CO) and hydrogen (H_2), known as syngas, using concentrated solar energy; and (3) the gas-to-liquid (GTL) unit, which converts syngas to liquid hydrocarbons or methanol.

The DAC unit has been commercialised by ETH's spinoff company Climeworks. Adsorption proceeds at ambient temperature and pressure for 180 min per cycle and desorption at 95°C and 0.1–0.3 bar for 43 min per cycle. The unit can process an airflow of 2,000 m^3 h^{-1} with 5.5 cycles per day, approximately 8 kg per day of CO_2, with a measured purity of 98 per cent and 20–40 L of water per day and contaminants below the 0.2 parts per million (ppm) detection limit.

The solar redox unit produces CO and H_2 through the thermochemical splitting of CO_2 and H_2O via a reduction-oxidation cycle driven by concentrated solar radiation. used non-stoichiometric ceria ($CeO_{2-\delta}$) as the redox material due Schäppi et al. (2022) to its rapid kinetics, crystallographic stability and abundance. The redox cycle at the heart of the solar redox unit comprises two steps. In the first endothermic step, ceria is thermally reduced to generate oxygen (O_2). In the second exothermic step, the reduced ceria is re-oxidised with CO_2 and/or H_2O to generate CO and/or H_2, respectively. Ceria is thus not consumed, and the net overall reactions are $CO_2 = CO + \frac{1}{2}O_2$ and $H_2 = H_2 + \frac{1}{2}O_2$, but with the fuel ($H_2$, CO_2) and O_2 generated in separate steps.

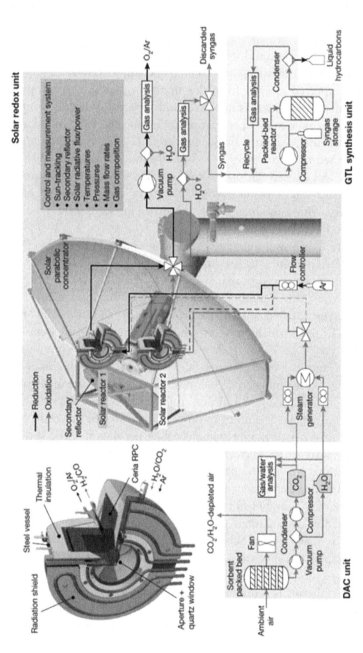

Figure 6.3 Simplified process chain of the solar fuel system

Source: Schäppi et al. (2022:64)

This important step prevents the formation of explosive mixtures and removes the need for high-temperature gas separation.

The solar redox unit can split pure CO_2, pure H_2O, and both H_2O and CO_2 simultaneously. A pure gas – argon (Ar) or air – guides fluid flow during the reduction step performed under vacuum pressures. Additionally, when splitting H_2O and CO_2 simultaneously, Ar or CO_2 is injected after the reduction step to repressurise the cavity before the oxidation step.

Downstream of the solar redox unit, the O_2 stream evolving from the reduction step is analysed and vented. The syngas stream is analysed and sent to the GTL unit, where it is compressed for storage in a 5 L buffer gas cylinder at up to 250 bar. The final syngas processing into methanol is a mature technology and uses a commercial Cu-ZnO-Al_2O_3 catalyst, yielding methanol with a purity of 65 per cent, the rest being water.

Depending on the catalyst used in the GTL unit, the desired H_2, the Cox molar ratio of syngas for methanol synthesis lies between 2 and 3, whereas the desired H_2: CO molar ratio of syngas for Fischer–Tropsch (FT) synthesis is approximately 2. In all cases, the syngas purity and quality are suitable for GTL processing and can be tailored for methanol or FT synthesis without the need for additional steps for correcting the composition and/or separating undesired by-products. In this study, the GTL unit was applied when processing solar syngas into methanol. FT synthesis of kerosene was performed with solar syngas obtained in two separate experimental set-ups using the same solar reactor design.

However, for commercialisation in the market, substantial process optimisation and upscaling are needed. For example, a multitude of solar dishes or a heliostat field focusing on a solar tower can be used for upscaling and concentrating the direct normal irradiation (DNI) to the solar flux concentration (C) required (C>2,000 suns). For example, a commercial-scale solar fuel plant could use 10 heliostat fields, each collecting 100 MW thermal of solar radiative power, to produce 95,000 L of kerosene a day (assuming an overall system efficiency system of 10 per cent), which is enough fuel for an Airbus A350 carrying 325 passengers on a London to New York City round-trip flight.

As this scientific verification indicates, jointly with scalability and technological feasibility, as both CO_2 and H_2O are obtained directly from the air, feedstock sourcing and fuel production are not dependent on water resources.

Considering salient costs and competitive perspectives, Schäppi et al. (2022) discuss the economic viability and policy requirements needed to bring this cutting-edge and revolutionary technology to market. In their work, they estimated a jet fuel cost in the range of €1.2–2 per litre. These cost values are sensitive to the energy efficiencies, the CO_2 costs (assumed €100 per tonne CO_2 captured from the air) and the manufacturing costs in the heliostat field, which typically represent half of total investment costs in this solar fuel system (assumed to be €100 m^{-2}). The compression and storage of CO_2 and syngas in the buffer tanks represent 9.5 per cent of the investment costs. Solar thermochemical fuels are most competitively produced in desert regions with a high DNI (>2,500 kWh m^{-2} per year).

Due to the high initial investment costs, solar thermochemical fuels require policy support. Schäppi et al. (2022) thus suggest an aviation sector support scheme, which would create a near-term market for the first generation of commercial solar fuel plants. Furthermore, solar drop-in fuels could use existing storage, distribution and utilisation infrastructures.

6.3 The Regenerative Strategy: A New Ecological Morality

6.3.1 Redefinition of Firm Purpose

The second element of the regenerative strategy is that it implies the redefinition of firm purpose in both temporal and content scopes (Bansal, 2019). Aguilera et al. (2022) advocate shifting the current short-term and myopic profit-oriented conception of firm purpose towards a moral integration of performance and progress, moving businesses from part of the problem to an active part of the climate emergency solution.

The World Economic Forum (2020) indicates that it is time to radically redefine the purpose of a firm – engaging all its stakeholders in shared and sustained value creation – by abandoning the traditional focus on shareholders to produce solutions for society and the environment instead of just economic profits. This reminds us of the importance of moral sentiments such as the pleasure of mutual sympathy when overcoming selfish behaviour and ambition (Smith, 1790). Therefore, according to George et al. (2021), this redefinition of company purpose implies moving from a goal-based purpose towards a duty-based purpose where a broader and explicit set of societal and

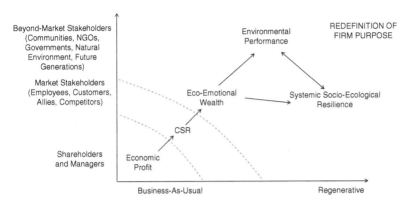

Figure 6.4 Regenerative strategy purposes
Source: Authors' own elaboration

environmental values and expectations are linked to economic, moral and ethical duties and the obligation to consider the welfare of future generations and approach sustainable development as intra- and inter-generational equity (Bansal, 2019).

George et al. (2021) propose a common understanding of firm purpose from a duty-based perspective and of related, traditional mission statements, visions and strategic intents with three new pillars: (1) new corporate values, such as dignity, plurality, solidarity, subsidiarity or reciprocity; (2) the key roles of social service; and (3) stewardship. The last pillar implies that a firm's product and process designs are environmental stewards of the planet and are obligated to consider the welfare of future generations in all decision-making processes.

Nevertheless, following three decades of research on the economic, financial and competitive effects of corporate environmentalism using research questions such as 'To what extent/under what conditions does it pay to be green?', 'How can we integrate environmental concerns/respect into business strategy?' or 'How can we fit environmental concerns with firm performance?', academics and practitioners should emphasise the socioecological dimension as follows: 'How does our company/organisation contribute to natural and social systems?', 'How can economic and business activities be integrated into systemic socioecological resilience?' To address these questions, firms must radically redefine their purpose. In this subsection, as Figure 6.4 illustrates, we develop three interrelated firm purposes in regard to real corporate environmentalism in the regenerative strategy: (1)

environmental performance focus (Sharma, 2022); (2) systemic socio-ecological resilience (DesJardine et al., 2019); and (3) new 'ecological emotional, or eco-emotional, wealth'.

This firm purpose redefinition implies that environmental performance is the aim of, not a means for, profit maximisation (Montiel et al., 2020). A firm's mission, vision and values should reflect and support this disruptive change. More specifically, Sharma (2022) and Montiel et al. (2020) propose a radical change in management research: moving from environmental management, internal organisational practices and strategies to environmental performance, measuring the real impact of business activities and strategies on the natural environment. Here, it is mandatory to combine company expertise and supply chain and stakeholder management with ecosystem impact; that is, using expertise from natural scientists across different disciplines such as chemistry, biology, physics, zoology, medicine and climate science, engineering or geography in a holistic, integrative and interdisciplinary analysis.

As Bansal (2019) advocates, there is no time: research is needed spanning the natural and social sciences developing disruptive technologies, due to the potential tipping points of planetary subsystems. As Sharma (2022:2) remarks, 'research has rarely measured whether environmental investments, practices, actions, and strategies have actually led to a reversal of resource depletion, cleaner air and water, a reduction in atmospheric carbon, the restoration of topsoil and aquifers, the preservation of biodiversity, and improved human health'.

This disruptive change implies moving from internal organisational impacts, such as reductions in energy or inputs, to an external point of view measuring how those internal environmental practices and policies impact cleaner air, water and soil, the reduction of CO_2 in the atmosphere, the restoration of aquifers, the preservation of biodiversity and so on. Accordingly, this puts the focus on the extent to which firms are restoring and accruing natural capital for future generations (Sharma, 2022).

Thus, Sharma (2022) proposes four main challenges for management academics and practitioners:

- Expertise in measuring ecosystem impact requires the co-work and joint expertise of natural scientists in a wide range of disciplines such as chemistry, biology, physics, zoology, medicine, environmental science and geography.

- Measuring actual environmental impact requires analysis in all global supply and related value chains under the logic of the product life cycle and industrial symbiosis. Therefore, unethical corporate behaviours, such as some types of greenwashing showing a sugar-coated, one-sided vision of reality, should be prevented.
- Different types of environmental impacts should be considered because they are relevant and important for different firm stakeholders.
- Finally, a single measure of an isolated environmental impact, without assessing the organisation's holistic ethical, social and environmental performance, may not be meaningful or acceptable for some stakeholders.

Specifically, Delgado-Ceballos et al. (2023) urge academics and practitioners to pass from traditional 'financial materiality' towards 'double materiality' when approaching the seventeen sustainable development goals of the United Nations in business activity. Materiality refers to the information that firms must provide to investors. In the sphere of environmental, government and social (EGS) indicators, financial materiality refers to the internal information that firms must provide to investors, usually focusing on the risks and opportunities that ESG factors may generate for them under 'business-as-usual' and 'environmental integration into business strategy' logics.

Nevertheless, in line with the radical redefinition of firm purpose, we propose the implementation of double materiality or 'stakeholder materiality' (Delgado-Ceballos et al., 2023), whereby companies must inform their external stakeholders of their real impact on society and the natural environment. This invites us to introduce the second purpose that firms following the regenerative strategy should pursue: systemic socioecological resilience. Paraphrasing former US President John F. Kennedy's famous First Inaugural Address on 30 January 1961, business academics and practitioners should 'Ask not what the society and natural environment can do for your business – ask what your business can do for the society and natural environment'. Firms can thus pass from being part of the problem, with passive behaviour while waiting for solutions, to being an active environmentalist and part of the solution, as citizens increasingly demand (Álvarez et al., 2020) and 'net positive' thinking implies (Polman & Winston, 2021). Figure 6.5 encapsulates this reasoning.

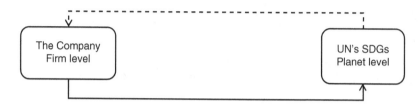

Traditional Sustainability Perspective:

How to integrate ESG-UN SDG into firm's strategy?
How to fit firm's profitability and environmental concerns?

The Company
Firm level

UN's SDGs
Planet level

Systemic Socio-Ecological Resilience:
How to integrate economic and business activity into the
social and natural system?

Figure 6.5 Towards systemic socioecological resilience
Source: Authors' own elaboration based on Delgado-Ceballos et al. (2023)

The second way to redefine a firm's purpose entails the concept of systemic socioecological resilience. Contrary to a traditional 'business-as-usual' environmental approach whereby management academics and practitioners tend to ignore the temporality in the causal relationship between corporate environmentalism and firm performance, companies following the regenerative strategy should understand that their most strategically and relevant benefits will be achieved in the long and very long term in the form of organisational resilience (Ortiz-de Mandojana & Bansal, 2016:1617), which as we have seen is defined as 'the incremental capacity of an organisation to anticipate and adjust to the environment'. Although generally associated with ecology, how ecological systems respond to exogenous disturbances (DesJardine et al., 2019) has also been explored in the fields of psychology, engineering, business and economics.

Resilience has been defined as the capacity to adapt and recover from disturbances that are perceived, within a system, to fall outside the range of normal and expected disturbances (Dentoni et al., 2021). Ortas et al. (2014) have defined adaptative resilience as the ability of a system to resist, avoid and recover from shock. In the field of sustainable supply chain management, Negri et al. (2021) have defined supply chain resilience as the ability of a system to survive, adapt and grow while preserving its structure and function. Resilience is thus the adaptative capability to prepare for and react to an unforeseen disruption and restore regular activities.

Specifically, organizational resilience fits the main organisational purpose described by Miles and Snow (1978) and Levinthal and March (1993), allowing them to operate dynamically as a complex adaptative system. Therefore, and beyond the well-known short-term focus on 'low-hanging fruit', Ortiz-de Mandojana and Bansal (2016) have tested among North American companies how social and environmental practices achieve organisational resilience-related benefits in the following fifteen years in the form of higher survival rates, reduced financial volatility and additional business growth opportunities.

As Hillmann and Guenther (2021) state, organisational resilience is gaining momentum in organisation studies, as it explains how companies address adversities and disruptive events, such as climate emergencies. To understand organisational resilience, DesJardine et al. (2019) propose two main factors: (1) a systemic perspective and (2) a balance between flexibility and stability. The systemic perspective implies that the unpredictable nonlinear property of change within complex systems is tempered by the properties of a resilient system, which reflects both stability, or, persistence, in maintaining its core organisational attributes and flexibility – innovating and adapting to these changes. In developing organisational resilience, DesJardine et al. (2019) propose the key role of strategic actions, such as corporate social and environmental activities that require long time horizons, large resource commitments, or significant adjustments to organisational structures and corporate governance mechanisms.

In this book, then, by exploring a disruptive regenerative strategy, we investigate a more complex, committed and integrative form of resilience that can be called systemic socioecological resilience, where ecological, social and organisational resilience are integrated into a complex adaptative system of real sustainable business models able to create social and environmental value and deliver net positive impacts (Polman & Winston, 2021) or positive socioenvironmental externalities, in line with recent developments by Dentoni et al. (2021) and Williams et al. (2021). This approach overcomes the existing divide between a firm's promises of sustainable business and its actual impact on the resilience of socioecological systems as a complex adaptative system. The resilience of a socioecological system can be defined as 'the buffering capacity of a system to cope with change and unforeseen disturbances while safeguarding the ecological systems on which human activity depends' (Williams et al., 2021:96). The development of this systemic socioecological resilience will drive firms to consider themselves an integral part of the socioecological system dynamics, adapting their activity to the cyclical and seasonal rhythm of the socioecological systems of which they are part (Hahn & Tampe, 2021).

Socioecological resilience is an emerging research topic in organisation and environment studies. It has two main dimensions (Dentoni et al., 2021): (1) the capacity to absorb disturbances, measured as the persistence of the relationships within a system despite important fluctuations among some of its agents; and (2) adaptative ecosystem management, the capacity to adapt to disturbances via thorough learning and proactive change and the recombination of evolved structures and processes in response to such change.

According to Dentoni et al. (2021), the resilience of a socioecological system can be achieved by firms through three main elements of cross-sectorial partnership: (1) the strategic elements: sensing the interconnectedness of issues and the stakeholders surrounding them (zooming out) as well as the tensions, resources and capabilities among them (zooming in) through the use of linguistic and disciplinary frames, transcending language and disciplinary silos; (2) the institutional elements of cross-sector collaboration: co-creating narratives transcending multiple logics, by which a partnership can foster deeper dialogue among its members, questioning aims, priorities and activities, and change when necessary; and (3) co-learning through distributed experimentation in many small-scale experiments, which allows learners to understand what truly works in their real, local context, preventing unintended consequences. In short, in the realm of regenerative strategies, cross-sectorial partnership means embeddedness.

Finally, the third path for redefining firm purpose implies adapting and moving the borrowed concept of 'socioemotional wealth' from the family firm research tradition (Gómez-Mejía et al., 2007) to the corporate sustainability arena, in line with Berrone et al. (2010) and Sharma and Sharma (2011). To this end, we propose a new concept of 'eco-emotional wealth' to be the driving force of both environmental performance and systemic socioecological resilience in a redefined firm purpose (see Figure 6.4) beyond the short term and profits, where a stable ownership structure produces a certain, patient capital and permanent financial resources, leading to intergenerational value creation. 'Socioemotional wealth' thus includes all the non-financial aspects of a firm, such as identity, the ability to exercise family influence and the perpetuation of family dynasty. In turn, in the corporate sustainability arena and in line with Berrone et al. (2010) and Sharma and Sharma (2011), eco-emotional wealth is both a key driver in a proactive environmental strategy and a higher motivation guided by an intergenerational value creation process. Eco-emotional wealth can be defined as the non-utilitarian value of the natural environment that guides individual intrinsic motivation, ethical and moral values.

Based on the microfoundations of strategy (Felin et al., 2012) and leadership theories (Little et al., 2016), we highlight the role of the emotions and sentiments of chief executive officers (CEOs) and top management as key driving forces in regenerative strategies' new corporate purposes. Kisfalvi and Picher (2003) have shown how a CEO's character and emotions influence top management team dynamics and strategy formulation, as decision-makers tend to do what feels right. They assert that 'emotions act as a qualitatively different heuristic that first selects from the realm of all possible options a subset of options that the decision-maker accepts as viable … Emotions make up a fourth category that should be added to the traditional decision-making perspectives of bounded rationality, power, and garbage' (Kisfalvi & Picher, 2003:60). In the same vein, highlighting the growing role of emotions in the workplace, Kluemper et al. (2011) examine how emotion management ability positively influences organisational citizen behaviour through motivation.

Delgado-García and De la Fuente-Sabaté (2010) have empirically analysed the influence of a CEO's affective traits, such as a long-term tendency to experience positive or negative emotions, on a firm's strategy and performance. Positive and negative affections lead managers to adopt different information processing strategies in their decision-making process. Thus, positive affections, such as being interested, excited, strong, enthusiastic, proud, alert, inspired, determined, attentive or active, condition processing strategies, rendering them simple and intuitive, thereby promoting creativity, the search for novel information, and non-conservative behaviour and decisions. In contrast, negative affections, such as being distressed, upset, guilty, scared, hostile, irritable, ashamed, nervous, jittery or afraid, lead to careful, error-avoiding and conservative behaviour and decisions. Delgado-García and De la Fuente-Sabaté (2010) empirically show in the Spanish banking sector how the positive affective traits of CEOs are negatively related to firm strategic conformity and to 'typical' firm performance. In our field of regenerative strategies, radical firm purposes such as systemic socioecological resilience and environmental performance can therefore be framed as 'non-typical performance' and far from firm strategic conformity; they are encouraged by CEOs' and top managers' eco-emotional wealth, as Figure 6.4 shows.

More recently, the empirical research of Wang et al. (2023) has identified CEOs' emotions and affectivity as the antecedents of firm corporate social responsibility (CSR) – a specific form of non-strategic conformity and non-typical firm performance. Wang et al. (2023) find that CEO affectivity, a relatively stable tendency to experience positive or negative emotions, influences CSR. They thus propose that CEOs' positive affectivity increases their firms' CSR engagement because (1) it broadens their scope of attention and action, expanding their awareness of their surroundings, which leads to a clearer understanding of the existence and demands of relevant multistakeholders; (2) it embraces more social-inclusive categories; and (3) it enlarges individuals' time horizons by fostering investment in resources with far-future outcomes. Accordingly, in terms of the regenerative strategy, this encapsulates the meaning of eco-emotional wealth, highlighting the importance of fringe stakeholders and future generations.

Thus, the new concept of eco-emotional wealth that we propose is embodied in a CEO and top management team that guides the new firm purposes – environmental performance and systemic socioecological resilience – beyond the short term and profits, agglomerating all the non-financial aspects linked to ecological preservation, pollution minimisation and reversion to bequeath the natural environment to future generations. This fits with the call of the World Economic Forum (2020) for a radical reappraisal of corporate purpose including broader societal and environmental aims and duties.

Eco-emotional wealth counteracts the negative psychological consequences of the climate crisis, such as the increasing eco-guilt, eco-depression and ecological grief recently detected among a growing mass of the adult population (Agoston et al., 2022), some of which fit the CEOs' negative affections analysed by Delgado-Garcia and De La Fuente-Sabaté (2010).

In fact, the origins of eco-emotional wealth could be rooted in some relevant issues first introduced by Adam Smith in his *Theory of Moral Sentiments*. How academics, business practitioners or citizens grasp social and environmental challenges leads them to the different negative emotions and sentiments that guide their behaviour, as Agoston et al. (2022) demonstrate. Recent media announcements, such as those by the founder and owner of outdoor clothing retailer Patagonia, Yvon Chouinard, who donated that company in 2022 to the fight against climate change, exemplify negative emotions, such as the eco-guilt that the climate emergency provokes, which can be contrasted to the opposite sentiment of eco-emotional wealth. Far from this being an isolated action, many of the richest people in the world, according to *Fortune* magazine, are donating or bequeathing part of their fortunes in favour of social and environmental causes. Hence, as Smith (1790:4) remarked concerning the propriety of individual action:

Even individual selfishness has evidently some interest in the fortune of others, rendering their happiness necessary to him, though he derives nothing from it except the pleasure of seeing it. Of this kind is pity or compassion, the emotion which we feel for the misery of others ... And hence it is, that to feel much for others and little for ourselves, that to restrain our selfish, and to indulge our benevolent affections, constitutes the perfection of human nature; and can alone produce among mankind that harmony of sentiments and passions in which consists their whole grace and propriety.

All in all, a new logic of firm purpose and shareholder features, with new ownership and governance structures, produces the necessary patient capital and permanent financial resources, leading to intergenerational value creation.

6.3.2 A New Stakeholder Perspective

In the capitalist tradition, wealth creation for corporate shareholders and the associated societal and environmental externalities have comprised the essential aim of a regular firm's mission (Friedman, 1970; Jensen & Meckling, 1976). Nevertheless, as mentioned earlier, ongoing grand challenges such as the climate emergency have led management scholars to claim that businesses must have a sustainable relationship with the natural environment on which they depend (Aguilera et al., 2022). This represents a disruptive change that overcomes the dominant assumptions of the 'business-as-usual' logic; that is, a new stakeholder management logic should be considered to redefine a firm's purpose, preserve the planet for future generations, and adopt moral managerial principles grounded in systemic socioecological resilience

Figure 6.6 A new stakeholders framework
Source: Authors' own elaboration

and eco-emotional wealth principles. As George et al. (2021) remark, a firm's mission and vision should be guided by a purpose following a benevolent and pluralistic approach to all firm stakeholders.

The stakeholder perspective thus provides an enriching forum for a variety of issues and debates at the intersection of business and society (Barney & Harrison, 2020). It passes from narrow stakeholder satisfaction to the wider engagement and participation of very different types of stakeholders as joint partners, co-creators with shared values, in line with Barney's (2018) new RBV logic on rent generation and appropriation. As Bridoux and Stoelhorst (2014) propose, firms should pass from an arm's-length approach where stakeholders are managed strictly according to their bargaining power to a fairness approach where stakeholders are treated based on fairness considerations.

As Figure 6.6 shows, a new perspective on stakeholder management avoiding the primacy of shareholders and managers and moving beyond the traditional management of well-established networks of external market stakeholders, especially customers, investors, suppliers, allies and rivals, is needed to develop disruptive solutions that address the climate emergency. Firms need to manage radical uncertainty by acquiring knowledge from a diverse and dispersed network of heterogeneous stakeholders, especially those outside firms at the periphery or fringe (Sharma & Vredenburgh, 1998) of their established stakeholders. The ability to generate profitability in the future will often require access to critical resources among a wider typology of stakeholders, both within and especially outside the firm. Competitive imagination demands disruptive skills from radical perspectives external to the traditional business sphere, which implies a new approach to stakeholder integration and engagement (Hart & Sharma, 2004). In the same vein, Dentoni et al. (2021) view cross-sector partnerships as effective organisational mechanisms in disruptive sustainable business models that create social and environmental value in support of systemic socioecological resilience and stakeholder embeddedness. Thus, disruptive sustainable business models depend on collaboration across a wider set of stakeholders in a socioecological system, where both private and public agents and cross-sector partnerships play a key role.

The current disruptive era also requires radical transactiveness, a dynamic organisational capability to pursue the identification, exploration and integration of the perspectives of fringe stakeholders (Hart & Sharma, 2004). Fringe stakeholders are those who have been traditionally forgotten in management practice: the impoverished, weak, isolated, non-legitimated or even non-human, such as the natural environment. These can offer firms disruptive change and help build the imagination needed to construct the future (Hart, 1995).

Hart and Sharma's (2004) radical transactiveness is therefore needed because it (1) allows two-way dialogue, engaging a firm with all stakeholders in a wide sense, influencing while being influenced by them; (2) produces radical knowledge and learning from fringe stakeholders that allow the firm to generate new value-creating strategies to address climate emergencies; (3) creates new, strong and trusted relationships with stakeholders, increasing the firm's legitimacy; and (4) enables imagining future competitiveness, which requires the divergent thinking that can mainly be supplied by beyond-market stakeholders. This demands the identification of unmet needs among existing customers as well as in new, yet-to-be-served and emerging markets. Accordingly, a new stakeholder management perspective requires putting the forgotten ones first – a conscious management effort to reverse the traditional rules inherent in the 'business-as-usual' logic. According to Hart and Sharma (2004), here competitive advantage will depend on a firm's ability to generate disruptive innovations and creative destruction through competitive imagination.

Recent developments in the most widely adopted theories in organisations and the environment, such as the RBV and institutional theory, call for a wider conception of a company's stakeholders and their integration and engagement with the company's activities and aim (Barney, 2018; World Economic Forum, 2020; Gibson et al., 2021;

McGahan, 2021). Indeed, the inclusion of traditionally excluded fringe stakeholders, such as communities, the natural environment or the voices of future generations, entails a revolutionary new stakeholder theory (Hart & Sharma, 2004; Gibson et al., 2021; McGahan, 2021) following a logic of polycentric governance, collaborative management and cross-sector partnership of business, government and civil society groups (Montiel et al., 2020).

Hence, Bridoux and Stoelhorst (2014) propose a co-creation stakeholder framework, called the fairness approach, which is more effective in attracting, motivating and retaining a firm's stakeholders in the value creation and appropriation process. This fairness approach can be manifested in three ways: (1) creating a strong nexus of stakeholders among different parties through organisational practices, such as open and honest information exchange, to resolve problems; (2) linking the firm to its stakeholders, relying not on legal enforcements but on trust and self-enforcement in the form of social sanctions; and (3) building relationships with stakeholders that tend to be long-lasting. Any disruptive transformation of business models through the regenerative environmental strategy requires this new fairness approach to managing firm stakeholders, obtaining the real engagement of all types of stakeholders in long-term shared value creation and appropriation.

That is, following the RBV and the postulates of Hart and Sharma (2004), a new profit-generation logic considering both the market and beyond-market stakeholders is needed (Barney, 2018) to overcome shareholder and manager primacy and address non-traditional business stakeholders beyond the market such as the natural environment, governments, communities and so on. Exploring profit generation and appropriation logic, Barney (2018) suggests that access to non-financial resources is more likely to be a source of such profits and is being increasingly provided by different types of stakeholders, who use their bargaining power to become residual claimants of firm profits. Accordingly, in the natural resource-based view (Hart, 1995), the strategic character of non-financial resources, such as many environmental resources and capabilities, is increasing because they are likely to be more socially complex, path dependent and causally ambiguous than financial resources. The new stakeholder management model of profit generation is, then, consistent with the growing importance of current phenomena such as ecosystems, multisided markets, open innovation schemes and clusters (Barney, 2018).

Therefore, the new resource-based theory of sustainable competitive advantage and profit generation is inconsistent with the traditional shareholder primacy of profit appropriation. This new theory requires a model of profit appropriation that relies on wider stakeholder profit generation and appropriation (Barney, 2018).

Furthermore, Gibson et al. (2021) extend the RBV by including the community as a strategic resource to be considered in tumultuous times, with the capacity to provide the enhanced corporate social and business legitimacy and reputation needed to build future, longer-term and sustainable competitive advantages (Martín-de Castro et al., 2020).

Considering the influence of institutions at different levels, Hoffman and Jennings (2021) explore new scenarios for Anthropocene societies, such as the role of institutional and political power in designing and reshaping for change in all spheres – cultural, economic, business, political, educational and so on. Also, the neglected 'voices' of non-human stakeholders, such as the natural environment, as well as of future generations should be considered in the social construction of societies, economies and businesses, as early postulates of sustainable development explicitly suggested (WCED, 1987; Hart, 1995).

This new, enriched and enlarged stakeholders' perspective also affects the mechanisms of corporate governance. Firms carrying out the regenerative strategy will require substantial investments with long- and very long-term implications, implying new multilevel coordination among different stakeholders – internal stakeholders, such as managers, workers or shareholders, and external stakeholders, public administrations, non-governmental organisations and so on – competing for scarce resources (Aguilera et al., 2021). All in all, it advocates greater integration of different firm collectives (owners, CEOs, top management teams or employees) in designing and implementing proactive environmental strategies. Indeed, the study by Aguilera et al. (2021) defines, as a promising research opportunity, the role of 'collective environmental entrepreneurship' in addressing the grand challenge of climate emergency.

6.3.3 *Redefinition of the Time Frame*

Time should play a key role in the construction and meaning of a theoretical construct and in the causal relationships among constructs, which implies an explicit consideration of temporality: 'what' are the constructs, and 'how' and 'why' they are related, as building blocks of theory building (George & Jones, 2000)? That is, time can modify the ways in which theoretical constructs and their relationships are conceptualised, thus also modifying theoretical propositions derived from them.

Generally, standard time can be understood as the intersection between cosmic time and a socially established calendar. However, time is embedded within the content of the subjective human experience in past, present and future perceptions. At the organisational level, critical situations suddenly emerging – such as the climate emergency in the case of our focal phenomenon – may alter the collective experience of time (George & Jones, 2000). Those authors have also highlighted the power of time aggregations of individuals, organisations and nations around an episode or episodes to which they give a particular meaning.

Based on this perspective of time, we sincerely believe that the current Anthropocene era and the climate emergency constitute a unique episode on Earth and in human history that confers a new meaning to business models and sustainable business models – as our disruptive proposal of the regenerative strategy provides – whereby the common rules of a 'business-as-usual' logic must be changed, and such changes must be hurried. This constitutes a discontinuous and revolutionary change in business conception and management research.

The 'what' of any theory, concerned with the creation and definition of constructs, changes over time (George & Jones, 2000). This is happening around our main episode – the current climate emergency. In the face of this grand challenge, the content and meaning of well-established constructs in the management literature, such as sustainable businesses, stakeholders or firm performance, are evolving radically, in a discontinuous manner, as previously corroborated by the evolutionary dynamics of environmental strategies and the regenerative strategy's redefinition of firm purpose and stakeholder management logic.

Especially relevant to the understanding of this feature of the regenerative strategy – redefinition of the time frame – is the 'how' of theory (George & Jones, 2000). This is concerned with the causal relationships and orders among constructs in theory building. The theorised antecedents and/or consequences of a certain phenomenon may or may not have immediate effects and can differ in terms of time dimension. Nevertheless, a time frame is vital for theory construction. Most constructs analysed in management studies are not related instantaneously and commonly follow a short-term orientation, usually one or two years. Nevertheless, most organisational behaviour and management choices have a long-lived effect as well as a time lag concerning causal relationships.

This second issue, time perspective, is particularly relevant for sustainable development research and environmental strategies. Sustainable development assumes that firms must make intertemporal benefit trade-offs to balance their short-term and long-term needs, known as 'temporal ambidexterity' or 'ambi-temporality' (Kim et al., 2019). Defining this duality, Kim et al. (2019) remark on the advantage of slack organisational resources for moving the focus towards long-term environmental investments. Slack resources provide clear opportunities for firms to redirect their investments to projects with uncertain and deferred outcomes. Thus, organisations facing severe resource constraints are unable to prioritise long-term benefits.

As Slawinski and Bansal (2012) remark, time plays a central role in organisational responses to climate change in two ways: (1) in organisational responses to climate change; and (2) in organisational time perspectives or the time horizons of investments.

Traditionally, a linear and simplistic conception of time has been categorised in the research on firm environmental strategies on a continuum from reactive, defensive and accommodating to proactive (Carroll, 1979) or from only reactive to proactive (Buysse & Verbeke, 2003). Thus, reactive firms are myopic in changing and envisioning the future, while proactive firms anticipate future changes and regulations. In the same vein, firms facing climate change can be categorised as carrying out two distinctive strategies (Kolk & Pinske, 2005): a compensation strategy, with a focus on external or internal emissions trading while waiting for new environmental innovations by other firms; or an innovation strategy, focused on carbon-preventing technologies, processes and products and organisational competency renewal. This time perspective implicitly assumes that only reactive or compensation responses to climate change focus on shorter payback periods and that only proactive and innovative responses make major investments in technologies with long payback periods. Nevertheless, prior work has not systematically assessed the role of time beyond that needed to respond to climate change: from reactive to proactive and, more importantly, from proactive to regenerative.

The second and least explored time consideration refers to the investment time horizon. In our case, this is the role of time in specifying the causal relationships among regenerative strategies and their organisational and systemic socioecological resilience consequences, as George and Jones (2000) highlight concerning the role of time in theory building. Conclusions from the qualitative empirical study of Slawinski and Bansal (2012) on the temporal perspectives of organisational responses to climate change show that advanced postures of integrated organisations towards the climate have a medium level of tolerance to uncertainty, a high extraction from the past and a long planning horizon – over twenty years – in comparison with the short planning horizons – less than five years – of less environmentally advanced firms. Nevertheless, the time tensions between the demands of today and the needs of tomorrow are recurrent issues in management studies and are accentuated in organisation and environmental management research.

Therefore, the time perspective is crucial in positioning a business in the face of the climate emergency. Never more than now have time, which is at the heart of the sustainable development construct, and intergenerational equity, which reminds us that current demands should not compromise the needs and wealth of future generations, been so significant. As Bansal (2019:11) claims, 'at no other time in history has research on sustainable development been more important'.

The inherent tensions between the demands of today and the needs of tomorrow are at the heart of sustainable business and development (Slawinski & Bansal, 2015). Hence, economic short-termism (Laverty, 1996) is a chronic problem for many companies, leading them to competitive disadvantages because of their lack of investments for the long run and their associated loss in organisational capabilities and workforce skills (see Figure 6.7).

Figure 6.7 shows the tensions and paradoxes in intertemporal choice. Investments in conventional technologies, characterised by incremental innovations, lower risk-taking and relatively small investments, are focused on short-term firm profitability. Meanwhile, sustainable development – and regenerative positioning – technologies imply radical innovations, high risk-taking and a higher volume of investment that produces profits in the long and very long term. Pursuing conventional rather than sustainable development produces greater performance in the short term up to time t. After t, sustainable development provides greater firm performance.

PERFORMANCE

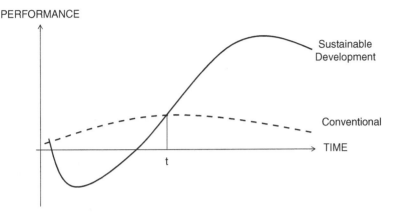

Figure 6.7 Organisational tensions of intertemporal choice
Source: Authors' own elaboration

According to Laverty (1996), economic short-termism exists for the following reasons:

- Flawed management practice. Management tools and practices discounting the future emphasise short-term economic performance, which impedes the development of organisational capabilities needed to maintain competitiveness.
- Managerial opportunism. Management choices often elide suboptimal personal intertemporal and private benefits, i.e. the well-known moral hazard problem.
- Stock market myopia. By pursuing stock price maximisation, managers can destroy long-run value when they sell off long-term assets to increase the current price of stock.
- Fluid and impatient capital. Capital markets for American firms are characterised by 'fluid capital', where funds move their investments according to perceptions of opportunities for near-term appreciation. In contrast, capital in Japanese and German markets is known as 'dedicated capital'. Jacobs (1991) thus remarks that 'impatient capital' increases US firms' capital cost due to the breakdown in long-term relationships among managers and their debt and equity sources.
- Information asymmetry. Since investors do not have a complete picture of long-term investments and prospects, short-term performance acts as a key indicator of firm profitability and management excellence.

Nevertheless, as this book proposes, new disruptive business models addressing the climate emergency, such as regenerative strategy, require a new long-term and very long-term perspective. In fact, all four main regenerative strategy features are interrelated in a deep way. Thus, to avoid economic short-termism, as Laverty (1996) claims, firms should redefine their purpose, moving beyond simple economic profits and towards climate-proofed management and business models (Nyberg & Wright, 2022).

According to Figure 6.7, this premise suggests that performance should include the concept of systemic socioecological resilience, moving from environmental management towards environmental performance with a clear and well-defined metric (Sharma, 2022). Additionally, a new stakeholder engagement logic must extend beyond the traditional primacy of shareholders, investors and managers and engage market and beyond-market stakeholders, fostering both intra- and intergenerational equity. Hence, Aguilera et al. (2022) highlight how the short-termism and selfish financial interests of powerful decision-makers are the key drivers of the growing risks of the climate emergency, and that the dominant short-termist behaviours that prioritise finance and power rewards are in clear contradiction to the interests of future generations and moral justice.

Finally, at the heart of sustainable development, as stated by the World Commission on Environment and Development (1987), is development that meets the needs of the present without compromising the ability of future generations to meet their own needs. The regenerative strategy suggests that this calls for a new time frame covering not only the short to medium term but especially the long and very long term. Managers must learn and be willing to manage intertemporal tensions. As Slawinski and Bansal (2012) have found, proactive sustainable firms can make climate change investments with a time horizon of twenty years or more.

To avoid economic short-termism, firms should make additional efforts to measure and disclose their environmental metrics, which will reduce market myopia and management opportunism. Accordingly, Sharma and Sharma (2019) propose the concept of 'patient capital'. According to them, in the context of family firms, patient capital has been positively linked to innovation because of their lower accountability for short-term financial results and higher motivation to perpetuate the business for future generations.

Some key features of patient capital are (Sharma & Sharma, 2019): (1) the willingness to forgo the maximisation of economic returns to achieve social and environmental impact; (2) a higher risk tolerance;

and (3) a longer time horizon for capital return. Thus, patient capital can be understood as 'an[y] investment that forgoes short-term return for long-term growth and achievement of nonfinancial objectives such as social and environmental impacts, and control of the business over generations' (Sharma & Sharma, 2019:12).

6.4 Concluding Remarks

In this chapter we have shown the main features of disruptive business models that can address the climate emergency through the regenerative strategy.

Following the logic proposed by Hardin (1968), the climate emergency can be understood as an extreme case of the well-known tragedy of the commons phenomenon, which requires two types of actions. The first one is to develop a cutting-edge climate technological innovation able to reverse the current climate emergency: atmospheric CO_2 capture and business utilisation. This requires first disruptive organisational technological prospection behaviour going further than the 'zero emissions aim' or the reduction of negative environmental externalities, to a 'beyond zero emissions aim' capable of creating positive and regenerative environmental externalities. The revolutionary climate innovation introduced in this chapter is the ability to capture – at an industrial scale – atmospheric CO_2 and to sequester or utilise it to produce synthetic CO_2-based fuel. It has been scientifically tested by the experiment at ETH Zurich University by Schäppi et al. (2022) and published in *Nature*. In this way, disruptive business models that formulate and implement a regenerative strategy would be part of the solution instead of being part of the problem.

Nevertheless, that is not enough. The climate emergency also requires a disruptive change in the ethical and moral values of the world's population (Hardin, 1968) covering all spheres: politics, culture, education, economic and business activities and so on. Focusing on the business sphere, a disruptive change in the ethical and moral values of investors, owners, managers and employees is necessary (Bansal, 2019; Nybergh & Wright, 2021; Sharma, 2021) to redefine, from a new stakeholder perspective, the firm's purpose under a new time frame.

The redefinition of firm purpose requires the interaction of three interrelated new constructs introduced in this chapter. The first refers to a new 'ecological emotional wealth' in the minds of key organisational actors, such as the CEO, top managers and shareholders. Their investment decisions must go beyond conventional and short-term 'financial materiality' towards a long-term 'double or stakeholder materiality', which includes all the non-financial aspects related to ecological preservation, pollution minimisation and reversion, and is connected to the moral obligation to leave a dignified natural environment to future generations. Acting as a new micro-foundation of firm strategy, this ecological emotional wealth guides the redefinition of firm purpose towards environmental performance measurement and managing the firm's negative environmental impacts. In fact, the focus on environmental performance drives the firm towards its final and significant purpose: systemic socio-ecological resilience. This follows the logic of a double materiality pointed to earlier and refers to the firm's contribution to and role in systemic ecological, social and organisational resilience as a complex adaptive system, where real business models are capable of creating social and environmental positive externalities.

Secondly, under this logic disruptive business models that adopt this new environmental morality require a fresh conception of stakeholder engagement that overcomes traditional stakeholder pressures to adopt a new stakeholder engagement logic (Barney, 2018; Gibson et al., 2021) and goes beyond the conventional primacy of shareholders, managers and customers to engage fringe stakeholders (Sharma & Vredenburgh, 1998), such as local communities, the natural environment, public administrations and even future generations.

Finally, under this new morality paradigm disruptive business models must face the climate emergency within a new time frame, which implies relevant and inherent tensions and paradoxes between the demands of today and the needs of tomorrow, pointing directly to the DNA of the concept of sustainable development.

References

Ágoston, C., Urbán, R., Nagy, B. et al. (2022). The psychological consequences of the ecological crisis: Three new questionnaires to assess eco-anxiety, eco-guilt, and ecological grief. *Climate Risk Management*, 37: 100441.

Aguilera, R., Aragón-Correa, J. A., and Marano, V. (2022). Rethinking corporate power to tackle grand societal challenges: Lessons from political philosophy. *Academy of Management Review*, 47(4): 456.

Aguilera, R., Aragón-Correa, J. A., Marano, V., and Tashman, P. A. (2021). The corporate governance of environmental sustainability: A review and proposal for more integrated research. *Journal of Management*, 47(6): 1468–1497.

Alvarez, S. A., Zander, U., Barney, J. B., and Afuah, A. (2020). Developing a theory of the firm for the 21st century. *Academy of Management Review*, 45(4): 711–716.

Bansal, P. (2019). Sustainable development in an age of disruption. *Academy of Management Discoveries*, 5(1): 8–12.

Barney, J. (2018). Why resource-based theory's model of profit appropriation must incorporate a stakeholder perspective. *Strategic Management Journal*, 39(13): 3305–3325.

Barney, J., and Harrison, J. (2020). Stakeholder theory at the crossroads. *Business & Society*, 59(2): 203–212.

Berrone, P., Cruz, C., Gómez-Mejía, L., and Larraza-Kintana, M. (2010). Socioemotional wealth and corporate responses to institutional pressures: Do family-controlled firms pollute less? *Administrative Science Quarterly*, 55(1): 82–113.

Bridoux, F., and Stoelhorst, J. (2014). Microfoundations for stakeholder theory: Managing stakeholders with heterogeneous motives. *Strategic Management Journal*, 35(1): 107–125.

Buyssee, K., and Verbeke, A. (2003). Proactive environmental strategies: A stakeholder management perspective. *Strategic Management Journal*, 24(5): 453–470.

Carroll, A. B. (1979). A three-dimensional conceptual model of corporate social performance. *Academy of Management Review*, 4: 497–505.

Chen, V. Z., and Hitt, M. A. (2021). Knowledge synthesis for scientific management: Practical integration for complexity versus scientific fragmentation for simplicity. *Journal of Management Inquiry*, 30(2): 177–192.

Delgado-García, J., and De La Fuente-Sabaté, J. (2010). How do CEO emotions matter? Impact of CEO affective traits on strategic and performance conformity in the Spanish banking industry. *Strategic Management Journal*, 31(5): 562–574.

Delgado-Ceballos, J., Ortiz-de-Mandojana, N., Antolín-López, R., and Montiel, I. (2023). Connecting the sustainable development goals to firm-level sustainability and ESG factors: The need for double materiality. *Business Research Quarterly*, 26(1): 2–10.

Dentoni, D., Pinkse, J., and Lubberink, R. (2021). Linking sustainable business models to socio-ecological resilience through cross-sector partnerships: A complex adaptive systems view. *Business & Society*, 60(5): 1216–1252.

DeSarbo, W. S., Anthony Di Benedetto, C., Song, M., and Sinha, I. (2005). Revisiting the Miles and Snow strategic framework: Uncovering interrelationships between strategic types, capabilities, environmental uncertainty, and firm performance. *Strategic Management Journal*, 26(1): 47–74.

DesJardine, M., Bansal, P., and Yang, Y. (2019). Bouncing back: Building resilience through social and environmental practices in the context of the 2008 global financial crisis. *Journal of Management*, 45(4): 2434–2460.

Ergene, S., Banerjee, B. S., and Hoffman, A. J. (2021). (Un)Sustainability and organization studies: Towards a radical engagement. *Organization Studies*, 42(8): 1319–1335.

Felin, T., Foss, N., Heimeriks, K., and Madsen, T. (2012). Microfoundations of routines and capabilities: Individuals, processes, and structure. *Journal of Management Studies*, 49(8): 1351–1374.

Friedman, M. (1970, 13 September). A Friedman doctrine: The social responsibility of business is to increase its profits. *New York Times Magazine*, 32–33.

George, G., Haas, M., McGahan, A., Schillebeeckx, S., and Tracey, P. (2021). Purpose in the for-profit firm: A review and framework for management research. *Journal of Management*, 49(6): 1841–1869.

George, J., and Jones, G. (2000). The role of time in theory and theory building. *Journal of Management*, 26(4): 657–684.

Gibson, C., Gibson, S., and Webster, Q. (2021). Expanding our resources: Including community in the resource-based view of the firm. *Journal of Management*, 47(7): 1878–1898.

Gladwin, T., Kennelly, J., and Krause, T. S. (1995). Shifting paradigms for sustainable development: Implications for management theory and research. *Academy of Management Review*, 20(4): 874–907.

Gómez-Mejía, L., Haynes, K., Núñez-Nickel, M., Jacobson, K., and Moyano-Fuentes, J. (2007). Socioemotional wealth and business risk in family-controlled firms: Evidence from Spanish olive oil mills. *Administrative Science Quarterly*, 52(1): 106–137.

Hahn, T., and Tampe, M. (2021). Strategies for regenerative business. *Strategic Organization*, 19(3): 456–477.

Hart, S. (1995). A natural resource-based view of the firm. *Academy of Management Review*, 20(4): 986–1014.

Hart, S., and Sharma, S. (2004). Engaging fringe stakeholders for competitive imagination. *Academy of Management Executive*, 18(1): 7–18.

Hepburn, C., Adlen, E., Beddington, J. et al. (2019). The technological and economic prospects for CO_2 utilization and removal. *Nature*, 575: 87–97.

Hillmann, J., and Guenthe, E. (2021). Organizational resilience: A valuable construct for management research? *International Journal of Management Reviews*, 23(1): 7–44.

Hoffman, A. J., and Jennings, P. D. (2021). Institutional-political scenarios for Anthropocene society. *Business & Society*, 60(1): 57–94.

IPCC. (2014). *AR5 Synthesis Report: Climate Change 2014*. Geneva: Intergovernmental Panel on Climate Change. www.ipcc.ch/report/ar5/syr.

IPCC. (2023). *AR6 Synthesis Report: Climate Change 2023*. Geneva: Intergovernmental Panel on Climate Change. www.ipcc.ch/report/sixth-assessment-report-cycle.

Jacobs, M. (1991). *Short-Term America: The Causes and Cures of Our Business Myopia*. Boston, MA: Harvard Business School Press.

Jensen, M., and Meckling, W. (1976). Theory of the firm: Managerial behaviour, agency cost and ownership structure. *Journal of Financial Economics*, 3(4): 305–360.

Kim, A., Bansal, P., and Haugh, H. (2019). No time like the present: How a present time perspective can foster sustainable development. *Academy of Management Journal*, 62(2): 607–634.

Kisfalvi, V., and Pitcher, P. (2003). Doing what feels right. The influence of CEO character and emotions on top management team dynamics. *Journal of Management Inquiry*, 12(1): 42–66.

Kluemper, D., DeGroot, T., and Choi, S. (2011). Emotion management ability: Predicting task performance, citizenship, and deviance. *Journal of Management*, 39(4): 878–905.

Kolk, A., and Pinkse, J. (2005). Business responses to climate change: Identifying emergent strategies. *California Management Review*, 47(3): 6–20.

Laverty, K. (1996). Economic 'short-termism': The debate, the unresolved issues, and the implications for management practice and research. *Academy of Management Review*, 21(3): 825–860.

Levinthal, D., and March, J. G. (1993). The myopia of learning. *Strategic Management Journal*, 14(S2): 95–112.

Little, L., Gooty, J., and Williams, M. (2016). The role of leader emotion management in leader–member exchange and follower outcomes. *Leadership Quarterly*, 27(1): 85–97.

Mac Dowell, N., Fennell, P. S., Shah, N., and Maitland, G. C. (2017). The role of CO_2 capture and utilization in mitigating climate change. *Nature Climate Change*, 7: 243–249.

Martín-de Castro, G., Amores-Salvadó, J., Navas-López, J. E., and Balarezo-Núñez, R. (2020). Corporate environmental reputation: Exploring its definitional landscape. *Business Ethics: A European Review*, 29(1): 130–142.

McGahan, A. (2021). Integrating insights from the resource-based view into the new stakeholder theory. *Journal of Management*, 47(7): 1734–1756.

Miles, R. E., and Snow, C. C. (1978). *Organizational Strategy, Structure and Process*. New York: McGraw-Hill.

Montiel, I., Gallo, P. J., and Antolin-Lopez, R. (2020). What on earth should managers learn about corporate sustainability? A threshold concept approach. *Journal of Business Ethics*, 162(4): 857–880.

Negri, M., Cagno, E., Colicchia, C., and Sarkis, J. (2021). Integrating sustainability and resilience in the supply chain: A systematic literature review and a research agenda. *Business Strategy and the Environment*, 30(7): 2858–2886.

Nyberg, D., and Wright, C. (2022). Climate-proofing management research. *Academy of Management Perspectives*, 36(2): 713–728.

Ortas, E., Moneva, J., Burritt, R., and Tingey-Holyoak, J. (2014). Does sustainability investment provide adaptative resilience to ethical investors? Evidence from Spain. *Journal of Business Ethics*, 124(2): 297–309.

Ortiz-de-Mandojana, N., and Bansal, P. (2016). The long-term benefits of organizational resilience through sustainable business practices. *Strategic Management Journal*, 37(8): 1615–1631.

Polman, P., and Winston, A. (2021). *Net Positive: How Courageous Companies Thrive by Giving More Than They Take*. Cambridge, MA: Harvard Business Review Press.

Shäppi, R., Rutz, D., Dähler, F. et al. (2022) Drop-in fuels from sunlight and air. *Nature*, 601(7891): 63–81.

Sharma, S. (2022). From environmental strategy to environmental impact. *Academy of Management Discoveries*, 8(1): 1–6.

Sharma, P., and Sharma, S. (2011). Drivers of proactive environmental strategy in family firms. *Business Ethics Quarterly*, 21(2): 309–334.

Sharma, S., and Sharma, P. (2019). *Patient Capital. The Role of Family Firms in Sustainable Business*. Cambridge, UK: Cambridge University Press.

Sharma, S., and Vredenburgh, H. (1998). Proactive corporate environmental strategy and the development of competitively valuable organizational capabilities. *Strategic Management Journal*, 19(8): 729–753.

Slawinski, N., and Bansal, P. (2012). A matter of time: The temporal perspectives of organizational responses to climate change. *Organization Studies*, 33(11): 1537–1563.

Slawinski, N., and Bansal, P. (2015). Short on time: Intertemporal tensions in business sustainability. *Organization Science*, 26(2): 531–549.

Smith, A. (1790). *The Theory of Moral Sentiments*. London: A. Millar (6th ed. 2006. São Paulo: Metalibri.)

Wang, L., Lin, Y., Jiang, W., Yang, H., and Zhao, H. (2023). Does CEO emotion matter? CEO affectivity and corporate social responsibility. *Strategic Management Journal*, 44(7): 1820–1835.

Whiteman, G., Walker, B., and Perego, P. (2013). Planetary boundaries: Ecological foundations for corporate sustainability. *Journal of Management Studies*, 50(2): 307–336.

Williams, A., Whiteman, G., and Kennedy, S. (2021). Cross-scale systemic resilience: Implications for organization studies. *Business & Society*, 60(1): 95–124.

World Commission on Environment and Development. (1997). *Our Common Future*. New York: Oxford University Press.

World Economic Forum. (2020). *The Global Risks Report 2020*. Geneva: World Economic Forum. www.weforum.org/reports/the-global-risks-report-2020.

World Economic Forum. (2022). *The Global Risks Report 2022*. Geneva: World Economic Forum. www.weforum.org/reports/global-risks-report-2022.

Wright, C., and Nyberg, D. (2017). An inconvenient truth: How organizations translate climate change into business as usual. *Academy of Management Journal*, 60(5): 1633–1661.

7 | *The Regenerative Strategy*
Facing the Climate Emergency

We are the first generation to feel the effect of climate change and the last generation who can do something about it.

Barack Obama, former US President

7.1 Exploring the Regenerative Strategy through Qualitative Research

Sustainable development is not merely a research topic; it constitutes a new research paradigm (Bansal, 2019). Thus, researchers need to broaden their research contexts – ecological, economic, technological and intergenerational logic – through transdisciplinary theoretical lenses, with theories from both physical systems and social and economic systems.

Following Bansal's (2019) methodological advice, one of the most effective ways to explore strategy and the natural environment in the age of disruption – as our regenerative strategy proposes – is through qualitative research using phenomena-driven research methods. As she declares, quantitative theory testing through regression models based on the historical data that are usually stored in available databases and secondary sources, given their inability to predict the future, offers little value.

In the same vein, Sharma (2022) highlights the utility of phenomena-driven research in gathering the essence and main features of a new corporate environmentalism. In fact, qualitative research is central in developing new theories. At its core, the process of qualitative analysis implies moving from data to the generation of new categories for new theoretical insights (Grodal et al., 2021). Thus, the novel empirical evidence and data found in pioneering business cases would be inductively interpreted and categorised by researchers, demonstrating and generating the new concepts and mechanisms that form, extend or reinterpret the foundations for theory building.

In this sense, carrying out qualitative research and following the postulates of grounded theory (Aguinis & Solarino, 2017; Grodal et al., 2021; Suddaby, 2006), as well as parallel developments of strategy thinking such as strategy-as-practice (Whittington, 1996), are useful paths for exploring several ways to put regenerative strategy into practice through qualitative research on selected cases of pioneering companies. Accordingly, this chapter illustrates the specific problems and contexts associated with the regenerative strategy and disruptive business models in addressing and reversing catastrophic, climate change-related tipping points. Based on the theoretical propositions and aims proposed in Chapter 6, we illustrate this through the pioneering company Carbon Engineering, which is developing the cutting-edge Direct Air Capture technology – with different uses in industry, such as carbon geological sequestration and enhanced oil recovery – and, more importantly, in the associated regenerative discourse, the creation of synthetic carbon dioxide (CO_2)-based fuel. Different qualitative research methods are employed as well as various data sources, such as secondary quantitative and qualitative data and reports from the focal company, industry, climate science and media documents, in addition to in-depth interviews with elite informants, one of the most important primary sources.

Due to the significance of these methodological clarifications and recommendations for qualitative research, to increase this work's rigour, transparency and replicability, in Sections 7.1.1–7.1.4 we analyse the purpose and method of qualitative research and related grounded theory to highlight an effective way of building new theory through case studies while placing methodological emphasis on our interviews with elite informants.

7.1.1 *Qualitative Research*

Scientific research on strategic management and organisations suffers from certain difficulties and controversies concerning its transparency, replicability and cumulative character (Aguinis et al., 2017). These issues are especially relevant for qualitative research. Nevertheless, studies adopting empirical qualitative methods to explore questions and emerging phenomena are critical in generating new insights for strategic management (Bettis et al., 2015). In fact, the development of theory through qualitative research is a central activity in organisational research (Eisenhardt, 1989).

In this vein, qualitative research results are especially suited to sparking debate on emerging issues, such as the strategy and business models for addressing climate and planetary emergencies. Although qualitative research can be built on deductive bases, inductive qualitative research, using more open-ended questions about unexplored emerging phenomena, such as those analysed in terms of the regenerative strategy, constitute an excellent way to provide new insights for strategic management and environmental studies. In fact, the most prominent research output journals on management and strategy, such as the *Strategic Management Journal* (Bettis et al., 2015) and the *Academy of Management Journal* (Suddaby, 2006), are encouraging new avenues for empirical qualitative research. The *Strategic Management Journal*'s website includes a useful guide to a variety of qualitative methods and encourages researchers in strategic management to use a range of different approaches to qualitative analysis, such as multiple case studies to build theory, methods concerning first-order and second-order analysis, qualitative research investigating 'how' questions, qualitative research to produce a strategy-as-practice framework, or qualitative comparative analysis (QCA).

According to Aguinis and Solarino (2017), transparency in qualitative research is necessary for three types of replication:

- Exact replication, which implies that a previous study is replicated using the same population and research procedures.
- Empirical replication, in which a previous study is replicated with the same procedures but a different population.
- Conceptual replication, when a previous study is replicated using the same population but different research procedures.

Qualitative research and the necessary methodological rigor achieved have been and continue to be subject to scrutiny and debate by scholars (Grodal et al., 2021). Hence, the categorisation process, the core purpose of qualitative research, must be transparent, showing how researchers generate theory from data. According to Grodal et al. (2021), categorisation is the process through which individuals group elements together to generate an understanding of their world. How the categorisation process achieves high levels of rigour for theory building is a central concern for researchers carrying out qualitative research.

To shed some light on and ensure transparency in qualitative methods, Grodal et al. (2021) define eight moves or steps that researchers should undertake during qualitative theory building to increase the rigour of their research. Specifically, the researcher raises the conceptual level of the analysis from pure description, and the phenomenal, to a more abstract theoretical level. These steps, in coherence with the two main mechanisms – constant comparison and theoretical sampling – of grounded theory, as exposed by Glaser and Strauss (1967), are as follows:

- Step 1: Asking questions. How researchers make sense of the focal phenomenon depends on their prior understanding of it and their initial goals. As Suddaby (2006) clarifies, in grounded theory analysis researchers cannot ignore existing literature and previous knowledge. Thus, our existing categories on environmental strategies are the foundations for the new disruptive regenerative strategy – a category that we try to elucidate in this research. Hence, this is the first move, in which researchers draw on their existing categories to select and approach their field settings with specific questions that they aim to answer. Additionally, asking questions is useful because it helps researchers manage the complexity and overload of empirical data.
- Step 2: Focusing on puzzles. Initial categories are formed by focusing on the part of the data most surprising/salient to the researchers – puzzles – because not all information is equally important for categorisation purposes. In this process, it is highly remarkable that observations do not always correspond to the existing knowledge of the focal phenomenon, as in the case of existing 'business-as-usual' environmental strategies. Here, salient data refer to the intensity of a feature that is at odds with the existing knowledge about a category, playing a critical role in new category formation. As previously stated in this book, the regenerative strategy possesses several salient features that invite us to adopt a new disruptive categorisation of environmental strategies.

  Indeed, as Grodal et al. (2021) highlight, strong qualitative research should focus on 'unexpected' data/evidence. Surprising and unexpected data – also called negative or unusual cases – are of great importance for theory building, even if there is only one case. Hence, this book explores a single pioneering case carrying out disruptive environmental business models: the Canadian firm Carbon Engineering.

The next steps, three to seven, focus on refining tentative categories and include further analysis and, possibly, added data collection, as

Glaser and Strauss (1967) emphasise in their proposed two complementary and key mechanisms of grounded theory – constant comparison and theoretical sampling:

- Step 3: Dropping categories. To avoid generating initially faulty, biased or irrelevant categories, the researcher should focus on categories that are more important and meaningful in explaining the focal phenomenon – in our case, disruptive business models for facing the climate emergency. Hence, dropping categories excludes any categories that are no longer relevant in explaining the focal phenomenon and entails dropping any categories generated during the initial raw data analysis that turn out to lack theoretical traction.
- Step 4: Merging categories. Merging two or more existing initial categories to create a higher-order or second-order category is performed because researchers initially tend to create elaborate and detailed categorisation structures for unfamiliar objects and phenomena. Nevertheless, to pass from just thinking phenomenally to theory building, researchers should merge these categories into superordinate categories to capture the essence of their meaning.
- Step 5: Splitting categories. Separating a category into two or more subordinate categories is the reverse process of merging categories. Nevertheless, as previously remarked, the qualitative method is not linear. Category formation does not progress uniformly from more categories to fewer categories; many times, the progress is from fewer to more categories and creating finer distinctions is often an important component of theory building.
- Step 6: Relating or contrasting categories. The iterative and qualitative process of constant comparison, in which data gathering and analysis are carried out simultaneously, processes several categories with the aim of identifying their relationships or the lack thereof. Hence, as we propose in several figures in Chapter 6, the relationships and differences between 'business-as-usual' environmental strategy categories and regenerative ones are revealed.
- Step 7: Sequencing categories. This involves temporally organising any categories that researchers have identified in the data. Effectively, the logic of our book and the content of its chapters' sequence categories identify and encode the causal relationships and path-dependent evolution of environmental strategies, following the pioneering work of Hart (1995). Sequencing is important in

qualitative research because categories and interrelationships allow processes and their temporality to be identified. Following Grodal et al. (2021), in our research we not only identify categories of environmental strategies, but also offer a novel and disruptive perspective on the relationships among the concepts and mechanisms in the regenerative strategy, a fundamental ingredient for theory building.

• Step 8: Developing or dropping working hypotheses. In this final move, researchers aim to create a new theory to explain the emerging focal phenomenon. Following Aguinis and Solarino's (2017) methodological advice for qualitative research, the determination of the saturation point is a key decision. This occurs when researchers consider that there are no new insights, discoveries or issues when collecting data or in data interpretation. Thus, this leads them to formulating an overarching theory and, by an interactive process with the data, either finding increasing evidence for it, leading to its elaboration, or finding contradictory or unsupportive evidence for it, leading to its abandonment.

In developing or dropping a working hypothesis, researchers formulate an overarching understanding of their data in an iterative process concerning these data that implies both elaborating propositions and hypotheses when supporting arguments and dropping them when contradictory or unsupportive evidence exists. This is a premise and a constant in qualitative research theory building: 'doubt and believe' (Grodal et al., 2021) or 'back-and-forth'. Although many researchers eliminate unsupported working hypotheses from public view prior to publication, nevertheless, as Aguinis and Solarino (2017) claim, for transparency and replicability in qualitative research, all the methodological steps, including this final one, should be described to the scientific community.

7.1.2 Grounded Theory

Grounded theory refers to a set of systematic inductive methods designed for qualitative research aimed at theory development. It was developed by Glaser and Strauss (1967) in reaction to the high degree of positivism dominating research in social sciences. Contrary to the 'grand theory' of natural sciences, social sciences do not fit with pre-existing and universal explanations for social behaviour. In the social sciences, far removed from the existing and external independence of scientific truth, truth is built with a pragmatic approach based both on the act of observation and on an emerging consensus within the community of observers in terms of how they make sense of what they have observed (Suddaby, 2006). This empirical reality is the pragmatic approach of social science.

Contrary to positivism, the grounded theory method is based on two main elements (Glaser & Strauss, 1967): (1) constant comparison, in which data gathering and analysis are carried out simultaneously; and (2) theoretical sampling, which implies that the data collection path is determined by the theory that is under construction.

Clarifying grounded theory, Suddaby (2006) highlights seven solutions to change common misconceptions:

- A literature review should be considered when carrying out grounded theory research. Although the danger of 'prior knowledge contaminating the researcher' could exist, a simple way to overcome this is to avoid research that adheres too closely to a single substantive area/theory.
- Grounded theory extends beyond the presentation of raw data, or phenomenological research, which emphasises the subjective experiences of actors, by focusing on how such subjective experiences can be abstracted into theoretical arguments about the causal relationships between actors/cases. Instead of focusing on raw data, grounded theory research tries to identify a higher level of abstraction through the constant comparative method until 'category saturation', a key element in grounded theory verification, is reached.
- Grounded theory is not concerned with hypothesis testing, content analysis or word count. Grounded theory does not entail theory testing because its purpose is simply to elicit fresh understandings of patterned relationships among actors and how they interpret reality. In fact, grounded theory should not contain explicit hypotheses to be tested. The researcher should discover and build theory from data through constantly comparative methods, evaluating any critical constructs arising against ongoing observations. Additionally, although content analysis is one of the methods for acquiring data in grounded theory, it implies much more than its title suggests or a word count.
- Grounded theory extends beyond routine applications of and formulaic techniques concerning data. Grounded theory is not mechanical;

it is an interpretative process, not a logico-deductive one. The researcher plays a very active role in this research process as a key creative component that cannot be replaced by any algorithm or software, which, while useful, cannot substitute for the researcher's interpretation of data. Overall, grounded theory research has a key creative component: becoming patient and tolerant of ambiguity. As Grodal et al. (2021) highlight, the creation of categories in qualitative research cannot be decoupled from the researcher who creates them or the context in which they were created.

- The previous statement suggests that grounded theory is far from perfect. As a practical approach to exploring and understanding complex social phenomena, its associated techniques are 'messy', which requires a deep knowledge of the empirical context and common problems arising when the researcher tries to determine the saturation point; Some researchers establish this at between twenty-five and thirty interviews. Nevertheless, for Glaser and Strauss (1967), the saturation point is determined by a combination of the empirical limits of the data, the integration and density of the theoretical postulates, and the analyst's theoretical sensitivity.

- Given these features, grounded theory is not easy to apply. Contrary to its apparent simplicity in terms of avoiding complex statistical treatment, a well-executed grounded theory study implies rich experience, hard work, creativity and sometimes luck. As an interpretative process, grounded theory heavily depends on the researcher's previous experience, sensitivity to tacit elements, intuition and creativity. Additionally, the constant comparative method implies an intimate and enduring relationship between the researcher and the contextual site – an explicit positioning of the researcher in the research process.

- Finally, grounded theory, despite its exploratory nature, requires a well-defined methodology. Hence, grounded theory studies should adopt transparent methods, for instance in theoretical sampling, constant comparison methods and data gathering, exploring how data are transformed into key conceptual categories, as well as elaborating how researchers combine the literature, data, their experience and so on. In the field of management and the natural environment, the work of Bansal and Roth (2000) on why companies go green constitutes a very good example of grounded theory and transparent and reliable methods.

7.1.3 *Qualitative Research Based on Case Study Research through Interviews with Elite Informants*

Theory building in case study research requires a careful roadmap. To carry out this relevant and complex task, we follow the prescriptions and methodologies proposed by Eisenhardt (1989).

A case study, as a research strategy, was first designed by Yin (1981, 1984), involving a case study typology design, different levels of analysis and replication issues, highlighting concerns with validity and reliability. Case studies can involve single or multiple cases and typically combine different data sources such as archival data, in-depth interviews with elite informants, questionnaires and direct observations (Eisenhardt, 1989). Evidence from cases can be quantitative, qualitative or both. Although these data can be used to test a theory or provide a description, in this research they are used to generate a new theory. For this purpose, Eisenhardt (1989) has proposed a roadmap that includes nine main steps. These are briefly explained in the following paragraphs.

The first step entails having a well-defined focus that includes an initial definition of the research question. In this vein, construct specification can help in the initial stages of theory-building research, allowing easier identification and even measurement. This stage is clearly linked to the extant literature.

The second step is focused on case selection. The focus on a specific population avoids environmental variation. However, in our research, as case studies are designed for theory building, we rely on theoretical sampling: cases are chosen for theoretical, not statistical, reasons. We choose a worldwide pioneering case to illustrate our emerging theory on disruptive environmental strategies for addressing the grand challenge of climate emergency by decarbonising the atmosphere.

Then, in the third step, the researcher designs data-gathering methods, usually different types of data, such as direct observations, archival data, both from inside and outside the focal organisation and, mainly, in-depth interviews with elite informants. Research reliability is thus achieved through the triangulation of several data sources. In this vein, Yin (1981) recommends the combination of qualitative and quantitative case evidence. Thus, qualitative data are useful for understanding the rationale of the quantitative evidence surrounding the theoretical argument(s). In this stage, multiple researchers simultaneously gathering evidence offer advantages and reliability to field research.

The fourth step implies beginning field research. For theory-building purposes, continuous overlaps of data gathering and analysis are the common rule. Some strong recommendations include the use of field notes and questions explicitly related to them or recurrent team meetings to share ideas and discuss fresh field evidence. Overlapping data analysis with data collection should be sufficiently flexible and adaptative to new insights and circumstances.

At the heart of building theory via case studies is the fifth step: analysis of within-case data. This involves detailed case study write-ups for each site, involving pure descriptions and raw data, key constituencies in the generation of insights. In this stage, a high volume of data is generated, which should be processed without any standard format of analysis. Narrative descriptions, figures and graphs, and videos are some examples.

Sequentially or in parallel, in the seventh step the researcher can search for cross-case patterns to avoid premature or even false conclusions because of information-processing biases. A possible technique is to select categories or dimensions and then check their within-group similarities, coupled with their intergroup differences. In our research, these dimensions are designed in our regenerative strategy, based on the literature review.

Eisenhardt (1989) continues building theory via case studies in the eighth step, which involves shaping hypotheses; that is, the proposition of tentative themes, concepts and potential relationships. In this highly iterative process, the researcher continuously compares the emergent model and features with the evidence from each case study. The key point is the continuous comparison of theory and data.

The next step is to enfold theory by comparing the emerging concept and features and propositions – in our case, the regenerative strategy, working in different contexts and facing different challenges – with the literature.

The final step, reaching closure, involves two important issues: when to stop adding cases and when to stop iterating between theory and practice. In both cases, theoretical saturation is the goal. It is reached when incremental learning becomes minimal, whether by adding new cases or iterating theory and new empirical evidence. The final output of this process could be a new concept, a new conceptual framework and/or new propositions or, possibly, a mid-range theory.

Overall, as Eisenhardt (1989) recognises, one of the main strengths of case study research is its utility for new theory generation when nothing or little is known about a phenomenon, such as the climate emergency and disruptive sustainable business models for addressing it. As Bansal (2019) advocates, at no other time in history has sustainable development research been more crucial.

When adopting a qualitative methodology in case studies, strategic management research traditionally identifies chief executive officers (CEOs) and top managers – elite informants – as the key informants for both questionnaires and in-depth surveys and in quantitative and qualitative research. As Basu and Palazzo (2008) recognise, many issues concerning firm strategy can only be provided by elite informants, who are thus necessary for theory building and testing.

Elite informants are not only CEOs and top managers, but also highly skilled professionals and people with substantial knowledge and expertise not possessed by others. Aguinis and Solarino (2017:1293) define elite informants as 'key decision-makers who have extensive and exclusive information and the ability to influence important firm outcomes, either alone or jointly with others – e.g. on a board of directors'.

Methodological issues to consider when carrying out qualitative research using interviews with elite informants are (1) the roles of informant and researcher, and their relationship; (2) the sampling procedures and saturation point determination; and (3) the data coding and analyses (Aguinis & Solarino, 2017), which include the research design, measurement, analysis, reporting of results and data availability.

Based on an extensive literature review on qualitative methodology, Aguinis and Solarino (2017) propose twelve transparency criteria in qualitative research, with the aim of increasing its exact, empirical and conceptual replication. They also offer rather interesting behaviourally anchored rating scales (BARS) for measuring transparency in qualitative research, ranging from 1 (criterion not mentioned) to 4 (criterion is met). Briefly and jointly with their associated BARS no. 4, the transparency criteria are as follows, according to the sequential path of the qualitative research process:

1. Qualitative method used in the research: The type of method chosen – case study, grounded theory, etc. – has certain derivatives for replication because the method's assumptions, beliefs and values affect theory, design, measurement, analysis and reporting, as well as results interpretation. This first criterion is met when the authors clearly identify their adopted qualitative approach.

2. Research setting: The physical, social, competitive and cultural circumstances under which the study is carried out affect its circumstances and potential bias. This criterion is met when the researcher offers a rich and detailed description of the research setting.

3. Position of the researcher: Her or his relationship with the focal organisation and informants/participants – insider/outsider – conditions the access to/collection of data and its interpretation and any potential subjectivity bias. To meet this criterion, the research must clearly explicate his or her position on the insider–outsider continuum.

4. Sample procedures: Qualitative research does not use probabilistic samples but entails the explicit selection of cases/participants – convenience, purposive, theoretical, etc. – and any potential for sampling bias. To fully meet this criterion, the researcher should describe the kind of variability pursued as well as how he or she identifies the participant(s) and/or cases.

5. Relative importance of the participant(s)/cases: This allows for identifying the cases/participants with similar features to the original study. If the researcher describes how each participant has been instrumental in developing or producing more themes, this criterion is met.

6. Documenting interactions with participants: Survey transcription and the documentation of other data sources – audio, video, notation, etc. – are crucial in qualitative research. Additionally, different means of documenting interactions may alter the information gathered. To meet this criterion, the researcher must document each interaction and all its associated content.

7. Saturation point: This is reached when the researcher considers that there are no new insights, discoveries or issues in collecting data and data interpretation. The precise measure used to conclude that the saturation point is reached should be clearly stated to meet this criterion.

8. Unexpected opportunities, challenges and other events: These will occur during the research process and involve examples such as access to new data, refusal of certain participants, etc., and how the researcher reacts to them. To meet this criterion, the researcher describes all unexpected opportunities, challenges and other events, how they were managed and their impact on the research.

9. Management of power imbalance: The different levels of control, authority and influence exercised by the researcher influence the utility of data gathering and any potential conclusions reached. Sensitive questions, endorsements from a prestigious institution, etc. influence the qualitative research process and insights. How the researcher has addressed any power imbalances with specific participants should be explained to meet this ninth criterion.

10. Data coding and first-order codes: This key step transforms raw data into categorised data to facilitate subsequent analyses (narrative coding, descriptive coding, etc.). This criterion is met when the research presents the full code list and describes the first-order coding method.

11. Data analysis and second- and higher-order codes: Explanation of the classification and interpretation of linguistic and/or visual material to produce statements about implicit and explicit dimensions and structures are carried out through the identification of the key relationships that tie the first-order codes together into a narrative or sequence, such as pattern coding, focused coding, axial coding, etc. As with the previous criterion, to meet it the researcher should present the full code list and make explicit the adopted second-order coding methodology.

12. Data disclosure: Raw material includes any type of information collected by the researcher before manipulation, such as transcripts, video recordings, etc. Criteria 10–12 permit other researchers to use similar analytical frames and tools and achieve similar conclusions. To meet this final criterion, the researcher should disclose the raw materials gathered and examined during the study.

7.1.4 Qualitative Research Carried Out at Carbon Engineering

Due to the unique and cutting-edge character of the technological climate innovations required to fight against the climate emergency, our qualitative research is focused on a single business case: Carbon Engineering (CE). Theoretical sampling, involving a unique case leading the grand challenge, led us to evaluate this pioneering company, the only one in the world that is capable of achieving this on an industrial scale and developed, in 2015–2017, two technologies, Direct Air Capture (DAC) and AIR TO FUELS (A2F). Through in-depth analysis of CE, we demonstrate that there is a real and technologically feasible possibility for companies to make a decisive contribution to the decarbonisation of society with real (scientifically proven) and scalable solutions.

Following qualitative methodological recommendations (Bansal, 2019), we have designed several information-gathering strategies:

- In-depth interviews with David Keith, founder and former CEO of CE, and Daniel Friedmann, CE's current CEO, an elite informant (Aguinis & Solarino, 2017), about the four regenerative strategy postulates. The aim was to enrich and compare information collected from scientific evidence, the media, non-governmental organisations (NGOs) and corporate reports. This online, semi-structured interview was conducted on 6 February 2023 in a recorded Microsoft Teams meeting with a length of one hour and concerned the following main topics:
  - Pioneering character of CE's technologies: Direct Air Capture and AIR TO FUELS.
  - 'Net Zero' and 'Net Negative' visions by 2050.
  - Personal feelings and values guiding the CEO's decisions in CE and future scenarios.
  - CE's unique purpose and values.
  - CE's business model elements and logic.
  - CE's partners, competitors and investors.
- As secondary information, we gathered personal details on the founder of the company, Professor David Keith. His personal and professional experience informed us on how the idea of carbon removal emerged. We also consulted his MIT book published in 2013, several of his scientific papers and the Harvard Business School business case on CE (Lassiter & Misra, 2013).
- Secondary information about CE regarding the company's history, financial and other information reports was collected from CE's website (https://carbonengineering.com), several reports by its media and communication manager, and the media's discussion of the company.

7.2 Putting the Regenerative Strategy into Action: Carbon Capture and Utilisation to Fight against the Climate Emergency

The Intergovernmental Panel on Climate Change (IPCC, 2014, 2023) foresees a highly improbable and rapid decarbonisation of the atmosphere that keeps the mean global temperature increase below 2°C by the end of the twenty-first century. Under this scenario, CO_2 DAC, or CO_2 removal technology, has taken centre stage (Keith, 2009; Qiu et al., 2022). The IPCC suggests that the remaining 420–1170 gigatonnes of CO_2 are expected to be depleted in between one and three decades under the current emissions rate, which implies the removal of excess CO_2 from the atmosphere amounting to approximately 200–1200 gigatonnes by the year 2100 through different CO_2 removal technologies. According to Qiu et al. (2022), DAC is gaining attention and recognition among the scientific community and policy-makers as a promising climate mitigation strategy.

One of the easiest and fastest ways to manage the atmospheric CO_2 captured is its storage in soil or geological sequestration. A forecast provided by CE (www.carbonengineering.com) suggests that the majority of atmospheric CO_2 captured will be sequestered into the Earth. Among the advantages of this, as CE's CEO Daniel Friedmann declared in his interview, are that 'The easiest and fastest way to achieve "net negative" CO_2 emissions is through carbon dioxide capture and soil sequestration.'

CO_2 capture and soil sequestration could represent, by themselves, a first step in the effective regenerative strategy for fighting the climate emergency. Additionally, according to Qiu et al. (2022), due to the homogeneous concentration levels of atmospheric CO_2 around the world, DAC facilities can be deployed in cost-convenient locations that provide abundant cheap and carbon-free energy and/or that are close to pipeline infrastructure, underground storage or utilisation facilities to reduce transportation costs. Nevertheless, as they describe, this practice has several trade-offs. For example, CO_2 sequestration in the soil increases terrestrial ecotoxicity and metal depletion levels per tonne of CO_2 sequestered.

One of the largest facilities for atmospheric CO_2 capture and storage is near Reykjavik, Iceland, and was inaugurated in 2021; there, the captured CO_2 is blended with saline water and stored in the soil. It is expected to capture and store 4,000 tonnes of carbon dioxide each year. This plant was designed by CE's rival company Climeworks, a start-up of ETH Zurich, Switzerland.

However, as mentioned, CO_2 capture and soil sequestration are only the first step towards the regenerative strategy. In our proposal of the regenerative strategy, carbon captured from the air should also be utilised in daily business activities, as feedstock for other business activities geared towards net zero emissions or even to create positive environmental externalities, such as net negative emissions. In this sense, two regenerative strategies using carbon captured from the air have recently become available and are undergoing increased scientific debate and scrutiny: (1) cement and concrete sequestration; and (2) CO_2-based synthetic fuel.

The first, CO_2-based cement and concrete building, is a technical way to decarbonise the atmosphere by both capturing CO_2 from the air and sequestering it in concrete, thereby reducing the CO_2 emissions of the traditional technological standard in the industry, which supposes, according to scientific evidence (Skocek et al., 2020), approximately 7 per cent of global anthropogenic carbon emissions into the atmosphere. Nevertheless, Friedmann's expert opinion offers a less optimistic perspective:

Concrete CO_2 sequestration is not a current solution to fight climate emergency due to its lack of worldwide scalability. CO_2 capture from the air requires megaton-scale plants incompatible with current concrete technological standards.

The second strategy, CO_2-based synthetic fuel, is attracting increased business and scientific attention and scrutiny due to its two prominent advantages: (1) worldwide scalability with currently compatible gas and oil industries and existing combustion engines; and (2) technical and economic viability. Both issues confirm it to be one of the most promising business actions for addressing the climate emergency.

In this sense, one of the first scientific demonstrations of the entire thermochemical solar fuel production chain, from water (H_2O) and CO_2 captured directly from the air to the synthesis of drop-in transportation fuels, such as methanol and kerosene – which currently represent approximately 8 per cent of anthropogenic CO_2 emissions – has been carried out by Schäppi et al. (2022) and recently published in *Nature*. It was carried out on the roof of ETH's Machine Laboratory Building in Zurich. Moving beyond the small-scale previous evidence, they worked with a modular 5 kW thermal pilot-scale solar system, operated under field conditions.

The rest of this chapter is devoted to introducing two business applications of CO_2 capture from the air: (1) enhanced oil recovery through DAC; and (2) CO_2-based synthetic fuel. Both of these have been developed for worldwide application on an industrial scale by the first-of-a-kind (FOAK) company CE.

7.3 The Regenerative Strategy at Carbon Engineering

7.3.1 Carbon Engineering's Origin, Current Development and Business Model

The Canadian company Carbon Engineering was founded in Calgary in 2009 by David Keith. He is a Harvard professor with a double appointment as Professor of Applied Physics at SEAS and Professor of Public Policy at the Kennedy School. He has the personal and professional background and profile of a mountaineer, Arctic explorer and son of a wildlife biologist, with a cross-disciplinary background in experimental physics, hardware engineering and public policy.

Keith and other scientists started to investigate Direct Air Capture as an additional tool for emissions reductions, due to the growing awareness that the world would not only need to bring emissions to zero, but would also need to remove carbon from the atmosphere. With support from a team of academic scientists, business leaders and strategic investors, Keith founded CE to shift a promising concept into real-world, hardware-driven engineering and design.

In 2013, CE's offices were located in the University of Calgary's Research Facility, a commercialisation hub for university technology. The main idea straddled academia and business. Hence, the company could benefit from Calgary, a hotbed of technological innovation, as well as power and petroleum processing plant construction in terms of attracting talented workers. The prototype plan for the DAC budget was C$15 million ($3 million more than expected; Lassiter & Misra, 2013). This prototype was an FOAK.

Following years of prototyping and technology research and development (R&D), in 2015 CE moved to Squamish, British Columbia, to build an operational pilot plant. CE first captured CO_2 from the air in 2015 and then produced the first batch of synthetic fuel in 2017.

CE was founded with a clear and concrete mission, as it declares on its corporate website: 'To develop and commercialize a technology that captures CO_2 directly out of the atmosphere at megaton-scale.'

One of the company's purposes was to create a unique, disruptive and sustainable business model capable of effectively – both on time and in terms of worldwide scalability – addressing the climate emergency, which encapsulates the regenerative strategy: linking two cutting-edge disruptive technologies, DAC and A2F, to a redefinition of the firm's purpose, new stakeholder engagement and a very long-term time frame. As the corporate website reports:

The CE business model is to licence our technologies to local plant developers and energy industry partners around the world to enable rapid and widespread deployment of Direct Air Capture technology. We've purposely chosen this model because it gives us the ability to deploy our solutions as quickly and broadly as possible and to start making a meaningful impact on the climate challenge.

In the rest of this chapter we show to what extent the main features of the regenerative strategy defined in Chapter 6 emerge in the pioneering case of CE. Thus, the cutting-edge technologies developed by the company are discussed (Direct Air Capture, enhanced oil recovery and AIR TO FUELS) and we illustrate its new and unique purpose: disentangling the concepts of the eco-emotional wealth of a CEO and entrepreneur as well as environmental performance and systemic socioecological resilience, to reveal the initiative of net zero emissions by 2050 in this case of the air transport industry. In addition, CE's stakeholders' engagement purpose, whereby the company, partners, key business actors in different industries, public and private administrations and institutions work together to reverse and regenerate the climate crisis, is assessed. Finally, the implications of CE's activities and business models for the very long term and future generations are discussed.

7.3.2 The Regenerative Strategy at CE: Cutting-Edge Technologies for Achieving Net Zero and Net Negative Emissions

To create net zero, net negative and positive environmental impacts, CE is developing several cutting-edge technologies. Two of the most prominent are its patented Direct Air Capture and AIR TO FUELS technologies. Both seek net zero emissions and, in some cases, net negative emissions or positive environmental impacts, although the development of a truly regenerative strategy can only be realised when both technologies are employed in a coordinated manner. While both technologies facilitate the fight against climate change, only their simultaneous deployment offers the potential for regenerative impact.

From an organisational point of view, clear prospector and explorer profile behaviour guides the company's policy, in conjunction with interdisciplinary executive and management teams and boards of directors, to take advantage of the natural sciences, engineering and economic and business fields; these are necessary to achieve the regenerative aims. We analyse all these relevant issues in what follows. As previously described, CE's 2013 DAC prototype plant has been deemed FOAK (Lassiter & Misra, 2013), corroborating the prospector and explorer pathway.

7.3.2.1 Direct Air Capture

Direct Air Capture is a cutting-edge technology that continuously captures CO_2 directly from the air using an engineered, mechanical system. The captured CO_2 is purified and compressed as gas for use or storage. Figures 7.1 and 7.2 show how DAC works.

DAC technology pulls in atmospheric air, then, through a series of chemical reactions, extracts the carbon dioxide from it while returning the rest of the air to the environment. This is what plants and trees do every day in photosynthesis, but Direct Air Capture technology does it much faster with a smaller land footprint and delivers the carbon dioxide in a pure, compressed form that can then be stored underground or reused.

DAC technology uses four major pieces of equipment, each of which has an industrial precedent and has been widely used in large-scale industries for years. This is how the technology is capable of achieving a megatonne scale with low scale-up risks and improved cost estimations.

The process starts with an air contactor – a large structure modelled on industrial cooling towers. A giant fan pulls air into this structure, where it passes over thin plastic surfaces that have potassium hydroxide solution flowing over them. This non-toxic solution chemically binds with the CO_2 molecules, removing them from the air and trapping them in the liquid solution as a carbonate salt.

Figure 7.1 Direct Air Capture technology
Source: www.carbonengineering.com

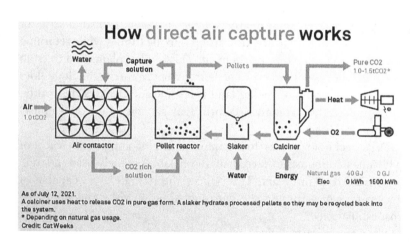

Figure 7.2 Direct Air Capture working process
Source: www.carbonengineering.com

The CO_2 contained in this carbonate solution is then put through a series of chemical processes to increase its concentration, purify and compress it so that it can be delivered in a gaseous form ready for use or storage. This involves separating the salt from the solution into small pellets in a structure called a pellet reactor, adapted from water treatment technology. These pellets are then heated in the third step, a calciner, to release the CO_2 in a purely gaseous form. The calciner is similar to equipment that is used on a very large scale in mining for ore processing. This step also leaves behind any processed pellets that are hydrated in a slacker, which are then recycled back into the system to reproduce the original capture chemical.

DAC technology possesses five main features that define it as an unlimited, scalable and rapid solution for reversing the climate emergency and decarbonising the atmosphere in a convenient way:

- Megatonne scale: CE has built its DAC technology by utilising known equipment and processes from other industries and then innovating and integrating them to create the cutting-edge DAC system. This fact implies scalability: the system can be built at large industrial scales with known supply chains and reliable equipment costs.

- Affordability: According to Keith et al. (2018), CE's DAC technology is capable of capturing CO_2 from the atmosphere for approximately US\$100 per tonne at a large scale. Additionally, a DAC plant would capture one million tonnes of CO_2 per year, similar to those under construction in Texas by CE's partner 1PointFive.

- Freedom of location: Due to the uniform distribution of atmospheric CO_2, DAC plants are location independent. Hence, they can be placed in abundance, use low-cost local energy to power their facility, or be sited wherever there are appropriate storage or utilisation sites. As they can be located on non-arable land, their facilities avoid competing for agricultural lands, overcoming other current solutions such as biofuels.

- Use of a closed chemical cycle: DAC technology captures CO_2 from the atmosphere in a closed chemical loop, reusing the same captured chemicals repeatedly. In this way, this technology is both non-volatile and non-toxic, meeting environmental health and safety standards with minimum waste and minor supplies of chemicals needed to operate.

- Emissions free: To power the system, DAC can use a flexible combination of renewable electricity, such as solar or wind, and natural gas. When natural gas is used, CO_2 from combustion is captured and delivered along with the CO_2 captured from the air, minimising emissions. Nevertheless, DAC technology is capable of reducing or eliminating the use of natural gas. Overall, then, DAC facilities can avoid the creation of new emissions, thereby achieving net zero emissions.

CO_2 captured from the air can be geologically stored or used for business purposes as feedstock. Hence, CE works with partners to deliver two types of large-scale industrial plants.

7.3.2.2 Storage Plants

DAC and storage plants offer an affordable solution for removing CO_2 from the air at a megatonne scale. They are location independent, so they can be built almost anywhere and in most climates. They have flexible configurations and can be sized to suit customer needs; however, their economics are most favourable on large industrial scales. CE's plants can be built to capture millions of tonnes of CO_2 per year.

Direct Air Capture and storage plants deliver the capture and permanent storage of atmospheric CO_2 at prices competitive in today's leading markets. There are a number of forms of CO_2 storage, but CE's main focus is on ensuring permanent carbon removal by burying the CO_2 deep underground through secure geological storage.

Many major scientific assessments have now concluded that the world will need large quantities of carbon dioxide removed from the atmosphere if we are to avoid the worst impacts of climate change. DAC with geological storage has the potential to deliver permanent carbon removal on a gigatonne scale.

Geological storage is the process of injecting and storing CO_2 deep underground in geological reservoirs, as Figure 7.3 shows. Also known as carbon sequestration, it has been used safely and effectively by industry for decades, with more than 200 million tonnes of CO_2 successfully stored in geological sites all over the world. Leading international bodies, such as the IPCC, have assessed this practice and concluded that when storage sites are properly regulated, selected and managed, CO_2 can be stored permanently for millions of years with very low risk. Suitable locations for carbon storage exist in many

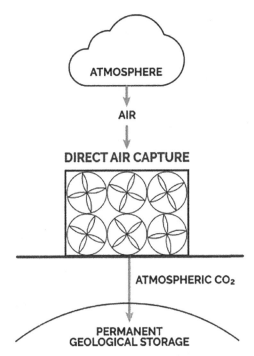

Figure 7.3 Permanent geological storage of carbon dioxide
Source: www.carbonengineering.com

regions worldwide and, collectively, have the capacity to store hundreds of years of CO_2 emissions underground.

Pairing DAC with geological storage is a safe and reliable way to permanently remove vast amounts of CO_2 from the atmosphere. Traditional use of fossil fuels extracts carbon from underground geological reservoirs. When used in cars, homes or power plants, carbon is released into the air in the form of CO_2, thus emitting the greenhouse gases that intensify climate change. DAC with secure geological storage can do exactly the reverse. By capturing atmospheric CO_2 and permanently storing it underground, this form of carbon removal can play a major role in greenhouse gas mitigation, creating, for the first time on an industrial scale, positive environmental externalities.

The main features of DAC with geological storage are as follows:

- It is a permanent solution for removing CO_2 from the air. According to the IPPC (2022), when geological storage is well regulated, selected and managed, CO_2 can be stored permanently for millions of years.

• It is measurable and verifiable through several monitoring technologies that have been successfully applied over decades of geological storage experience, ensuring its measurement, monitoring and verification.

• It is a safe and reliable form of storing CO_2. It has been a well-known, regulated and established technology for decades.

There are two different types of storage options: (1) standalone geological storage; and (2) enhanced oil recovery.

7.3.2.2.1 Standalone Geological Storage

CO_2 removed with DAC can be securely stored in saline formations or depleted oil and gas wells to deliver permanent carbon removal.

Saline formations are large layers of rocks with porous spaces that are isolated deep underground and contain saltwater. The practice of storing CO_2 in saline formations has been examined extensively by industry, academics and government agencies and has been found to offer a long-term solution for CO_2 storage with immense capacity.

Depleted oil and gas fields that are no longer productive also make ideal geological storage sites due to their established trapping and storage characteristics and the availability of extensive geological data from when they were operational wells.

Permanently storing atmospheric CO_2 in saline formations and depleted oil and gas wells allows for the achievement of what is known as CO_2 removal, constituting a necessary first step in the regenerative purpose. A DAC facility built in this way has the sole purpose of removing CO_2 from the atmosphere. In the near term, this provides a tool for reducing the net amount of CO_2 that is being released into the atmosphere and help reach net zero faster. In the future, if CO_2 emissions can be reduced dramatically, these facilities could be used to reduce and return the overall level of CO_2 in the air to safe levels.

7.3.2.2.2 Enhanced Oil Recovery

Atmospheric CO_2 captured by DAC plants can be permanently stored in oil reservoirs during oil production.

Injecting CO_2 into oil reservoirs is a common practice known as enhanced oil recovery (EOR) that has been performed by the oil and gas industry since the 1970s. While historically EOR has not been performed to achieve environmental benefits, when the CO_2 used has been removed from the atmosphere using DAC technology, it can dramatically reduce the overall carbon footprint of the oil produced; in this way, firms can achieve low carbon emission fuels, net zero emissions or even net negative emissions.

Additionally, new laws and regulations, such as California's Low Fuel Standard, are now offering guidance and incentives to experienced operators to ensure that CO_2 is stored permanently during the process. When performed this way, the permanent injection of atmospheric CO_2 into a reservoir can partially or completely counteract the emissions from the oil produced. Alternatively, if the quantity of atmospheric CO_2 permanently stored is greater than what is produced through the refining and use of the oil, this activity can produce fuels for transportation while generating net negative emissions. For readers familiar with life-cycle analysis, this means that depending on factors such as the pattern of the well and the operation of the oil reservoir, DAC with EOR can produce fuels with low, zero or even negative life-cycle 'carbon intensity'.

As CE has declared and Figure 7.4 shows, if the amount of CO_2 injected and stored is equal to the amount produced when the oil is refined and used, the full process is carbon neutral. If more CO_2 is injected than is produced, the process results in a net reduction of CO_2 in the atmosphere, allowing the company to create positive environmental externalities, as the regenerative strategy advocates.

7.3.2.3 AIR TO FUELS

A2F technology, developed to its full extent, is the crucial element for achieving a true regenerative strategy that drives disruptive changes on a large scale. A2F plants combine CE's DAC technology with hydrogen generation and fuel synthesis capability to deliver nearly carbon-neutral synthetic fuel. At these facilities, atmospheric CO_2 is captured from the air and converted into synthetic crude. This synthetic crude can then be processed into the gasoline, diesel and jet fuel that work in existing vehicles and transportation infrastructure without any modifications.

Due to an unlimited feedstock – atmospheric CO_2 – A2F plants can deliver global-scale quantities of much cleaner fuels to meet growing market demand. These fuels can form an important complement to

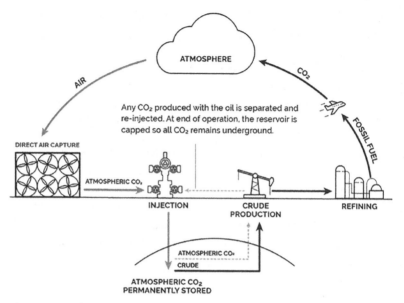

Figure 7.4 Enhanced oil recovery
Source: www.carbonengineering.com

electric vehicles by providing clean liquid fuel for transport sectors that are difficult to electrify and that require the high energy density of liquid fuels, such as long-haul transport, marine and aviation.

CE expects that the transportation industry of 2050 will run on an energy mix unlike that of today. Operators are demanding increasing quantities of low-carbon energy sources and renewable fuels, and the sector is searching for next-generation technologies to help reduce emissions and achieve climate targets. CE's A2F process provides a highly scalable solution that can help address these growing needs.

CE's process delivers synthetic, low carbon-intensity fuels – such as gasoline, diesel and jet fuel – out of air, water and renewable electricity. This cutting-edge technology can produce synthetic fuels that are drop-in compatible with today's infrastructure and engines and are almost completely carbon neutral. The process integrates four growing fields – renewable electricity generation, DAC, green hydrogen production and sustainable fuel synthesis – to deliver a highly scalable, clean fuel solution. It delivers drop-in ready fuels that have a low life-cycle carbon intensity and are cost competitive with biofuels.

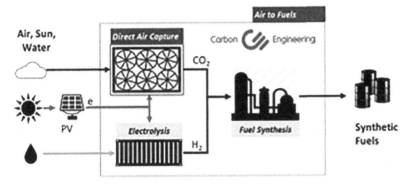

Figure 7.5 AIR TO FUELS plant technology
Source: www.carbonengineering.com

As a leader in large-scale DAC technology and with its A2F pilot plant, which first produced clean fuel in 2017, CE is uniquely positioned to deliver this solution. It is open to partnering with best-in-class suppliers and partners in renewable electricity generation, green hydrogen, fuel synthesis and plant development in commercial projects.

CE's A2F solution entails three major steps (Figure 7.5): (1) the DAC process captures and concentrates CO_2 from atmospheric air; (2) clean electricity (such as that from solar photovoltaics) is used to electrolyse water, splitting it into hydrogen and oxygen; and (3) the CO_2 and hydrogen are reacted to produce hydrocarbons that can directly, or with refining, be converted into drop-in compatible gasoline, diesel and jet fuel.

The main features and benefits of this cutting-edge technology are as follows:

- Low life-cycle carbon intensity: It can deliver fuels that have a low life-cycle carbon intensity, even net zero. Burning this fuel releases the CO_2 that was captured to create it, but the process adds very few new CO_2 emissions to the atmosphere, resulting in a virtuous circle of negative emissions.
- Drop-in compatible: These fuels are drop-in compatible with today's refineries, infrastructure and engines, so they do not generate the financial and environmental costs of completely replacing world transportation elements.
- Highly scalable: Using atmospheric CO_2 as a feedstock, these fuels can be produced in global-scale quantities at any location on Earth to meet the growing demand for low carbon-intensity fuels.

- Competitive cost: The fuels are cost competitive with biodiesel. While currently more expensive than the production cost of conventional fossil fuels, when paired with regulatory incentives for low carbon-intensity fuels, such as the Low Carbon Fuel Standard regulations, this cost becomes competitive in leading jurisdictions today. Furthermore, given the probable assignment of negative environmental externalities associated with CO_2 emissions, soon the production costs of conventional fossil fuels and emission costs will alter their currently competitive situation, even without taking into account the foreseeable governmental subsidies for clean technologies.

According to CE, operators are demanding increasing quantities of low-carbon energy and renewable sources, and the industry is searching for next-generation technologies to help reduce emissions and achieve climate targets. CE's A2F process provides a highly scalable solution capable of facing the climate emergency.

CE, as it declares in its mission and business model, seeks to license its DAC and A2F technologies to partners and allies around the globe in a multitude of industries.

7.3.3 Prospector and Explorer Behaviour: Achieving Positive Environmental Externalities

In conjunction with technologically and economically cutting-edge climate technologies capable of decarbonising the atmosphere, such as DAC and A2F, one of the most prominent features of the regenerative strategy, a disruptive corporate environmental position, should be able to overcome the existing divide between natural sciences and management and organisational studies (Bansal, 2019; Aguilera et al., 2022; Sharma, 2022). In this sense, CE's board of directors and management team have the potential to carry out regenerative strategies, as they are made up of profiles that come not only from the business sphere but also from the basic science and legal environment.

CE's prospector and explorer behaviour (Miles & Snow, 1978; Levinthal & March, 1993) has been detailed in technical terms in Section 7.3.2.2 on its DAC and A2F technologies. Furthermore, its own history and envisioned future developments corroborate this proactivity.

In 2015, CE constructed an end-to-end DAC pilot plant, demonstrating the technology's viability to the world. Pilot-scale equipment for all four core modules within its carbon removal technology – air contactor, pellet reactor, slaker and oxy-fired calciner – was designed with its vendors and partners to accurately replicate the performance of commercial-scale modules. Recent scientific works published in the leading natural science journal *Nature* (Shäppi et al., 2022), among others, have replicated and tested DAC technology and have also been published by CE's founder (e.g. Keith, 2009, 2013).

Two years later, in 2017, CE incorporated fuel synthesis capability into its DAC pilot plant, creating an A2F pilot plant based entirely on industrially scalable technologies. This allowed it to produce liquid fuels on site from CO_2 captured from the air and enabled the continued testing and refining of the fuel synthesis process. Recent scientific works on CO_2-based synthetic fuels have been published in science journals, including Qiu et al. (2022).

More recently, in 2021, CE built a Direct Air Capture Innovation Centre concurrently with its design and engineering work regarding the first commercial plants to utilise DAC technology. This facility has become CE's permanent R&D and advanced development platform, where the team will continue to optimise and innovate its technologies. Using data from its pilot plant and Innovation Centre, and in partnership with 1PointFive, CE is currently completing the engineering design for full-scale commercial facilities.

CE's business model is to license its technology to local plant development partners around the world to enable the rapid and widespread deployment of DAC technology. Currently, in 2023, the first large-scale commercial plant to utilise DAC technology is under construction. It is being developed in partnership with 1PointFive and will be in the Permian Basin in Texas. It is expected to capture one million tonnes of CO_2 from the air annually once complete.

CE is also exploring commercial facilities in other key markets. Although its A2F technology is not its main priority, it has plans to develop further DAC and A2F plants in several locations in Canada, the United Kingdom, the United States and Europe.

Explorer and prospector behaviour, as the core business in CE's DNA, are also exemplified in the network of its partners, who through co-creation develop, apply and improve DAC and A2F technologies. Among them are 1PointFive, Airclub, BBA, Carbon Ireland, Carbon Removal, Huron Clean Energy, Nordicdac Group, Low Carbon Ventures, Storegga and Virgin Red.

7.3.4 Redefining the Firm's Purpose, Stakeholder Engagement and Time Frame

In Section 7.3.3 we illustrated the science and technology side of CE's proposal. Here, we introduce the managerial side of CE to assess its proposal in light of the main characteristics of the regenerative strategy: (1) the redefinition of firm purpose, putting into practice eco-emotional wealth, environmental performance and systemic socioecological resilience; (2) wider stakeholder engagement in CE's mission, vision and strategy, reaching both market and beyond-market or fringe stakeholders with a special impetus on the natural environment and global population; and (3) a very long-term perspective with a special focus on future generations, realising the ultimate and real meaning of sustainable development.

7.3.4.1 Redefining the Firm's Purpose

From a position apparently far removed from short-termist shareholders and managerial primacy and thus a focus on only economic profit, CE declares that its focus is on the environment, fitting the theoretical foundations of the regenerative strategy: systemic socioecological resilience, which extends beyond private company benefits, and a planetary scale, helping to resolve the climate emergency. Indeed, on CE's website, the first sentence is 'We believe humanity can solve climate change.' Additionally, the company continues:

Creating this future will require leadership, collaboration, and creativity and will involve a diversity of new technologies, business ideas, and social innovation. Getting there is a challenge, but also an imperative.

7.3.4.1.1 Eco-emotional Wealth

As we propose with regenerative strategies, new disruptive environmental business models and firm purposes can only emerge from the deep personal values and beliefs of environmental entrepreneurs, CEOs and top management teams, as encapsulated in the concept of eco-emotional wealth introduced in Chapter 6.

In academia, in a recent editorial of a special issue published in the *Journal of Business Ethics* on 'corporate greenhouse gas emissions' data and the urgent need for a 'science-led just transition', Bush et al.

(2023) highlight two relevant issues: (1) the transition to sustainability should be led by science, as we propose in the regenerative strategy; and (2) climate change mitigation constitutes an ethical issue with significant implications for policy-makers, businesses, human livelihood, equal development opportunity for emerging economies and intergenerational fairness. This ethical issue constitutes what we conceptualise as eco-emotional wealth.

In this sense, as David Keith (2013:XIII–XIV) declares in the introduction to his book:

Wilderness has shaped my life. From weekend canoe trips to long solo ski expeditions in the high Arctic. I am fortunate to have spent about a year of my life travelling in the big wilds far from roads. My thinking was shaped by a family interest in environmental protection: my father played an early role in the science and regulation of DDT, and his brother helped lead the creation of birding as a social activity separate from scientific ornithology. I am an oddball environmentalist ... I am also a tinkerer and a technophile.

He continues (Keith, 2013:XVI–XVII):

A fuzzy love of nature is uncontroversial ... For me, the challenge is to craft an environmental ethic that recognizes non-utilitarian values in the natural world without asserting that these values trump all others and without making naïve claims of a sharp distinction between nature and civilization.

This constitutes a declaration of the personal ethical principles that have inspired his professional and academic life and impregnated his scientific activity. Indeed, Professor Keith was given the Heroes of the Environment 2009 award in the Scientists & Innovators section by *Time* magazine (Morton, 2009). As *Time*'s award text justifies, 'Professor Keith is researching tools that are immodest in the extreme: planet-size ideas for planet-size problems.'

Additionally, as published on Keith's personal website, he also took first prize in Canada's national physics prize exam and won MIT's prize for excellence in experimental physics, expending more than twenty-five years of his life on the interface between climate science, energy technology and public policy.

Additionally, on CE's corporate website, the company elaborates on its commitment to the future and the planet, which the regenerative strategy's eco-emotional wealth highlights:

Believe we can create a future in which our children and neighbours inherit the same planet we've enjoyed, where we delivered prosperity and well-being avoiding environmental impact.

7.3.4.1.2 Firm Environmental Performance

As Sharma (2022) remarks, most advanced corporate postures towards sustainability imply leaving environmental management and prioritising environmental performance, not just as a means to achieve firm profitability but as an aim by itself.

The idea of double materiality (Delgado-Ceballos et al., 2023), where companies must account for and inform their external stakeholders of their real impact on society and the natural environment, leads us to deem environmental performance the final aim of companies carrying out the regenerative strategy. As Busch et al. (2023) remark, corporate greenhouse gas emissions data are at the core of the regenerative strategy because (1) they allow us to investigate the main sources of climate change and its causal mechanism; and (2) monitoring is the best way to achieve agreed company targets.

To do this, a company's top management, as well as technical positions, should be occupied by an eclectic team of natural science and managerial profiles. CE possesses the requisite scientific and technical expertise and profiles that can effectively guide the company, its mission, vision and strategy formulation towards environmental performance.

7.3.4.1.3 Systemic Socioecological Resilience

Systemic socioecological resilience starts with the adequate measurement of a company's impact on the natural environment through environmental performance, with the aim of understanding the negative, net zero and net negative emissions of its business activities into the atmosphere.

The climate crisis and CO_2 emissions to the atmosphere represent a well-known problem identified in the economic literature tradition, with a special application in environmental issues: the 'tragedy of the commons'. As we saw in Chapter 1, this theory was initially conceptualised in 1833 by William Forster Lloyd and used for the first time by Hardin (1968) in a paper published in *Science* to link this problem to a technological solution and a fundamental extension of human morality, in consonance with the *Theory of Moral Sentiments* of Adam Smith mentioned in Chapter 6.

In general terms, the tragedy of the commons explains how individuals' tendency to make decisions is based on their personal needs, regardless of the negative impact that may have on others. In some cases, an individual's belief that others will not act in the best interest of the group can lead them to justify their selfish behaviour. The potential overuse of a common-pool resource – a hybrid of a public and a private good – can also influence individuals to act with a short-term interest in mind, resulting in the use of an unsustainable product and disregard of the harm it could cause to the environment or general society.

Regarding environmental degradation and pollution, although the tragedy of the commons is shared across soil and spring water, rivers and lakes, pollution, ocean degradation and especially atmospheric pollution is where it manifests in its maximum expression, because the atmosphere belongs to the whole population on Earth. CE's CEO Friedmann explained to us this problem and the potential lack of commitment by countries:

Atmosphere has no nation's borders, which implies that individual action taken by a local or national government or individual actor will imply only costs and not benefits, due to atmospheric CO_2 is equally distributed around the globe, independently from any specific location … If we would talk about soil or lake or river pollution and degradation, local or national action and investment in solving that 'domestic' problem can be seen as appropriate due to both cleaning costs and environmental benefits will be belonging to this domestic and restricted area.

In Hardin's (1968) analysis of the tragedy of the commons, applied to population growth or nuclear war problems, he advises that those dilemmas had no technical solution but required a fundamental extension of human morality. In the twenty-first century, climate science-based solutions such as those provided by DAC and A2F can address the climate emergency. However, as Hardin reminds us, a planetary joint solution, guided by a 'human green or natural' morality, is needed to change the way humans behave towards the natural environment. This is precisely the core of our regenerative strategy. It requires the following:

- A science-technical solution: Atmospheric decarbonisation through DAC and other technologies, such as A2F.
- A new human morality: We have encapsulated this in the disruptive business model's parameters: (1) redefining firm purposes in

terms of eco-emotional wealth, environmental performance and systemic socioecological resilience; (2) considering a new and wider stakeholder engagement including market and fringe stakeholders – communities, natural environment, etc.; and (3) maintaining a very long-term perspective, including future generations.

Several of CE's corporate slogans and statements manifest this disruptive solution path:

We believe humanity can solve climate change.
  Creating this future will require leadership, collaboration, and creativity and will involve a diversity of new technologies, business ideas, and social innovation. Getting there is a challenge but also an imperative.

Furthermore, as Friedmann declared in his interview:

The purpose that makes Carbon Engineering unique and differentiates from 'business-as-usual' solutions is that we create scalable climate solutions for hard to abate atmospheric carbon dioxide.

As an example of CE's systemic socioecological resilience, the company is engaged in a planetary technological project entitled 'Making net-zero aviation possible. An industry-backed, 1.5°C-aligned transition strategy' (Uppink et al., 2022) within the Mission Possible Partnership, which includes the World Economic Forum, We Mean Business Coalition, Energy Transitions Commission, MPP Aviation Sector Lead and McKinsey, as well as sixty-eight other aviation, technological and gas and oil companies from around the globe. They have forecast the future using different scenarios and accounting for how different complementary technologies and human behaviour (such as DAC, sustainable aviation fuels, electric engines, novel propulsion aircrafts and demand-side measures) could collectively and effectively address the climate emergency to achieve net zero emissions by 2050, which the world needs to do in order to avoid the most harmful effects of climate change. In terms of industry, by far one of the hardest to decarbonise is the transport industry due to several factors, such as the limited decarbonisation options, the high costs for renewable alternatives and high demand growth.

  Overall, CE's declared purpose, its DAC and A2F technologies, and its joint actions in seeking a solution to decarbonise and realise net zero in the aviation sector by 2050 invite us to suggest that this company pursues a real systemic socioecological resilience commitment. It declares that CO_2 captured from the air is equivalent to forty million trees working together, showing clearly the environmental performance of the company in terms of the natural environment. Hence, the firm's operational efficiency and productivity are directly transformed into environmental performance and positive environmental externalities.

7.3.4.2 Holistic Stakeholder Engagement

The second key feature of the regenerative strategy is wider stakeholder engagement, both in the external market and beyond the market or on the fringe, including competitors, customers, allies, investors, public administrations, NGOs, communities, the media, and even the natural environment and future generations.

CE's business model, as a technological licenser of DAC and related technologies such as A2F and EOR as worldwide scalable and quick solutions to the climate emergency, implies deep collaborations and business co-creation values among CE and its partners, such as Greyrock Energy in California and 1PointFive in Texas.

As previously described, via its unique purpose, mission and founders and the CEO's statements, CE's major priority and motive is to put 'humanity' and 'the natural world' at its heart. Additionally, the integration of scientists in the top management team and board of directors at CE manifests the effective integration of often forgotten 'fringe' scientists in the firm's strategic decision process, which is mandatory for creating disruptive business models capable of addressing the current climate emergency, as Sharma (2022) and Hardin (1968) advocate.

Previous arguments on the tragedy of the commons that characterises the fight against the climate emergency have stated that the solution can only be approached with joint planetary action: only one planet and atmosphere for all. Hence, planetary citizenship engagement is the only plausible solution to the climate emergency.

The Mission Possible Partnership shows how CE works with more than seventy private and public companies from different industries, as well as public and private worldwide institutions, to fight the climate emergency by putting into action different technological solutions, such as atmospheric decarbonisation with DAC. Only joint planetary action and commitment, involving worldwide industry, governmental agencies, natural science and global citizenship, can reverse and address the current climate emergency.

7.3.4.3 A Very Long-Term Perspective

In conjunction with CE's history and present situation, its future actions and aims are relevant. On its corporate website, two future datasets are described, in the long term (2035) and very long term (2050). The first milestone, 2035, will be the date for its extensive plant rollout:

Carbon Engineering's global deployment partner, 1PointFive, has announced a scenario of deploying 100 DAC facilities by 2035, each with an expected capacity of up to 1 million tonnes per year. At 100 million tonnes per year, this scenario creates a carbon capture capacity equivalent to the emissions from approximately 21.5 million standard cars or the carbon removal work of approximately 4 billion trees. The company estimates that up to 135 DAC facilities could be deployed by 2035 with an increase in global policy initiatives and demand in the voluntary market.

By 2050, 'we believe Direct Air Capture facilities have the potential to be playing a mainstream and significant role in the global effort to achieve net zero emissions and restore safe levels of CO_2 in the atmosphere'.

Additionally, CE declares:

Believe we can create a future in which our children and neighbours inherit the same planet we've enjoyed, where we delivered prosperity and well-being avoiding environmental impact.

Thus, CE's vision and objectives envision deploying DAC and A2F facilities in leading markets with the highest corporate and government targets and the strongest policies that favour its permanent sequestration of atmospheric CO_2 and clean fuel production. As global markets move to cut emissions and reduce dependence on fossil fuels, there is an immense opportunity to deploy DAC and A2F facilities around the world to deliver clean fuels for transportation and help drive emissions to zero through permanent carbon removal. By 2050, CE expects DAC facilities to have the potential to play a mainstream and significant role in the global effort to achieve net zero emissions and restore safe levels of CO_2 in the atmosphere. Furthermore, its mission and vision encapsulate a unique purpose: future generations, at the heart of sustainable development and the regenerative strategy, 'our children', are included.

CE's disruptive regenerative strategy, which implies a very long-term perspective, requires a different typology of investors and shareholders who do not prioritise economic profits and short-termism. One of the first and principal investors in CE was Microsoft co-founder Bill Gates. Nevertheless, this relationship has come from afar. As Keith (2013) declares, some of Harvard's research grants to him came from Bill Gates, for whom Keith acts as an occasional informal adviser on climate change and energy technologies.

CE relies on a mix of private and public money and project finance. According to Lassiter & Misra (2013), in 2009 CE obtained $35 million from Gates, Canadian financier Murray Edwards and others to conduct process design, R&D and prototyping in Calgary, Alberta. In 2013, CE closed a $3 million follow-on round from private investors to develop its first pilot-scale plant to capture CO_2 from the air on an industrial scale.

7.4 Reasons for Caution: Putting Our Feet on the Ground

Now the case of CE has been presented, it is time to analyse to what extent this company is actually moving towards the regenerative strategies that constitute the main argument in our work.

Beyond the science and technology of CE's proposal that we have already described, throughout the book we have maintained that the advance towards regenerative strategies implies a radical change in business logic or 'environmental morality': the company's purpose, holistic stakeholder engagement and very long-term vision.

Despite the environmentalist stance that initially characterised the company and to which we have referred in Section 7.3.4.3, CE's business seems to have moderated its initial environmentalist impetus. This can be deduced from what Friedmann himself indicated in the conversation we had with him. For Friedmann, the main focus of CE's business is carbon sequestration and DAC technology, but the technology that constitutes a further step in the field of regenerative strategies, A2F, still seems to be in its emergent and infant stages. This initial impression is corroborated by the company's own statement in its 2022 yearly review (https://carbonengineering.com/news-updates/year-review-2022):

Since day one, our focus has been on deploying DAC at large scale and low cost.

Construction has begun for the first large-scale commercial facility to utilize CE's technology in the United States. Located in Ector County, Texas, the plant is being deployed by our U.S. partner, 1PointFive, and is expected to capture up to 500,000 tonnes of carbon dioxide per annum, with the capability to scale up to one million tonnes per annum (Mtpa). Once fully operational, it will be the largest in the world – expected to surpass existing DAC facilities by 100x.

We began engineering for large-scale DAC facilities at a second site in the U.S., in Kleberg County, Texas. Once complete, CE will have produced the required materials to replicate megatonne-scale DAC trains within multi-megatonne facilities.

We introduced a new global deployment approach with 1PointFive, which leverages decades of infrastructure engineering and project expertise as a subsidiary of Occidental, an international energy company. This model standardizes the design of plants and helps deliver complete, operationally ready commercial DAC facilities to projects with local partners.

Therefore, in light of these public statements, it appears that A2F technology is not even in the medium term with regard to the company's priorities today. In other words, there is a strong focus on the development of DAC technology, which offers the least uncertainty and the most immediate returns.

As its own website (https://carbonengineering.com/news-updates/year-review-2022) indicates, thanks to its DAC technology CE has benefited significantly from funds coming from the recently approved Inflation Reduction Act and from agreements with the aviation industry regarding carbon removal credits:

Aviation visionary – Airbus – signing an agreement to purchase 400,000 tonnes of carbon removal credits from CE's U.S. partner, 1PointFive.

Only months later, Airbus was joined by seven major airlines in signing agreements to explore a future supply of DAC-based carbon removal credits.

Ultimately, while there is no doubt that DAC technology is an unprecedented breakthrough and can (and should) play a major role in decarbonisation efforts, the use of captured carbon to create a synthetic, clean and scalable fuel with A2F technology would be an even greater breakthrough in the field of regenerative strategies.

Therefore, taking the main characteristics of regenerative strategies as a reference, we can conclude the following.

In terms of redefining the company's purpose, CE shows progress towards the regenerative strategy, although it seems to remain strongly linked to fossil fuel-based businesses, as instead of investing in DAC+A2F, it continues to advance in what it sees as the priority applications of DAC technology. These are standalone geological storage, according to which the CO_2 removed with DAC can be securely stored in saline formations or depleted oil and gas wells to deliver permanent carbon removal, and EOR, according to which the atmospheric CO_2 captured from DAC plants can be permanently stored in oil reservoirs during oil production.

It does not even seem to be an option for CE to abandon the fossil fuel industry, as proposed by Hoffman and Ely (2022). In this sense, the separation of sustainable businesses from those still linked to fossil industries (in what those authors call triage) could be an alternative in a regenerative direction.

In terms of holistic stakeholder engagement, there is also no doubt that CE, with its DAC technology, is taking an important step in stakeholder engagement from a broad point of view, provided we understand humanity or global citizenship as a beneficiary of capturing CO_2 from our atmosphere. However, if we look at stakeholder engagement from a more concrete point of view, although CE's management exemplifies the combination of expertise from many different fields, by strategically choosing to stay in a business related to the fossil fuel industry, it fails to engage deeply with the socioecological system of which the company is a part, something it would be closer to achieving if it were to make a firm commitment to A2F technology, which could potentially have more far-reaching applications in the social arena.

If we analyse the very long-term orientation that characterises regenerative strategies, we can observe that although CO_2 capture can be understood as a technology aimed at mitigating greenhouse gases (which must necessarily have a beneficial effect in the long term), CE nevertheless gives priority to businesses that provide it with medium-term benefits in the form of carbon removal credits or access to greater oil resources (EOR technology), leaving (as mentioned) A2F technology (with more uncertainty in its development and more oriented towards the long term) playing a residual role.

In short, taking all of that into account, we suggest that CE is pursuing a regenerative strategy that is still far from reaching the full regenerative potential that we propose in this book, and still needs to take strategic steps towards reaching systemic socioecological resilience and fulfilling its stated vision of 'solving climate change'.

A window for optimism towards a fully regenerative strategy is the 'Making net-zero aviation possible' initiative, which aims to address the climate emergency by reducing greenhouse gas emissions, streamlining them into a central challenge by combining seven strategies to decarbonise one of the most polluting industries and difficult tasks to carry out: the aviation sector and reaching net zero by 2050. Framing the problem of aviation emissions and the climate crisis as the extreme case of the tragedy of the commons (Hardin, 1968), the only solution resides in joint actions among firms across industries, climate science cutting-edge solutions, global citizenship and government and public institutions on a planetary level. From a technological point of view, in 'Making net-zero aviation possible' the necessary combination of several cutting-edge technological solutions to achieve net zero emissions by 2050 is proposed, such as CE's DAC and A2F technologies, continued and enhanced fuel efficiency improvements, as well as battery electric, hydrogen, power-to-liquid and other biofuels. Jointly with these, several changes in business and citizen morality are necessary to foster eco-emotional wealth, such as behavioural changes: reducing business travel via videoconferencing, or a moral shift from short-haul flights to high-speed rail. Overall, the document focuses on how the aviation sector can achieve net zero emissions by 2050 (that is, three decades away, or very long-term positioning: the next generation); highlights transparency in terms of the measurement of CO_2 emissions by companies and the sector as a business priority (environmental performance focus); and remarks that the common aim can only be achieved if polluting companies around the globe work together on cutting-edge solutions, in coherence with new global citizenship environmental values and preferences and with the supervision, advice and support of governments and public administrations, in an effort to gain wider stakeholder engagement, beyond the traditional business sphere or on the fringe (Sharma & Vredenburgh, 1998). Thus, the climate emergency – the natural environment, global citizenship and governments and public administrations – and the next generation – 2050 – comprise a recent solution, proposed by the latest IPPC report (2023), which would constitute a regenerative strategy.

7.5 Concluding Remarks

In this chapter we have tried to illustrate the main features of disruptive business models that can address the climate emergency through regenerative strategies.

Conscious of the planetary and immediate consequences of the current climate emergency in conjunction with the well-known tragedy of the commons phenomenon that characterises atmospheric pollution and its potential solutions (Hardin, 1968), our qualitative research and theoretical sample have been driven by the pioneering and unique character of the Canadian company Carbon Engineering.

CE has been chosen to illustrate the regenerative strategy because, currently, it constitutes a unique case in the world. It was the first – in 2015 and 2017 – to capture CO_2 from the air at a megatonne, industrial scale in conjunction with the production of synthetic CO_2-based fuel. Both technologies can be disruptive technological solutions for the climate emergency for three main reasons: (1) scientific and economic science has recently proven them (Shäppi et al., 2022); (2) their scalability as DAC and A2F technologies under licence can be put into action on a planetary level – they are compatible with existing gas and oil infrastructure and combustion engines (transportation means, industry, etc.); and (3) they constitute an immediate way to decarbonise the atmosphere that, in conjunction with other technological solutions, can achieve net zero or even net negative carbon emissions. As the IPCC (2023) report remarks, what is done in this decade will mark the following centuries.

Hence, it could be technologically possible to fight the climate emergency, even the extreme case of the tragedy of the commons, because today an emerging technology developed by CE offers a technical solution to this problem. Nevertheless, as Hardin (1968) and Busch et al. (2023) suggest, the preservation and regeneration of the natural environment for current and future generations require a profound change of mind among business leaders and policy-makers: a new morality and ethic, recognising 'non-utilitarian values in the natural world' (Keith, 2013), for both present and future generations, which we call the eco-emotional wealth driver. They also require the three main features of the regenerative strategy: a disruptive firm's purpose – environmental performance and systemic socioecological resilience; wider stakeholder engagement – including all types of external stakeholders, even the natural environment and global citizenship; and a very long-term horizon, including future generations. We have analysed these in Section 7.4.

Through the analysis of the case of CE, we have observed how starting from a disruptive technology that is already in place makes it possible to complete great advances in the fight against climate change. However, this case also serves to illustrate a realistic view of the situation by showing how difficult it is for companies to apply the main tenets of regenerative strategies and to make significant changes in the ways they do business. As we will see in Chapter 8, the transition to a socioecologically resilient economy is not only achieved with the right technology, but also requires far-reaching social changes and decisive actions by governments and institutions.

References

Aguilera, R., Aragón-Correa, J. A., and Marano, V. (2022). Rethinking corporate power to tackle grand societal challenges: Lessons from political philosophy. *Academy of Management Review*, 47(4): 456.

Aguinis, H., Cascio, W., and Ramani, R. (2017). Science's reproducibility and replicability crisis: International business is not immune. *Journal of International Business Studies*, 48(6): 653–663.

Aguinis, H., and Solarino, A. M. (2017). Transparency and replicability in qualitative research: The case of interviews with elite informants. *Strategic Management Journal*, 40(8): 1291–1315.

Bansal, P. (2019). Sustainable development in an age of disruption. *Academy of Management Discoveries*, 5(1): 8–12.

Bansal, P., and Roth, K. (2000). Why companies go green: A model of ecological responsiveness. *Academy of Management Journal*, 43: 717–736.

Basu, K., and Palazzo, G. (2008). Corporate social responsibility: A process model of sensemaking. *Academy of Management Review*, 33(1): 122–136.

Bettis, R., Gambardella, A., Helfat, C., and Mitchell, W. (2015). Qualitative empirical research in strategic management. *Strategic Management Journal*, 36(5): 637–639.

Busch, T., Cho, C., Hoepner, A., Michelon, A., and Rogelj, J. (2023). Corporate greenhouse gas emissions' data and the urgent need for a science-led just transition: Introduction to a thematic symposium. *Journal of Business Ethics*, 182: 897–901.

Delgado-Ceballos, J., Ortiz-De-Mandojana, N., Antolín-López, R., and Montiel, I. (2023). Connecting the sustainable development goals to firm-level sustainability and ESG factors: The need for double material. *Business Research Quarterly*, 26(1): 2–10.

Eisenhardt, K. (1989). Building theory from case study research. *Academy of Management Review*, 14(4): 532–550.

Glaser, B., and Strauss, A. (1967). *The Discovery of Grounded Theory: Strategies for Qualitative Research*. New York: Aldine.

Grodal, S., Anteby, M., and Holm, A. (2021). Achieving rigor in qualitative analysis: The role of active categorization in theory building. *Academy of Management Review*, 46(3): 591–612.

Hardin, G. (1968). The tragedy of the commons. *Science*, 162(3859): 1243–1248.

Hart, S. (1995). A natural resource-based view of the firm. *Academy of Management Review*, 20(4): 986–1014.

Hoffman, A. J., and Ely, D. (2022). Time to put the fossil-fuel industry into hospice. *Stanford Social Innovation Review*, 2022(Fall): 28–37.

IPCC. (2014). *AR5 Synthesis Report: Climate Change 2014*. Geneva: Intergovernmental Panel on Climate Change. www.ipcc.ch/report/ar5/syr.

IPCC. (2023). *AR6 Synthesis Report: Climate Change 2023*. Geneva: Intergovernmental Panel on Climate Change. www.ipcc.ch/report/sixth-assessment-report-cycle.

Keith, D. (2009). Why capture CO_2 from the atmosphere? *Science*, 325(5948): 1654–1655.

Keith, D. (2013). *A Case for Climate Engineering*. Cambridge, MA: MIT Press.

Keith, D., Holmes, G., St. Angelo, D., and Heidel, K. (2018). A process for capturing CO_2 from the atmosphere. *Joule*, 2: 1573–1594.

Lassiter, J., III, and Misra, S. (2013). Carbon Engineering. Harvard Business School Case 814-040, October 2013. (Revised November 2016.) www.hbs.edu/faculty/Pages/item.aspx?num=45759.

Levinthal, D., and March, J. G. (1993). The myopia of learning. *Strategic Management Journal*, 14(S2): 95–112.

Miles, R. E., and Snow, C. C. (1978). *Organizational Strategy, Structure and Process*. New York: McGraw-Hill.

Morton, O. (2009, 22 September). Scientists & Innovators: David Keith. Heroes of the Environment 2009. *Time*. https://content.time.com/time/specials/packages/article/0,28804,1924149_1924154_1924428,00.html.

Qiu, L., Diaoglou, M., de Boer, H., Wilcox, B., and Suh, S. (2022). Environmental trade-offs of direct air capture technologies in climate change mitigation toward 2100. *Nature Communications*, 13(1): 3635.

Shäppi, R., Rutz, D., Dähler, F. et al. (2022). Drop-in fuels from sunlight and air. *Nature*, 601(7891): 63–81.

Sharma, S. (2022). From environmental strategy to environmental impact. *Academy of Management Discoveries*, 8(1): 1–6.

Sharma, S., and Vredenburgh, H. (1998). Proactive corporate environmental strategy and the development of competitively valuable organizational capabilities. *Strategic Management Journal*, 19(8): 729–753.

Skocek, J., Zajac, M., and Haha, M. (2020). Carbon capture and utilization by mineralization of cement pastes derived from recycled concrete. *Scientific Reports*, 10: 5614.

Suddaby, R. (2006). From the editors: What grounded theory is not. *Academy of Management Journal*, 49(4): 633–642.

Uppink, L., Ganguli, M., and Riedel, R. (eds) (2022). Making net-zero aviation possible: An industry-backed, 1.5°C-aligned transition strategy. Mission Possible Partnership. https://missionpossiblepartnership.org/wp-content/uploads/2023/01/Making-Net-Zero-Aviation-possible.pdf.

Whittington, R. (1996). Strategy-as-practice. *Long Range Planning*, 29(5): 731–735.

Yin, R. (1981). The case study crisis: Some answers. *Administrative Science Quarterly*, 26(1): 58–65.

Yin, R. (1984). *Case Study Research*. Beverly Hills, CA: SAGE.

8 | *Concluding Remarks*

The future of humanity, and indeed all life on Earth, depends on us.

Sir David Attenborough, scientist and science communicator

The important thing for the government is not to do things that individuals are already doing, and to do them a little better or a little worse, but to do those things that are currently not being done at all.

John Maynard Keynes, economist

8.1 Introduction

In this final chapter, readers will find a brief review of the main content that has been covered throughout the book.

In addition, we wanted to leave for the end a series of reflections derived from everything that we have discussed in the text. Thus, we wanted to highlight the role played in the fight against the climate emergency by two issues, in our opinion fundamental: business education; and a stakeholder that is frequently underappreciated by scholars in the field of management, the entrepreneurial state.

As we elaborate in this chapter, we believe that a profound change is necessary in the education of future management professionals. In accordance with a more humanist management proposal and a greater awareness of the organisations–natural environment relationship, here we detail the educational proposals that stand out for presenting the new management values that this book aims to highlight and that begin by redefining the company's internal mission of regenerative strategies.

The chapter ends with a brief reflection on the role that the entrepreneurial state must play in the definitive boost of the technologies that can help us face the climate emergency, not only by supporting companies and solving market failures, but also by creating markets and taking risks that no other agent is willing to. From our perspective, the climate emergency demands it.

8.2 Climate Emergency and Disruptive Business Models

This research calls for a disruptive shift in business models towards a regenerative strategy capable of reversing the current climate emergency. For that purpose, it is essential to show and convince business leaders and policy-makers of the scientific truth of the climate emergency. This was precisely the aim of the milestone Chapter 5, where we make clear two of the main theses of our work:

- Not climate change, but climate emergency.
- It requires immediate action – we do not have much time.

In this vein, management researchers and business practitioners must overcome two existing divides: (1) between science and management; and (2) between the firm and the natural environment.

Our book introduces the reader to the phenomenon with a review of the last three decades of work devoted to discovering, integrating and fitting together business activity and concern for the natural environment. Thus, Chapter 2 first discusses the pioneering studies in climate science that warned of the relationship between the amount of CO_2 in the atmosphere and the increase in the Earth's temperature, from which it was possible to establish a relationship between the concentration of CO_2 and the use of fossil fuels in the production of energy. Based on this evidence, the responses of governments and multinational institutions, and, very specifically, the world of business practice and academia, were then analysed, highlighting the evolution of the environmental strategy concept from the early 1990s to the present day.

Analysing how the environmental strategy concept has been understood and how its meaning has evolved over time is useful in signalling the main issues and topics traditionally included in the academic debate, as well as the prospects for its future conception, in conjunction with the main theories used to frame the phenomenon: the natural resource-based view (Hart, 1995), institutional theory (Bansal & Roth, 2000), the new stakeholder view (Barney, 2018; Gibson et al., 2021; McGahan, 2021) and the microfoundations of strategy (Barney & Felin, 2013). Each of these highlights firms' and managers' motivations, beliefs and behaviours, which help us to understand how companies strategically behave and integrate environmental concerns, integrating and complementing their logic, motivations and reasoning.

Continuing the review of traditional approaches to the firm and the natural environment, Chapter 3 is devoted to introducing the reader to firms' various environmental strategic postures, from reactors to proactive environmental postures, linking them to the most traditional research on strategy (Miles & Snow, 1978) and learning and innovation (Levinthal & March, 1993) in a critical review based on deconstruction. This process of deconstruction allows us to clearly differentiate the strategic positions that can be considered 'business as usual' from those that are not, highlighting, in this sense, the role of regenerative strategies, which constitute one of the main arguments around which the book revolves.

Expressing a parallel logic, Chapter 4 reviews business models. Traditionally, business models have been used and have appeared since the 2000s to offer answers to radical competitive challenges, such as the globalisation of markets and the appearance of low-cost rivals in the aviation industry, and radical innovations, such as information and communications technologies and the internet, e-business and e-commerce. For their part, sustainable business models aim to balance business activity, economic profit and respect for the natural environment, while environmentally sustainable business models (also known as circular business models) seek to shift the principles and postulates of industrial symbiosis and a circular economy to the microeconomic perspective of business (Geissdoerfer et al., 2018). In addition, while social business models aim for social profit maximisation, in contrast to non-profit organisations, they also seek the repayment of invested capital (Yunus et al., 2010).

Overall, the reviews carried out in Chapters 3 and 4 lead us to consider the common 'business-as-usual' logic of traditional strategic and management thinking as insufficient for dealing with the current grand challenge of the climate emergency. The strategic logic behind business model construction is a useful tool, but it is not enough to address climate crises. In this sense, the regenerative strategy logic (Hahn & Tampe, 2021) that we propose in this book integrates previous social and environmental business models, taking into consideration not only circular economy principles and social equity issues, but also future generations.

Awareness of the planetary limits and the immediate consequences of the current planetary emergency is scientifically analysed in Chapter 5, where we examine the decisive impact that human activity has had on the natural environment throughout human history, highlighting the importance of the so-called Anthropocene in this respect. From a perspective based on the energy uses that our civilisation has adopted over time, we emphasise the intensive and widespread use of fossil fuels as a determining element in the climate crisis that threatens us. Thus, in addition to reviewing the main consensuses in relation to planetary tipping points, we propose another series of critical scenarios that should be taken into account to manage climate risk appropriately.

Chapters 6 and 7 are devoted to the analysis of the key concept of regenerative strategies. In Chapter 6, we define regenerative strategies and elaborate on their main characteristics. Thus, we refer to the important role played by disruptive technologies, the redefinition of firm purpose, the broader vision of stakeholders that these strategies entail and their very long-term orientation, among other aspects, including the concept of eco-emotional wealth. We address the question of 'What is new?' by exploring a disruptive business model encapsulating the regenerative strategy. Our answer proposes a dual set of disruptive changes in the business sphere:

• Disruptive climate science innovations capable of reversing and regenerating the current climate crisis. These are only possible by overcoming the existing divide between science and management studies.
• Disruptive management innovations, in line with Hardin's (1968) moral and ethical change, entailing that three business redefinitions are needed. The first is the redefinition of firm purpose, which has been analysed through three new constructs: (1) eco-emotional wealth that changes rationality and logic among top management, workers, investors and citizens; (2) the effective measurement of a firm's environmental performance, not just a means of economic profits but an aim in itself; and (3) systemic socioecological resilience, the only way to fight against the climate crisis, which extends beyond organisational limits. The second redefinition is a wider stakeholder engagement perspective, highlighting external, especially fringe stakeholders, such as global citizens, governments and the natural environment. Finally these is a very long-term perspective, emphasising business's effects on future generations.

In Chapter 7, we put regenerative strategies into action by introducing a pioneering business case in the fight against the climate emergency.

Through a qualitative research design, we assess the case of Carbon Engineering, a company that is currently developing cutting-edge technologies, such as Direct Air Capture (DAC) and AIR TO FUELS (A2F), thereby capturing, sequestering and more importantly applying captured CO_2 in the production of synthetic fuel. Regenerative strategy principles are tested in practice by showing a realistic and pragmatic view of the real progress of the most advanced technologies in the fight against climate change. In this sense, the Carbon Engineering case implies several disruptive technological and managerial issues and illustrates the regenerative strategy because it currently constitutes a unique case worldwide. The company was the first – in 2015 and 2017 – to capture CO_2 from the air at a megaton industrial scale in conjunction with the production of synthetic CO_2-based fuel. These two technologies can be a disruptive technological solution to address the climate emergency for three main reasons: (1) their scientific and economic viability has recently been proven (Shäppi et al., 2022); (2) their scalability: DAC and A2F technologies under licence can be put into action on a planetary scale, as they are compatible with existing gas and oil infrastructure and combustion engines (transportation, industry, etc.); and (3) they constitute an immediate way to decarbonise the atmosphere that in conjunction with other technological solutions can achieve net zero and even net negative carbon emissions.

In this way, it could be technologically possible to fight against the climate emergency, even in an extreme case of the 'tragedy of the commons', because an emerging technology developed by Carbon Engineering offers a technical solution to this problem. Nevertheless, as Hardin (1968) and more recently Busch et al. (2023) suggest, the preservation and regeneration of the natural environment for current and future generations require a profound change of mind on the part of business leaders and policy-makers, with a new morality and ethic, recognising 'a nonutilitarian value in the natural world' (Keith, 2013), for both present and future generations. This reflects what we term the 'eco-emotional wealth' driver and the three business definitions of the regenerative strategy: a disruptive firm's purpose – environmental performance and systemic socioecological resilience; wider stakeholder engagement – including all types of external stakeholders, even the natural environment and global citizens; and a very long-term horizon – including future generations. We analyse these in Section 8.4.

8.3 A Radical Change in Business Education

The required disruptive changes in the economy and businesses require joint efforts across both the public and private spheres, via citizens and policy-makers, and especially in terms of changing minds in the educational sphere. In this sense, in this section we introduce the compelling need for a radically new perspective in business education to create a new generation of responsible business leaders.

The traditional and typical business-as-usual logic, critically reviewed in other chapters of this book, impedes an adequate approach to and the necessary disruptive business changes for addressing the current climate and planetary emergency. The disruptive social and environmental entrepreneurship logic that this emergency requires can be reshaped through the key role played by education in general and by business education specifically.

However, as Nyberg and Wright (2022) remark, different forms of management research and practice are in denial of the critical consequences of the climate emergency. These authors highlight several types of climate denial and the key role played by traditional business research and teaching in business schools. Thus, business and management scholars are uniquely positioned and even obligated to contribute to real and disruptive changes in sustainable business models that are capable of addressing the current planetary emergency. In their words, 'management research needs to be "climate-proofed" and unfettered from its assumptions of "business-as-usual"' (Nyberg & Wright, 2022:716) to bridge the existing gap between climate science and management research.

Nyberg and Wright (2022) describe three different forms of climate denial on the agenda of management research and business schools:

- Literal denial, which implies an explicit rejection of the existence of both climate change and its anthropogenic nature, has been a dominant logic during the recent decades, promoted and funded by several gas and oil companies and associations, as discussed previously with the case of ExxonMobil.
- Implicatory denial. In this case, the existence of climate change is assumed, but the denial of its urgency contradicts one of the leading theses of this book: the climate emergency and the vast scientific evidence for it. As seen in this book, a great majority of management research carried out during the last three decades has adopted this

logic to integrate environmental concerns and climate change into the dominant logic of capitalism and 'business as usual'.

- Interpretative denial frames climate change as a relevant issue and a new context to consider in business strategies, threats and opportunity analyses. Resilience and sustainability logics modify business models to anticipate and prepare firms and industries for climate change-induced extreme weather events, but always emphasising Porter's well-known slogan 'Green and Competitive' (Porter & van der Linde, 1995) by fitting the traditional profit-maximisation logic to the natural environment. At its heart, the 'business-as-usual' logic is maintained.

Therefore, climate and planetary emergencies require a new, radical and disruptive economic and business logic to address these practices of denial. In this sense, management scholars and business schools have a great responsibility in framing the grand challenge of climate emergency. Here we introduce some remarkable business education initiatives: the United Nations (UN) initiative Principles for Responsible Management Education (PRME); the Sustainable Innovation MBA launched by the UVM Grossman School of Business at The University of Vermont; and European alliances for dealing with climate change, such as Business Schools for Climate Leadership, led by a number of highly respected business schools, and the Una Europa alliance and its new European bachelor's in sustainability, offered by a range of European universities. In addition, given the importance in our work of the personal values of future managers in the search for regenerative strategies, we present the 'Management as a Calling' programme, taught at the Stephen M. Ross School of Business at the University of Michigan by Professor Andy Hoffman.

8.3.1 *Principles for Responsible Management Education*

PRME is a UN-supported initiative founded in 2007. This voluntary initiative, with over 800 signatories worldwide, is the largest organised relationship between the UN and management-related higher education institutions. As Alvarez et al. (2020) have highlighted, businesses should play a key role in solving the grand challenge of the climate emergency. The PRME initiative recognises the key role of business schools, as well as management and leadership development institutions, as the most influential actors in the world, in reshaping the knowledge, skills and behaviours of future business and management leaders.

PRME's vision is to create a worldwide movement and drive thought leadership on responsible management education, and its mission is to transform management education and develop the responsible decision-makers of tomorrow to advance sustainable development. It works closely with the UN Global Compact to ensure that management schools and businesses collaborate on common aspirations and create a collective impact. As Antonio Guterres, UN Secretary-General, states, 'The PRME initiative was launched to nurture responsible leaders of the future. Never has this task been more important. Bold leadership and innovative thinking are needed to achieve the Sustainable Development Goals' (www.unprme.org/about).

The UN Global Compact (Independent Group of Scientists, 2019) constitutes a blueprint for integration of the UN's Sustainable Development Goals (SDGs) into the curricula, research and partnerships of business education faculties and schools. Launched in June 2020, it is driven by the 'decade of action' announced by the UN that same year, seeking effective implementation of the seventeen SDGs by 2030.

In this vein, PRME seeks to realise the SDGs through responsible management education. Adhering to PRME are organisations and institutions such as the Association to Advance Collegiate Schools of Business (AACSB), the European Foundation for Management Development (EFMD) and the Association of MBAs (AMBA). Furthermore, two of the most prestigious organisations analysing and ranking universities and business schools consider these principles. Thus, since 2019 *Times Higher Education* has included a new 'social impact ranking system' for universities based on the SDGs. Additionally, the *Financial Times* business school rankings now include corporate social responsibility measures.

The PRME SDG Compass is a four-stage model that offers business school leaders, administrators, professors and researchers a systematic guide to integrating SDGs in higher education institutions. The first stage aims to understand the current situation of SDG integration in a curriculum via a mapping exercise. In the second stage, the scope of mapping is determined, defining priorities and setting goals for curricula, research and partnerships. In the third stage, the institution can choose to broaden and/or deepen SDG integration via two delivery mechanisms, integrating them into existing structures and programmes or creating new ones. Finally, the fourth stage is devoted to communication and continuous improvement.

Overall, higher education institutions adhering to the UN Global Compact's SDGs should declare their willingness to progress in terms of their implementation of the following principles (Independent Group of Scientists, 2019:8):

- Purpose: 'We will develop the capabilities of students to be future generators of sustainable value for business and society at large and to work for an inclusive and sustainable global economy.'
- Values: 'We will incorporate into our academic activities, curricula, and organisational practices the values of global social responsibility as portrayed in international initiatives such as the United Nations Global Compact.'
- Method: 'We will create educational frameworks, materials, processes and environments that enable effective learning experiences for responsible leadership.'
- Research: 'We will engage in conceptual and empirical research that advances our understanding about the role, dynamics, and impact of corporations in the creation of sustainable social, environmental and economic value.'
- Partnership: 'We will interact with managers of business corporations to extend our knowledge of their challenges in meeting social and environmental responsibilities and to explore jointly effective approaches to meeting these challenges.'
- Dialogue: 'We will facilitate and support dialogue and debate among educators, students, business, government, consumers, media, civil society, organisations and other interested groups and stakeholders on critical issues related to global social responsibility and sustainability.'

8.3.2 Business Schools for Climate Leadership Alliance

As it declares on its website (http://BS4CL.org), Business Schools for Climate Leadership (BS4CL) is a unique alliance of eight of the leading European business schools to help present and future leaders in combatting the climate crisis facing the planet. The founding members recognise the responsibility of higher business education to drive and accelerate change towards the goals of the Paris Agreement and the UN Framework Convention on Climate Change.

The alliance comprises Saïd Business School at the University of Oxford, Cambridge Judge Business School, HEC Paris, IE Business School in Madrid, IESE Business School in Barcelona, INSEAD in Fontainebleau, IMD Business School in Lausanne and London Business School. It covers more than 55,000 students and executives per year, with alumni exceeding 400,000 business leaders.

As business schools concerned with the planetary emergency, among their objectives its members assume a sense of urgency regarding and awareness of businesses' role in climate change mitigation and adaptation in their outreach activities, consistent with Nyberg and Wright's (2022) recent call. This radical change requires deep collaboration across industries and generations, to accelerate the business response to the climate emergency; research collaboration, to identify the best practices and avenues of research; impact, through joint outreach to the alumni of their degree programmes; and influencing the leadership of organisations and institutions across society at large.

As Professor Mauro Guillen, Dean of Judge Business School, declared in 2022: 'Until recently, business schools were seen as part of the problem of climate change, but now we want to be part of the solution. The challenge of climate change can't be solved without the involvement of companies, and a great portion of that relies on business education' (Valls, 2022).

As an initial step, academics from the eight founding business schools collaborated closely to deliver a climate change toolkit, first unveiled at COP26, the 2021 United Nations Climate Change Conference in Glasgow, Scotland. Prior to this launch, a series of webinars were held to share relevant content via the participation of members from multiple business schools. The toolkit is organised around eight challenges or topics, each led by a business school that is a member of the alliance, as follows:

- Inequality and climate change, INSEAD.
- Decarbonisation of business, HEC Paris.
- Global Strategy in a Transformed World, Strategy and Geopolitics, IESE Business School.
- Innovation and Technology as a Solution to Climate Change, IE Business School.
- Business Transformation and Climate Change, IMD Business School.

- Risk Management and Transition to Green Energy, Saïd Business School.
- What Businesses Need to Know about Climate Change and Nature, Cambridge Judge Business School.
- Business Value and Climate Standards, London Business School.

8.3.3 Sustainable Innovation MBA at UVM Grossman School of Business

One of the worldwide pioneering business schools offering radical new perspectives on business education is the UVM Grossman School of Business, under the leading role of its dean, Professor Sanjay Sharma.

The Sustainable Innovation MBA (SI-MBA) programme was initially headed by Professor Sanjay Sharma and Professor Stuart Hart. It is suited to emerging changemakers who believe that business can, and must, become a transformational force for good. It was listed as the Best Green MBA by the Princeton Review for 2018, 2019 and 2020.

During the one-year full-time programme, SI-MBA students learn from sustainable business leaders in conjunction with academics and researchers to transform businesses into a force for good, addressing the numerous calls for business academic action (Alvarez et al., 2020; Nyberg & Wright, 2022) and constituting a unique ecosystem that attracts changemakers. The capstone experience of the SI-MBA programme is completing a practicum project – a hands-on, full-time consulting engagement within an existing or emerging enterprise. Recent host organisations have included Ashoka, Ben & Jerry's, Burton Snowboards, Facebook, Pepsico, REI Co-op and Seventh Generation.

8.3.4 European Bachelor's in Sustainability, Una Europa Alliance

The European bachelor's in sustainability launched by the Una Europa alliance is an initiative of eleven leading universities across Europe that aims to draw on their collective strengths to create a truly European inter-university environment, a University of the Future.

This alliance was formed by Université Paris 1 Panthéon-Sorbonne (France), Complutense University of Madrid (Spain), The University of Edinburgh (United Kingdom), KU Leuven (Belgium), Freie Universität Berlin (Germany), University College Dublin (Ireland), Helsingfors

Universitet (Finland), Universiteit Leiden (Netherlands), University of Zurich (Switzerland), Alma Mater Studiorum – University of Bologna (Italy) and Jagiellonian University (Poland). These institutions have been educating Europe for over 1,000 years, and together they teach over 500,000 students and include almost 100,000 university staff, with digital learners numbering in the millions.

The mission and vision of Una Europa (www.una-europa.eu) include five priority areas of development: cultural heritage, data science, European studies, one health and sustainability. These act as the thematic 'glue' that binds the eleven universities together.

The sustainability priority area aims to address the interdependent UN SDGs in an effective manner with a new approach that requires deep inter-university collaboration, as well as other actors, such as civil society, governments, non-governmental organisations and the media. In line with the previously discussed PRME goals, Una Europa promotes the interaction of all disciplines in the fields of the sciences, social sciences, health sciences, engineering, arts and humanities, as the best way, as Sharma (2022) remarks, to link research and teach the connections and interdependencies among the seventeen SDGs. This alliance aims to transform itself into a single transnational campus that generates cross-disciplinary knowledge and societal interaction and to educate the next generation in making the 2030 Agenda part of daily life.

Among the Una Europa teaching initiatives in sustainability, we can highlight the design of a future European bachelor's in sustainability, to be launched in academic year 2023–2024, in which both co-authors of this book are involved as members of the Complutense community. On a transdisciplinary basis, this bachelor's degree connects natural sciences to social sciences, offering to future students several paths close to natural sciences, economy, politics and sociology itineraries, all across intercampus and inter-university mobility bases.

8.3.5 'Management as a Calling' Programme

As detailed on its website (https://businessimpact.umich.edu/mana gement-as-calling-program), the 'Management as a Calling' programme, led by Andy Hoffman (Holcim (US) Professor of Sustainable Enterprise at the University of Michigan, with joint appointments in the Stephen M. Ross School of Business and the School for Environment & Sustainability), was founded on the conviction that we need to cultivate leaders who are willing to challenge accepted norms and create a new vision for the firm. It takes the perspective that business education has not kept pace with the challenge of creating business leaders who will serve the world. Thus, the modern business school format is leaving a gaping moral hole at the centre of business education. Citing Harvard Business School professor Rakesh Khurana, the programme argues that the professional and moral ideals that once animated and inspired business schools have been conquered by a perspective suggesting that managers are merely the agents of shareholders, beholden only to the cause of profit share. Therefore, now is the time to focus on the intellectual and moral training of future business leaders, to redefine the role of business in society into one that serves society's needs and solves the systemic problems that the market, in many ways, caused in the first place. As both programmes state, to make a meaningful career that also serves society – employees, customers, the community, the natural environment – rather than merely asking 'What career track gives me the most opportunity for professional development?' students may also ask themselves 'What pursuits will bring me closer to making a meaningful contribution to others in my business, my community and my society?' or 'What kind of a future do I imagine, and what role do I want to play in making it a future we all want to see?'

The novel structure of the programme revolves around the idea that students themselves can create their own personal mission through specialised readings, self-reflection and peer mentoring and feedback. All this involves contact with nature and is devoid of technology and technological devices. In short, it is an immersion programme that challenges the more conventional conceptions of traditional MBAs and puts the moral dimension at the centre.

8.4 Towards Sustainable Business and Economy

Henderson (2020) proposes reimagining capitalism. For her, business as usual is not a viable option. We must pass from the past conceptions of a firm's corporate social responsibility voluntary actions to frame disruptive business models operating under environmental limits within a thriving society. She proposes four main challenges for businesses: (1) creating shared value for firm, society and the natural environment; (2) building a purpose-driven organisation; (3) rewiring finance, moving beyond short-termism and profit-only logic; (4) building cooperation to approach grand challenges; and (5) rebuilding our institutions and fixing our governments via the development of new laws and regulations.

Effectively, as we have exposed, the climate emergency is an extreme case of the 'tragedy of the commons', which requires a coordinated and collaborative approach at national and supranational levels, among governments, businesses and global citizens. In this vein, Henderson (2020) remarks that reimagining capitalism requires moving businesses towards radically rethinking the role of government by balancing the power of markets and multinational companies with a democratic, accountable government and a strong civil society.

Moving a step beyond the role of governments and citizenship, Adler's (2022) essay on 'Capitalism, socialism and the climate crisis' proposes a more radical solution to address the current climate emergency that gives a key role to governmental action and citizenship: 'democratic socialism'. In democratic socialism, we would democratically govern both our firms and our economy.

According to Adler (2022), the two common assumptions of capitalism – profit maximisation and negative environmental externalities – can be reversed by democratising the governance of firms. In this way, companies with democratic governance can make better trade-off decisions and internalise some relevant externalities. In parallel, to prevent capitalist competition in product and factor markets, which would be economically inviable for democratic firms addressing the climate emergency, the pool of a country's economic factors must be managed democratically, collectively and strategically towards shared economic, social and environmental goals. He states that the democratic governance of companies is currently carried out by many large firms and chief executive officers because 'they in public defend the superiority of markets and competition over coordination and planning, inside their own corporations, where they could leave their various business units to compete with each other, they instead treat corporate resources as a single pool, and they draw the corporation's various business units into a strategic management process for deciding how to use those resources to achieve the best outcomes for the corporations as a whole' (Adler, 2022:5). The second issue, the democratic, collective use of a country's economic factors, has an antecedent in the West – the economic mobilisation for World War II, when in the United States and the United Kingdom, the business sector acquiesced to government control over production, distribution, prices and wages, whereby their governments financed and directed most of these countries' investments. Adler (2022) proposes four system requirements for fulfilment of this aim: (1) the strategic management of the economy must be democratic; (2) a massive wave of innovations is needed to overcome the climate crisis; (3) product reorientation towards eco-efficiency is required; and (4) there must be high levels of citizen and worker motivation.

Overall, although Adler (2022) does not expect much additional support for his programme, even from the more progressive sectors of the business community, the evidence discussed in Chapter 7 on international, intra-industrial, private and public alliances for net zero emissions in the aviation sector indicates that Carbon Engineering shares common issues with the two principles exposed in his 'democratic socialism' solution to the current climate crisis.

Accordingly, our proposal can be summarised in Figure 8.1, which illustrates the main disruptive changes that businesses must make to fight against the current climate crisis.

The views of Henderson (2020) and Adler (2022) highlight the importance of a particularly relevant stakeholder group in the fight against the climate crisis: namely, governments. The role of governments and public resources has been traditionally silenced in the management literature, and this silencing continues in management education, where the rhetoric of the wealth-creating entrepreneurial business person and magical thinking (Klein, 2015) is incessantly repeated. According to this logic, there will always be a great entrepreneur who will – single-handedly and with only the power of her or his brilliant mind – provide solutions for a better life for humankind.

However, this is far from the truth. Of course, individual initiative and entrepreneurial creativity are necessary, but the world as it is today would not exist without a risk-taking entrepreneurial state. One need only look at the work of Mazzucato (2022) to observe how state initiative is behind many of the great inventions that currently sustain our way of life.

State funds have supported many of the innovations driving the information technology revolution, even as creativity and entrepreneurship flourish spontaneously in Silicon Valley. The features that make the iPhone a smartphone were financed with public funds, from the internet to the touch screen to the global positioning system (GPS).

Tesla, Tesla Solar and SpaceX, all led by Elon Musk, have benefited from $4,900 million in federal, state and local government support, and both SpaceX and Blue Origin (founded by Jeff Bezos) are drawing on NASA's accumulated technological know-how.

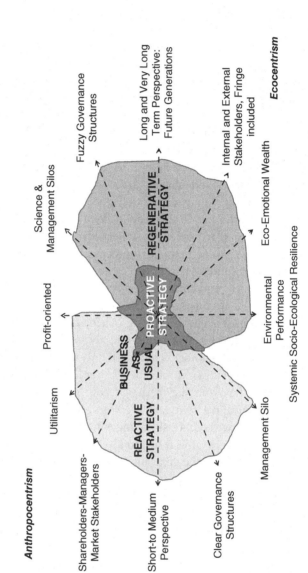

Figure 8.1 From reactive strategy, to business as usual, to regenerative strategy
Source: Authors' own elaboration

In short, these are just a few examples of how much we owe to the entrepreneurial power of states, which dynamise the economy and take risks that no one else will. As Mazzucato (2022) suggests, venture capital funds are not truly very risk-loving; therefore states, in taking risks, also make mistakes, but this does not mean that their impetus is not essential in certain areas and critical moments where risk and uncertainty are unaffordable for a private initiative. Hence, the task of the government is not just to solve market failures, as is often argued, but to make decisions that create the markets of the future, to take the risks necessary to do so and to promote technological change where necessary by creating appropriate innovation structures and systems.

This is the problem that underlies the main case presented in this book. That is, the most regenerative technological alternative (AIR TO FUELS technology), although viable and technologically proven, is not playing the central role desirable in a context marked by the climate emergency. Private companies, in this case Carbon Engineering, do not receive sufficient incentives to invest in A2F technology, either because it risks consuming their core business or because they prefer to make short-term profits with technologies that are more familiar to them.

Thus, it may be time for the state to take the initiative. If not now, when?

References

Adler, P. (2022). Capitalism, socialism, and the climate crisis. *Organization Theory*, 3(1): 1–16.

Alvarez, S. A., Zander, U., Barney, J. B., and Afuah, A. (2020). Developing a theory of the firm for the 21st century. *Academy of Management Review*, 45(4): 711–716.

Bansal, P., and Roth, K. (2000). Why companies go green: A model of ecological responsiveness. *Academy of Management Journal*, 43(4): 717–736.

Barney, J. (2018). Why resource-based theory's model of profit appropriation must incorporate a stakeholder perspective. *Strategic Management Journal*, 39(13): 3305–3325.

Barney, J. A. Y., and Felin, T. (2013). What are microfoundations? *Academy of Management Perspectives*, 27(2): 138–155.

Busch, T., Cho, C., Hoepner, A., Michelon, A., and Rogelj, J. (2023). Corporate greenhouse gas emissions' data and the urgent need for a science-led just transition: Introduction to a thematic symposium. *Journal of Business Ethics*, 182: 897–901.

Geissdoerfer, M., Vladimirova, D., and Evans, S. (2018). Sustainable business model innovation: A review. *Journal of Cleaner Production*, 198: 401–416.

Gibson, C., Gibson, S., and Webster, Q. (2021). Expanding our resources: Including community in the resource-based view of the firm. *Journal of Management*, 47(7): 1878–1898.

Hahn, T., and Tampe, M. (2021). Strategies for regenerative business. *Strategic Organization*, 19(3): 456–477.

Hardin, G. (1968). The tragedy of the commons. *Science*, 162(3859): 1243–1248.

Hart, S. (1995). A natural resource-based view of the firm. *Academy of Management Review*, 20(4): 986–1014.

Henderson, R. (2020). *Reimagining Capitalism in a World on Fire*. New York: PublicAffairs.

Independent Group of Scientists appointed by the Secretary-General. (2019). *Global Sustainable Development Report 2019: The Future Is Now – Science for Achieving Sustainable Development*. New York: United Nations.

Keith, D. (2013). *A Case for Climate Engineering*. Cambridge, MA: MIT Press.

Klein, N. (2015). *This Changes Everything: Capitalism vs. the Climate*. New York: Simon and Schuster.

Levinthal, D., and March, J. G. (1993). The myopia of learning. *Strategic Management Journal*, 14(S2): 95–112.

Mazzucato, M. (2022). *El Estado emprendedor: La oposición público-privado y sus mitos*. Barcelona: Penguin Random House.

McGahan, A. (2021). Integrating insights from the resource-based view into the new stakeholder theory. *Journal of Management*, 47(7): 1734–1756.

Miles, R. E., and Snow, C. C. (1978). *Organizational Strategy, Structure and Process*. New York: McGraw-Hill.

Nyberg, D., and Wright, C. (2022). Climate-proofing management research. *Academy of Management Perspectives*, 36(2): 713–728.

Porter, M., and van der Linde, C. (1995). Green and competitive: Ending the stalemate. *Harvard Business Review*, 73(5): 120–134.

Shäppi, R., Rutz, D., Dähler, F. et al. (2022) Drop-in fuels from sunlight and air. *Nature*, 601(7891): 63–81.

Sharma, S. (2022). From environmental strategy to environmental impact. *Academy of Management Discoveries*, 8(1): 1–6.

Valls, M. P. (2022, December). *Empresa y Sociedad*, episode 4. www.ivoox .com/podcast-empresa-sociedad_sq_f11209697_1.html.

Yunus, M., Moingeon, B., and Lehmann-Ortega, L. (2010). Building social business models: Lessons from the Grameen experience. *Long Range Planning*, 43(2–3): 308–325.

Index

Printed in the United States
by Baker & Taylor Publisher Services